BOYS AND

English-Can_____ ____dren and the First World War

*Boys and Girls in No Man's Land* examines how the First World
War entered the lives and imaginations of Canadian children.
Drawing on educational materials, textbooks, adventure tales,
plays, and Sunday-school papers, this study explores the role of
children in the nation's war effort.

Susan R. Fisher also considers how the representation of the
war has changed in Canadian children's literature. During the
war, the conflict was invariably presented as noble and thrilling, but recent Canadian children's books paint a very different
picture. What once was regarded a morally uplifting struggle,
rich in lessons of service and sacrifice, is now presented as pointless slaughter. This shift in tone and content reveals profound
changes in Canadian attitudes not only towards the First World
War but also towards patriotism, duty, and the shaping of the
moral citizen.

SUSAN R. FISHER teaches in the Department of English at the
University of the Fraser Valley.

SUSAN R. FISHER

# Boys and Girls
# in No Man's Land

## English-Canadian Children
## and the First World War

UNIVERSITY OF TORONTO PRESS
Toronto Buffalo London

© University of Toronto Press Incorporated 2011
Toronto Buffalo London
www.utppublishing.com
Printed in the U.S.A.

ISBN 978-0-8020-4224-9 (cloth)
ISBN 978-0-8020-1123-8 (paper)

Printed on acid-free and 100% post-consumer recycled paper with
vegetable-based inks.

---

**Library and Archives Canada Cataloguing in Publication**

Fisher, Susan, 1948–
    Boys and girls in no man's land : English-Canadian children and the
First World War / Susan R. Fisher.

    Includes bibliographical references and index.
    ISBN 978-1-4426-4224-9 (bound)     ISBN 978-1-4426-1123-8 (pbk.)

    1. World War, 1914–1918 – Children – Canada.   2. Children and war –
Canada.   3. Children – Canada – Social conditions – 20th century.
4. Children – Canada – History – 20th century.   I. Title.

D639.C4F58 2011     940.3'161     C2010-905770-8

---

University of Toronto Press acknowledges the financial assistance to its
publishing program of the Canada Council for the Arts and the Ontario
Arts Council.

 Canada Council   Conseil des Arts
for the Arts      du Canada        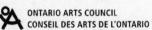 ONTARIO ARTS COUNCIL
CONSEIL DES ARTS DE L'ONTARIO

This book has been published with the help of a grant from the Canadian
Federation for the Humanities and Social Sciences, through the Aid
to Scholarly Publications Program, using funds provided by the Social
Sciences and Humanities Research Council of Canada.

University of Toronto Press acknowledges the financial support for its
publishing activities of the Government of Canada through the Book
Publishing Industry Development Program (BPIDP).

*For my parents, whose fathers were Canadian soldiers of the Great War*

# Contents

# Acknowledgments

I would not have been able to undertake this work if it were not for the rich resources made available to scholars across the country through the Canadian Institute for Historical Micro-reproductions (CIHM), now part of Canadiana.org. Many of the documents and sources I have used were available in Vancouver through the CIHM collection at the University of British Columbia.

I am also indebted to people at other libraries and archives. Paula Brennan and Kulwant Gill at the University of the Fraser Valley tracked down many interlibrary loan requests. The knowledgeable archivists and librarians at the British Columbia Archives, the Canadian War Museum, Library and Archives Canada, the General Synod Archives of the Anglican Church of Canada, and the United Church of Canada / Victoria University Archives helped me find materials. I am also indebted to Karl Larson at the Archives of the Salvation Army for all his assistance. Eiran Harris of the Jewish Public Library of Montreal searched English and Yiddish publications of Canada's Jewish community for children's material on the war. Barbara Geiger of the Regis College Library assisted me with items from the *Canadian Messenger of the Sacred Heart*; Alison Morrow assisted me with the *Catholic Register*. John Tooth of the Manitoba Department of Education, Citizenship and Youth helped me obtain copies of the Manitoba Empire Annuals. Leslie McGrath of the Toronto Public Library answered several queries. Dr C. Lloyd Brown-John, who found a cache of First World War materials in an abandoned barn, sold me several books and photocopied some sheet music for me.

I am grateful to the University of the Fraser Valley for the sabbatical term that enabled me to complete this project. Diane Nosaty of the Instructional Media Services Department of the University of the Fraser Valley helped me to prepare illustrations. The university also provided funds for a research assistant, a role that Amy McCall filled most efficiently and helpfully. In the summer of 2008, I taught a class at UFV in which we read and discussed some of the materials examined in this book. I am very grateful to the English 360 students for their thoughtful comments on children's war literature, and for their imaginative presentations of the patriotic playlets of Edith Groves.

Throughout the process of getting from idea to book, Siobhan McMenemy of University of Toronto Press has been efficient, kind, astute, and practical. Frances Mundy and Ken Lewis of the Press provided alert and attentive copy-editing of the sort that every writer hopes for. The readers of this manuscript made valuable suggestions and asked important questions; their work has made this book much better than it would otherwise have been. Whatever errors or problems remain are entirely my own responsibility.

I would also like to thank Eva-Marie Kröller for her encouragement and her example.

My greatest thanks are owed to my family for their patience with, and confidence in, this project. I am especially grateful to my husband, Gordon, for his help and companionship.

BOYS AND GIRLS IN NO MAN'S LAND

English-Canadian Children and the First World War

# Introduction

Children are rarely mentioned in Canadian histories of the First World War. This silence could lead one to believe that while the war raged across the seas, Canadian children simply went about the business of being children – studying, playing, doing chores. To some extent children did indeed do so, just as adults on the home front were not wholly engrossed by the war but of necessity went on working, cooking meals, raising crops and families. Nonetheless, Canadian children were, as Jonathan Vance has put it, 'vital foot soldiers in the crusade against the kaiser's Germany' (*Death* 234). They participated in the home-front war effort, raised money for war refugees, studied war in school, and spent their leisure hours playing war games and reading war stories.

Some young Canadians even went to the battlefields.[1] In principle, an adolescent had to be eighteen to join up, and nineteen to go to the front, but it is clear that many recruiting officers did not question too deeply the lad who lied about his age. The census of 1911 had included persons over the age of fourteen in its count of the gainfully employed, indicating the Canadian adolescent was already considered an adult in some respects; thus, it is not surprising that boys were ready to enlist and the military was ready to accept them. Still, the very fact that an age requirement did exist, however loosely applied, indicates an understanding that boys under eighteen were not old enough to fight and die for their country. In the early years of the war, there was very little public concern about underage soldiers, despite the frantic attempts of some mothers to retrieve their boys. It was not until mid-1917 that a special unit, the Young Soldiers Battalion, was created in order to keep in England and away from the front those Canadian soldiers found to be underage. (Canada's last known survivor of the Great War, Corporal John Babcock, was a member of this battalion: he had enlisted when he was just fifteen ['Canada's'].) But boys were placed in the special battalion 'only at the whim of the unit officers,' and it seems that many underage soldiers continued to fight (Cockerill 140). The story of Robert Clarence Thompson of Picton, Ontario, demonstrates that a determined boy could get to the front. When Thompson first enlisted, at the age of thirteen, he lasted only a month before his father got him out, but then in early 1916, still just fourteen, Thompson enlisted again. He fought at Vimy in 1917 and then was discovered to be underage and sent home; he joined up yet again and 'was quickly promoted ... to sergeant major' (138). He was fifteen years old when he 'led his company at the Battle of Mons and was in his sixteenth year when the armistice was signed.' Tim Cook estimates that there may have been as many as 20,000 soldiers under the age of nineteen in the Canadian Expeditionary Force, and of these, perhaps 2,270 died in the war (72). In its records, the Commonwealth War Graves Commission has identified more than a thousand underage Canadians among the fallen, fourteen of whom were just fifteen years old when they were killed (71).

But the underage soldiers, especially the very young ones, were exceptional in that they managed to act on their fantasies of war and get to the battlefields. The vast majority of young Canadians stayed home. Still, the war came to them. The most dramatic instance of the war's effect on Canadian children was the Halifax Explosion of 6 December 1917, in which 482 of the nearly two thousand fatalities were persons under the age of fourteen (MacDonald 291). But many other children in Canada were also injured by the war. About 10,000 of the more than 60,000 Canadian men who died on the battlefields left behind widows and an unknown number of children (Morton, *Fight* 228). To lose a father or other close relative is, as psychiatrist Lynne Jones has concluded from her study of Bosnian children in the 1990s, 'the greatest disaster' children can experience in wartime, perhaps even more grievous than actually being in the midst of battle (210). Even children whose fathers and brothers survived would not have been immune: through networks of extended family and community relationships, virtually every household in the country was in some way exposed to the losses of war. The death of a father in the First World War would have been not only an emotional loss; often it spelt financial disaster for the family. Some war widows were forced to give up their children because they could not afford to raise them alone; some died in the influenza epidemic that swept across Canada in the fall of 1918, and their children were left parentless. In Ontario alone, nearly six hundred children became permanent wards of the Soldiers' Aid Commission (Raynsford 57). They were raised in the hostels operated by the Commission or sent to board with farm families; some were cared for in foster homes. Well into the 1930s, soldiers' children were still receiving aid from the Commission.

A second group of children was also seriously affected by the war: those left in penury when their fathers joined up. Of the more than four hundred thousand Canadians who were sent overseas, about a fifth were married (Morton, 'Supporting' 195). Most of these married soldiers, one assumes, had children at home in Canada. At the beginning of the war, Sir Robert Borden's government had moved quickly to reassure volunteers that their families would not suffer. In August of 1914, the government revived the Canadian Patriotic Fund (CPF) and made it responsible for assisting soldiers' families. This privately funded body, which became the 'largest single charity that Canadians had yet created,' collected large sums of money from private citizens (194). But it was intended to supplement, not replace, the soldier's pay. In principle, the soldier's family could count on two sources of income: a separation allowance, which was paid (on a scale that varied with rank) directly to the soldier's dependants, and assigned pay, which was the amount the soldier chose to have sent home out of his paycheque. However, given the complexity of a payment system in which 'a soldier and his family depended on four distinct pay offices,' and 'the potential for error and delay by ill-qualified personnel in a pre-electronic era,' many wives and other dependants (such as infirm parents or widowed mothers) found themselves effectively without an income (Morton, *Fight* 46). It was the role of the CPF to help out in such situations. The fund was supposed to show a 'flexible

1 Isaac Sambrook in the uniform of Princess Patricia's Canadian Light Infantry, with young child, ca 1915. On his attestation papers, Sambrook listed his profession as masseur. He was married and had two children; the child in this image may be his son Osmund. Sambrook survived the war and came home. Courtesy of Glenbow Archives, image NB-50-62.

generosity,' but in fact inefficiencies and middle-class prejudice interfered with its mission ('Supporting' 204). Whether a family would get CPF funds depended on a home visit by members of the branch donations committee or by their wives or daughters. In effect, the visit was both a means test and a morality check: wives deemed extravagant or immoral did not receive aid (206). The consequence of these limitations, both in the operations of the CPF and in the army pay system, was very real hardship for many soldiers' children. The hardship did not end with the war. Some returned soldiers were able to re-establish themselves in the civilian economy, but some could not: 'Largely disabled emotionally and physically by the tragedies of war, depressed by the brutalizing effects of close combat, frequently dependent on alcohol, these veterans would continue throughout their lives to require help and support for themselves and their families' (Raynsford 35). Some veterans were simply no longer fit to be husbands and fathers: 'Over two thousand cases of desertion were reported in the first three years after the war' (55). The children of these men, like the children of the fallen soldiers, became 'silent casualties of a war fought halfway across the world' (55).

Yet, for all its sorrows, the war brought excitement to Canadian children. Schools and Sunday schools organized a seemingly endless round of activities to engage children in the war effort. Fundraising concerts, projects to make 'comforts' for the soldiers, campaigns to raise money for war causes – such enterprises filled afternoons, evenings, and holidays for many Canadian children. To judge by their letters and by their contributions, Canadian children threw themselves with earnest enthusiasm into this work and felt themselves valued participants in the great national and imperial cause.

How did it happen that a war taking place so far away pervaded the lives of Canadian children, making its baneful presence felt in the primary classroom, the Sunday school, and the nursery? Why did educators, parents, churchmen, and publishers enlist children in supporting what we now feel was so cruel and savage a war? The French historian Stéphane Audoin-Rouzeau, in *La Guerre des enfants, 1914–1918: essai d'histoire culturelle*, sees the involvement of children in the Great War as intimately linked to the 'total war' mentality:

... it was not just the nation but human civilization that seemed at risk; it was a certain conception of man that was at stake. Henceforth, the 'totalization' of war became a necessity, and the price to pay was no longer important. There resides the key to this surprising violence introduced into the domain of childhood, the key to why children were integrated into the war: what need was there for children to survive if France – if Civilization – were to lose the war and therefore disappear? Children were called upon to participate in the sacrifices that adults had consented to; in a struggle of this kind, children could not be spared. Total war was therefore destined to offer children a special place ... (13)[2]

Audoin-Rouzeau's study focuses on France and, to a lesser extent, Germany and Britain, but what he has to say applies also to Canada. Here, too, despite our distance from the battlefields, there was a mentality of 'total war.' The full force of the nation's productive power in industry, agriculture, and resource extraction was harnessed for the war effort. And so was the work of children. This meant not only their labour in fundraising or gardening or making comforts but also the moral work of shaping themselves into adults of good character. It included too the symbolic role that children were assigned in the discourse of war. There was indeed, to use Audoin-Rouzeau's phrase, a 'special place' for Canadian children in the First World War.

From the outset, children had served as the iconic victims of German militarism. During the first weeks of the invasion of Belgium, German soldiers killed some 6,500 civilians in Belgium and Northern France (Horne and Kramer 430). Although there has been much debate about the extent of the 'German atrocities,' as the actions against Belgian civilians were soon labelled, the recent work of historians John Horne and Alan Kramer has established that they did indeed take place. But on the foundation of the actual atrocities was erected an edifice of propaganda. As George Mosse has noted, in the depiction of enemy atrocities 'no holds were barred' (172). In anti-German propaganda, according to Horne and Kramer, 'the commonest myth of all was one that expressed a shared sense of violation: that of the baby or child whose hand had been severed by a Teutonic brute' (202). They list numerous examples of refugees who recounted having seen Belgian or French children with bandaged limbs; supposedly these children had been mutilated by the Germans so that they could never bear arms (202-3). While the Germans undoubtedly did harm children in the invasion of Belgium – some children were killed, many were orphaned, and many lost their homes – there is no reliable evidence that any were deliberately maimed. Nonetheless, the child with severed hands became 'the key Allied myth of 1914' (204). This, of course, was a myth of great utility, for it symbolized as no other story could the 'barbarism' of the Germans.[3] The violated child became a simple, irrefutable, and enduring justification for the war. A pamphlet for women voters published by the Union government in 1917 provides eyewitness accounts (quoted from the Bryce Commission Report) of the 'fiendish slaughter of children' ('German' n.pag.); this material was intended to persuade Canadian women that they must support the Union government and its policy of conscription.[4] In 'The Little Refugee' (1919), a story by Canadian author Jean Blewett, a soldier returns home on Christmas Eve, carrying a Belgian child whose arms have 'been severed at the wrist' and whose 'little body is scarred with bayonet wounds' (28-9). The sight of the child causes the soldier's mother, a Quaker, to renounce her pacifism:

> Mother, the mutilated lad in her arms, stood up as if taking part in a sacrament. 'God bless Great Britain! I – I didn't know she fought for this,' her tears falling on the face of the Belgian child. (29)[5]

A similar image appears in 'Emile, the Belgian Boy,' a story published in the King's Own, the Presbyterian Sunday-school paper. A German soldier cuts off the arms of Emile, who has tried to defend his mother. The German is unrepentant: '"One fighting man the less!" the villain called out to his men and went laughing on' (27 Oct. 1917: 170).[6]

While the notion that the Germans had deliberately maimed Belgian and French children was a myth, there were, of course, many real child victims of the war. Indeed, the Great War created so many that for the first time 'children as war victims became an international issue on the American and European agenda,' and concern about the child victims of the Great War, especially the many refugees, led to the founding of such specialized relief agencies as Save the Children (Janfelt 880). Part of this response was motivated by genuine concern about the physical and psychological damage wrought by the war on children. Part of it was also a recognition, in the age of photography, that child victims made good publicity. Dominique Marshall, in her study of humanitarian agencies and children's rights, has pointed out that 'depictions of suffering children were prominent' in the publications of relief agencies 'as they could represent the endangered innocence of whole nations' (187).

The injuries and suffering of child war victims in Europe, both real and symbolic, threw into relief the precious value of children at home in Canada. The Canadian child, intact and healthy, symbolized everything that was worth defending. As one Canadian recruiting poster put it, 'The thin Khaki line keeps the fate of Belgium from your hearth and home' ('Canadian Posters'). If Canadians did not do their part in driving back the Germans, Canadian children could meet the same fate as Belgian ones. The child as symbol of home was exploited in sentimental ditties like 'I Want My Daddy':

> I want my Daddy, I'm as lonely as can be
> I want my dear old Dad tho' he's far away from me
> When I kissed him as we parted, there was a tear drop in his eye.
> 'Good luck to the boys of the Allies,' we sang, then we said good
>     bye.

This song, written by Morris Manley of Toronto, was the 'great song hit' of Little Miss Mildred Manley, 'Canada's Greatest Child Vocalist.' Another Canadian song of this kind was Hobb Lynne's 'My Daddy's Gone to War,' in which a little girl sings to her playmate, 'My daddy he has gone to war, Has your dear dad gone too / My daddy he has gone to fight, Fighting for me and you.'

A related symbolic function of the child was to sanitize the war effort. As war workers, patriots, and make-believe soldiers, children helped to elevate war enthusiasm above the jingoism of the recruiting rally or the crude excitement of the mob. Children in small uniforms, waving flags at parades, smiling on posters and in advertisements, lent their innocence to the enterprise of war. In 1917, a Victory Bond poster featuring a little blonde child helped to raise $419 million dollars in two weeks ('Canadian

Posters'). Fred Landon, the chief librarian of London, Ontario, writing in the *Ontario Library Review* in November 1917, recognized presciently that this poster would be a valuable document in any future archive of the war:

> Take, for instance, that very handsome Victory Loan poster, the little girl with her blocks, with arms upraised, imploring, 'Oh, daddy, please do, buy me a Victory bond.' What a picture to be used in explaining to children of the future what the war meant to Canadians of to-day. (52)

Landon did not elaborate, but surely his point was that Canadians believed they were fighting in order to protect children like the appealing little girl. Moreover, the poster demonstrated that the war was reaching into every corner of Canadian life, even that inner sanctum of the home, the nursery.

Children also had symbolic power as the representatives of the future, as 'symbols of the continuity between generations' (Mosse 137). In the short term, they constituted the pool of future soldiers, a reserve force ready to take the place of the fallen. In the long term, they were the inheritors of the post-war world. In Canada, this view of children as the future was closely linked to the national self-image as a young country about to emerge into glorious maturity and prosperity. Because Canadian children embodied this future, protecting the nation was a struggle to be waged not only on the battlefields but also on the home front, in schools and in Sunday schools. As Paula S. Fass has pointed out, 'Children are pivotal to how a culture defines itself and its future' (7). In post-war Canada, children themselves were to be a war memorial. This view was nowhere expressed more plainly than in the introduction to the 1919 anthology *The Great War in Verse and Prose*, published by the Ontario Department of Education:

> Those who have fallen ... will be commemorated by public monuments, by tablets of bronze, or brass or marble in public buildings, by 'storied windows richly dight.' They deserve this. But, before God, they deserve at our hands a better monument – even the monument of a purer, nobler Canada, more intelligent, more united, more sober, more kindly, more God-fearing. Dying for

2  Victory Loan poster. Courtesy of Archives of Ontario.

Canada, they have recreated Canada. Let us be worthy of those
whose deaths have kept us free. (Wetherell xiii-xiv)

Children and young people were the raw material – the stone,
the bronze – for the most important monument to the war dead:
a better Canada.

This book about Canadian children and the First World War
began when, during the course of other research on the war, I
discovered a number of recent children's books about the war. I
was astonished: how had the carnage of the Western Front made
its way into children's literature? As I read through the modern
war books, I could not help but discern in some the distorting
light of presentism, making these fictional Canadian children of
the First World War seem altogether too knowing, too skeptical,
too modern. But was this a fair assessment? What had Canadian
children really thought and felt and experienced during the
war?

To answer these questions, I turned to children's books, magazines, textbooks, and teaching materials from the war years. It
soon became evident that the war represented in these wartime
materials was very different from the one depicted in most modern books. It also became evident that what had been written for
children during the war had to be understood in a larger context. What did Canadian children know about the conflict? What
else in their lives exposed them to information or propaganda?
How did the war – its sorrows and its demands for work and
sacrifice – impinge on their everyday lives? Gradually, a book
that was intended as a comparison of two eras of war writing for
children evolved to include something else: a study of Canadian
children during the First World War. The main emphasis, however, remains literary, not only because that is where my interest
began, but also for the practical reason that while many books,
magazines, pamphlets, and textbooks have survived, other aspects of Canadian children's war experience, such as the patriotic gardens they tended and the socks they knitted, have not.

It is inevitable that a study of this kind is shaped as much by its
limitations as by its reach. The most important of these is the focus on materials in English. Partly, this was a practical decision,
but it also reflects the very different experience of the war in

francophone Canada. While French Canada initially manifested some enthusiasm for the war, Canada's francophone citizens did not, by and large, see it as their war. The nationalist tensions of the period – the anger over Regulation 17 in Ontario, which prohibited teaching in French after Grades 1 and 2, and then the bitterness of the conscription crisis – were aggravated by the government's mishandling of recruitment in French Canada (which one historian has described as 'a story of frustration, incompetence, and negligence' [Dutil 118]). The result was not only a low rate of enlistment in Quebec but also a marked lack of interest in recruiting children for the home front. For example, while in Ontario the Ministry of Education required that the war be integrated into the curriculum, in Quebec there was no such directive (Djebabla and Mesli 127). Focusing on materials in English also means that I have not examined publications in the languages of immigrant communities, such as the German-language publications of Canada's Mennonites.

The second limitation is that, for children's war writing produced in Canada (as opposed to what came from Britain and the United States), I have relied largely on the Sunday-school papers of the Anglican, Presbyterian, and Methodist churches and of the Salvation Army. As I discuss more fully later, these Protestant denominations published the only magazines aimed at Canadian children. There were no secular alternatives. Other faiths and denominations did not publish materials for children. The Baptist Church used periodicals produced by the Presbyterians and Methodists (Lowe). The Yiddish paper *Kenneder Adler* had a children's column, but it did not print any materials about the war (Harris). The *Canadian Messenger of the Sacred Heart*, published by the Jesuits, included fiction aimed at the whole family, but it had no children's column until the 1930s (Power). Similarly, the *Catholic Register*, while it did publish letters from children, included very little for them about the war.

Another limitation has to do with what has survived. Advertisements and reviews identify some books Canadian children were reading during the war. I have tracked down these books, copies of which can still be found in libraries and second-hand bookstores. But almost certainly there were other materials – for example, flimsy books for very small children – that were simply too fragile to endure or too trivial to review or to save. Materials for children have not always been regarded as important enough to take up space in public collections, and even some serious-minded war materials for children have nearly disappeared. For example, the fifty-six numbers of the multi-volume *Children's Story of the War*, issued in pamphlet form throughout the war, were sent to every school library in British Columbia; thousands of copies must have been in circulation, yet only a single one has survived in the province's libraries. The publications I discuss represent only a provisional survey of what Canadian children read during the war, and other materials may yet surface.

In contrasting how writers from two different eras approach the same topic, there is always the temptation to pronounce on who gets it right or who understands it better. I have at times yielded to this temptation, concerned as I am with the tendency to project onto children of the past ideas and attitudes that only adults of the present can possess. Yet I hope that I have been able to show not that some war books are 'good' and others are 'bad' but rather that the First World War, as understood and experienced by Canadians, especially Canadian children, has changed. The American scholar of children's literature Anne Scott MacLeod has observed that 'children's books do not mirror their culture, but they do always, no matter how indirectly, convey some of its central truths' (*American* viii). I hope that by looking more closely at what Canadian children have read about the war, we can glimpse some of those 'central truths,' not just about the First World War but also about patriotism, childhood, and the nation.

**Preparing for War**

In the early twentieth century, there were few homegrown publications for Canadian children. Much of what they read originated in Britain, where, in the closing decades of the nine-teenth century, there had been rapid growth in the publishing of books and magazines for children. Children's publications had emerged in Britain as 'essentially a new enterprise, arising in tandem with the educational reforms of 1870 and 1880, and the advent of new printing technology which made it possible to produce cheap books and periodicals on a large scale' (Rey-nolds xv-xvi). Coincident with these phenomena was the rise of a new 'doctrine of imperialism,' not merely as a matter of policy but as an ingredient in national identity. From the 1880s onward, 'imperialist propaganda saturated British society' and thus its publications for children (Moyles and Owram 5). The *Boy's Own Paper* (begun in 1879) and the *Girl's Own Paper* (1880) were only the earliest and most successful of the many children's periodicals, so popular in Britain and in the Dominions, that retailed this new imperialism.

Much has been written about the values that the *Boy's Own,* the *Girl's Own,* and their many lesser imitators promoted.[7] Some of these periodicals were sensational, some moralistic: the *Boy's Own* and the *Girl's Own,* for example, were published by the Religious Tract Society in order to wean children from the 'pernicious literature' of the commercial juvenile papers (quoted in Altick 362). While these periodicals varied widely in literary quality and educational value, all to some degree presented the same messages about the superiority of the British, the strength of the Empire, and the glory and necessity of war.[8] British adventure books and stories of the period were, as Patrick Dunae has put it, 'without exception dedicated to the imperial idea' ('Boys' 106). Dunae argues that the 'imperial idea' became even more forceful and militaristic towards the end of the nineteenth century. A more 'bellicose, boisterous mood of imperialism' emerged that, during the years of the South African War (1899–1901), found expression in reports on battles and stories about heroic actions and military leaders – a clear foretaste of what such publications would provide for children during the Great War (112). Moreover, the errors and defeats of the South African War led to 'anxiety about the next generation of men,' and 'new publications, entirely devoted to inspiring boys with the need to defend their imperial heritage, proliferated' (Reynolds 58). As publishers quickly realized, this concern with 'rearing a new breed of more masculine boys made for good business' (59). Mark Moss, in his study of Ontario before the First World War, demonstrates convincingly the overwhelming importance of British adventure reading for Canadian boys, and its unequivocally martial tone (73–89).

While Britain was the chief source of militaristic reading material, some did originate in Canada. The books of Ralph Connor (Charles Gordon), while not overtly imperialist, certainly promoted the English public-school ideal of the 'muscular and moral male,' especially through the depiction of sporting matches (Mangan 186–7). A thirteen-year-old reader of a Canadian Sunday-school paper explained why Connor was his favourite author: 'I like the books because they are full of adventure. The heroes in his books are strong, broadminded men who are not afraid of hardships' (*King's Own*, 26 Dec. 1914: 208). In the pre-war period, it was not just leisure reading that promoted militarism and manliness. Textbooks, physical training, boys' organizations, sports, games, and toys all in their various ways glamourized war, cultivated patriotism, and stirred the desire for adventure. Moss concludes that young Ontario men volunteered in 1914 because they had been brought up to be 'warriors for the Canadian nation' (3). One important ingredient in creating this outlook was Scouting, with its 'militaristic thrust' (115). Founded in 1907 and brought to Canada soon after (Baden-Powell enlisted the governor general's support in establishing Canadian Scouting in 1910), the Scout movement caught on rapidly: by July of 1912, it boasted 40,000 members across the country (G. Brown). In *The Canadian Boy Scout* (1911), Lord Baden-Powell claimed that Scouting was not militaristic: 'From the national point of view our aim is solely to make the rising generation into good citizens. We avoid military training …' (ix). Baden-Powell was distinguishing his movement from the militarist culture of German education, but the supposedly non-military purpose of Scouting is belied by Baden-Powell's constant use of military examples and anecdotes. For example, when he argues for the value of cleanliness, to prove his point he compares the high rate of death by disease among the British in South Africa to the relatively low losses suffered by the Japanese in the Russo-Japanese war: the Japanese soldiers stayed healthy because of their habit of regular bathing (202). Frequent examples drawn from his own war experiences in South Africa remind young readers that Baden-Powell acquired his skills and manliness not in peacetime work but on the battlefield. He also holds up the example of valiant Canadian fighters such as Adam Dollard and General Brock (280–2). The Scouts are instructed to 'train yourselves so that if at any time your country or your Empire needs your help by land or by sea, you will not be cowards or shirk your duties, but will be ready to come forward and take your share in defending your home and liberty' (283). Any boy who participated in Scouting could not have helped but imbibe a reverence for war as the ultimate proving ground of manhood.

By the end of the first decade of the twentieth century, Canadian children were being exposed to patriotism and militarism in a wide variety of contexts – home, school, church, community. As I discuss in chapters 2 and 3, the patriotic attitudes so evident in wartime publications and activities for children did not appear in 1914 *ex nihilo* but rather were a continuation and expansion of pre-existing values. Even the idea of war with Germany was not new, for German invasion had featured in many boys' stories in the first decade of the century (Cadogan and Craig, *Women* 26–31).

**War Stories**

When war broke out, the major genres of children's literature readily absorbed this compelling new subject. In the boys' adventure tale, nothing essential changed: authors shifted locales, adapted stock characters (the Oriental villain, for example, giving way to the Teutonic one), and updated the weaponry. The animal story transferred its familiar messages about loyalty and compassion from the barnyard or forest to the battlefield. The girls' story, while continuing to deliver romance, friendship, fashion, and glamour, demonstrated how 'even a girl' could make an important contribution to the struggle. The book of heroes, a genre that in the pre-war days had been 'ubiquitous,' now drew its exemplars of self-sacrifice and courage from the daily war news (J. MacKenzie 200).

Despite the straitened conditions of wartime, British publishers like Thomas Nelson and Sons, Jack, Blackie, and Amalgamated Press continued to issue an astonishing array of books, magazines, and annuals for children, many now with war-themed stories and adventures. Large numbers of these made their way to the Canadian market. Some were imported; others were published in Canada through the Toronto offices of the major British firms.

But the British publishers did not have the Canadian market to themselves. In the early twentieth century, 'the Canadian book market was inundated with products' from not only Britain but also the United States (Litt 330). Even much of what was published in Canada originated elsewhere: by 1910, the Toronto publishing industry had in effect become 'a commercial satellite of the British and the Americans' (Parker 909). During the war, Canadians actually read more books about the conflict – both fiction and non-fiction – from the United States than from Britain (Vipond 107). One measure of just how important American books were for young Canadian readers during this period is the long list of Horatio Alger books advertised in the Eaton's catalogue for Spring/Summer 1917 – six times the number of G.A. Henty books on offer. When war broke out, American publishers, like their British counterparts, saw its potential for adventure tales and romances that would appeal to young readers and soon began issuing new war-related titles in popular series like the Boy Scouts. There were even new series focused entirely on the war, such as the Boy Allies and the Red Cross Girls. These American books were soon making their way into Canadian bookstores and libraries.

But for Canadian war stories – that is, written by Canadians and published in Canada – there was virtually only one source: the Sunday-school papers. In late nineteenth- and early twentieth-century Canada, the Protestant churches 'played a very strong role in the publication of periodicals for children' (Weller 44). The Methodist church issued 'a vast array of Sunday-school periodicals' (Clarkson and O'Leary 356); in 1880, the Methodist Book and Publishing House was 'the largest publishing establishment in the Dominion, largely on account of its immensely popular periodicals' (357). Its various Sunday-school papers all 'presented a fairly consistent focus and message,' which Neil Semple, in his history of Canadian Methodism, sums up as 'loyalty to the nation, the monarchy, and, particularly before and during World War I, to the empire' (380). By the time of the war, the magazines published by the Protestant denominations were the most important children's publications in Canada.

Among these were two published by the Presbyterians: *Playmate* for the juniors (issued in cooperation with the Methodists), and the *King's Own* for boys and girls under sixteen (published by the Methodist Publishing House for the Presbyterian Church). While the annual reports of the Presbyterian

Church's Publishing Committee do not provide any circulation figures for these papers, membership in the *King's Own* readers' club, The Order of the King's Own or TOKO, is one gauge of the magazine's readership: in 1915, there were 1,500 members in Canada (*King's Own*, 2 Jan. 1915: 4). Since becoming a member entailed writing a letter to the magazine, one can assume that the members represented only a small proportion of the total readership.

The Anglicans also had children's periodicals. Before 1916, the Sunday School Commission of the Church of England in Canada had distributed *Our Empire*, an illustrated paper from Britain published by the Society for the Propagation of Christian Knowledge. But when, in 1916, wartime restrictions on paper forced the Society to suspend publication, the Anglican Church in Canada launched its own 'story paper,' the *New Young Soldier and Crusader*. By 1918, circulation was 36,000 (Report of Sunday School Commission 277). There was also an Anglican paper for the 'juniors,' *Child's Own*. The *Letter Leaflet* of the Woman's Auxiliary to the Missionary Society of the Church of England in Canada had a children's corner in each issue. With a circulation of 17,000, the *Letter Leaflet* must have reached many homes.[9]

Another Sunday-school paper with wide circulation was the Salvation Army's *Young Soldier*. Although the Army is now regarded chiefly as a social outreach organization, it was, in the years of the war, the church of many Canadians. It was not a large denomination – only some 19,000 adherents according to the 1911 census – but it was a visible and active one. As a revivalist church, the Salvation Army had many innovative ways of reaching out to potential converts, ranging from its famous brass bands to the 'Hallelujah Runaway,' in which an army captain would suddenly dash off from an open-air meeting, with other Salvationists racing behind at top speed, thereby enticing curious bystanders to follow them right into a Salvation Army citadel (Moyles, *Blood* 17). The Army also used its publications to attract new members, most famously the *War Cry*, which, with its 'boldness, blunt editorials, witty reporting, colourful descriptions,' appealed to many Canadian readers, not just Salvationists (30). Like the *War Cry*, the *Young Soldier* was both an internal publication and a means of recruitment. Young members of the Army sold it on the street corner, and some of these 'boomers,' as the Army paper sellers were called, sold as many as two dozen copies a week. In October of 1917, the editor reported that the paper's circulation was 16,151; he called upon Salvationists to see that 'every boy and girl attending the Company Meeting is supplied with a copy' so that 6,000 more would be in circulation each week (27 Oct. 1917: 3). Thus, despite the relatively small number of Salvationists, the Army's publications had considerable reach. Moreover, the Salvation Army's children's magazine is of special interest because of its position on the war. It published a considerable number of war items; indeed, during the first two years of the war, it published more news about the war than did other Sunday-school papers. Yet, while papers of the other Protestant denominations moved ineluctably towards embracing the war as a holy struggle against the savage Hun, the Salvation Army's *Young Soldier* steadfastly maintained that war was evil and unchristian. Even in 1917, an editorial urged young readers to 'look at the world as one big country, and pray that God will save all the people in it. This may seem much to do, but it is the message that Jesus Christ would have this fourth war-Christmas bring to us. Pray even for our enemies!' (22 Dec. 1917: 5). Given the military style adopted by the Salvation Army in its uniforms, ranks, and terminology (the individual churches were sometimes known as barracks), it is surprising that the *Young Soldier* was the only Sunday-school paper to resist the war theology of the times.

The emphasis on church publications in this study reflects not only the energetic commitment that the Protestant churches made to periodical publishing for children but also the churches' educational and social prominence in many Canadian communities. In Toronto in this period, according to J.M.S. Careless, 'next to the home, and well ahead of the school, the church remained the firmest middle-class social institution. It was not only a place of worship and of Sunday school, of mission and charitable endeavours, but a recreational resort as well, for church guilds, choirs, bazaars and magic-lantern shows' (166). What children learned about the war from the Sunday-school papers was reinforced by involvement in church-based war work: for example, many of the patriotic entertainments and other fundraising activities that children participated in were organized by the Sunday schools.

Although the Sunday-school papers were published in Toronto, their reach was national. The letters columns of these periodicals indicate that children across the country, from the Maritimes to Vancouver Island, were regular readers. Letters came from such places as Oxford Mills, Georgetown, and Cobden in Ontario; New Waterford in Nova Scotia; Bon Accord in New Brunswick; Sperling, Manitoba; Kindersley in Saskatchewan; Cranbrook and Pender Island in British Columbia. In the Presbyterian *King's Own*, there was even a letter from a young Earle Birney in Banff, Alberta. Similarly, the reports on Sunday-school activities indicate a readership based not just in urban congregations but also in a range of small towns and rural communities.

As for other kinds of books and periodicals, they too reached children outside major cities. Again, letters in the Sunday-school papers of the period provide evidence that rural children, like those in cities, had access to such relatively new books as L.M. Montgomery's *Anne of Green Gables* (1908), Gene Stratton-Porter's *Girl of the Limberlost* (1909), Marshall Saunders's *Beautiful Joe* (1893), and Marian Keith's *The Silver Maple* (1908). If they were able to obtain this kind of popular fiction, then they could have obtained books about the war when they began to appear on the market. Indeed, any household that received the Eaton's catalogue had access to the latest war books from Britain and the United States, both adult and juvenile.

Children could also have obtained war books from the library. In this period, the public library was no longer an amenity that only city-dwellers enjoyed. In 1918, the *Ontario Library Review* published circulation data for more than four hundred public libraries in the province; in communities both large and small, children's books accounted for about a quarter to a third of the circulation (3.1: 12–15). Even a community as small as Lanark (pop. 628) reported on the circulation of its books for boys and girls. If these small public libraries were able to purchase the books recommended by the *Library Review*, then they could have supplied children's war books to the boys and girls in their community. But it must be acknowledged that the situation in Ontario was not typical. During the war years, most Canadian children did not have access to a public library. As late as 1933, the authors of a national survey on Canada's libraries estimated that 80 per cent of Canadians were 'utterly without library service of any kind' (quoted in Bruce and Hanson 431). Children, of course, did not restrict their reading to juvenile titles. Anne Scott MacLeod has observed that American children in the late nineteenth and early twentieth centuries were reading 'a great grab bag of material, good, bad and mediocre, adult and juvenile, books and magazines' (*American* 116). The same was true of Canadian children: according to Leslie McGrath, writers for adults like Nellie McClung and Ralph Connor 'had a readership among children' (404). In letters to the Sunday-school papers, children mentioned all sorts of titles, from American series like Horatio Alger and Elsie Dinsmore to such serious if not unequivocally adult books as *Nicholas Nickleby, Treasure Island, The Man from Glengarry,* and *Little Women.* The same sort of catholic taste applied to war books too. John Oliver, aged ten, reported in the letters column of the *King's Own* that he was reading H.W. Wilson's *The Great War* (29 Jan. 1916: 20). Issued in series form from 1914 to 1919 and subtitled 'The Standard History of the All-Europe Conflict,' Wilson's book was not aimed at children. Ralph Connor's best-selling war novels *The Major* (1917) and *The Sky Pilot in No Man's Land* (1919) were not children's literature either, but they were doubtless consumed by the many young readers who had enjoyed *The Prospector* and *The Man from Glengarry.*

What might children have gleaned from the adult war books that was different from what juvenile war literature offered? In the adult war novels there was more realistic detail about the fighting. The heroes were men who were actually in the trenches, not boy heroes who had improbable escapades (though many war novels had their share of improbabilities). There was also more romance in the adult novels: in Connor's *Sky Pilot in No Man's Land,* for example, the hero enjoys a reprieve from the front when he and his new wife enjoy a honeymoon in Scotland. But nothing in Connor's novel would have cast doubt on the honour and integrity of the Canadian soldier, or on the rightness of the Empire's and Canada's cause. Moreover, Connor's protagonist goes to war but is not tarnished by the rough habits and vulgar speech of the men he fights beside. The example of his nobility in fact lifts up the others. The bitter realism that we now associate with the fiction of the First World War – British works such as Robert Graves's *Good-bye to All That* (1929) and Siegfried Sassoon's *Memoirs of an Infantry Officer* (1930) and, on the Canadian side, Charles Yale Harrison's *Generals Die in Bed* (1928) and Philip Child's *God's Sparrows* (1937) – came long after the war. It is easy to forget that such war books were controversial. Harrison's book, for example, excited so much anger among Canadian veterans that they asked the government to ban it (Vance, 'Soldier' 30). Given this reaction, it seems unlikely that such war books would have found their way into the hands of young people; at least, parents and librarians would not have made them available. Harrison's novel is now marketed in Canada at the Annick Press website as for 'age 15+' – a fact that suggests much about how ideas about children's reading and the war have changed in the past seventy-five years.[10]

In discussing wartime children's literature, I refer at times to the backdrop of collective thinking about the war in Canadian society at large. How the war was discussed in publications for adults has obvious bearing on how it was presented to children. But this is a two-way street, for children's literature (broadly defined, including textbooks and other educational materials) illuminates the attitudes of society at large. What was written for children can be understood as 'a stylized version of the discourse' reserved for adults:

> ... it permits us to apprehend what constituted, in a sense, the hard kernel of national cultures of war, what each nation judged to be the most indispensable to teach children and to make them understand. The study of what they were 'taught' about the war permits us to reach into the heart of the cultural machinery of societies at war. (Audoin-Rouzeau 12)

In other words, children's literature about war reveals the essence of national thinking more plainly than does other war writing. Moreover, it was also more 'static,' remaining relatively unchanged throughout the course of the war (12). The reports on war dogs, the girls' stories, and the boys' adventure tales, for all that they are in their various ways limited, simplistic, and formulaic, nonetheless contain some clear truths about how Canadians viewed the war.

They also demonstrate what George Mosse has called the 'process of trivialization, cutting war down to size so that it would become commonplace instead of awesome and frightening' (126). Any representation of children playing at war literally reduces the size of combatants. Toys like tin soldiers, pretend guns, dolls, and child-sized uniforms are inherently trivializing both because they are miniatures of the real thing and because they partake of the domestic and commercial worlds. As Mosse points out, such toys and props 'inure[d] men and women to reality' (139); they enabled war to be represented as a harmless, even 'happy and joyous,' pastime that children could pursue (142). The narrative patterns employed in children's leisure-time reading about the war were similarly trivializing: they subsumed the unspeakable horrors of mass death within familiar plot structures that guaranteed a happy or at least reassuring ending. These war stories were aimed at an audience of children, but the adults who wrote and bought them must not have been immune to their comforting effect. While the lighthearted tone of children's war literature might seem sacrilegious and a strange contrast to the elevated rhetoric of sacrifice so essential to other Canadian writing about the war, Mosse asserts that such trivialization 'helped people confront war, just as its glorification did' (143).

This book begins with an examination of children's war work and the teaching of the war in Canadian schools. Then, in the second section, it turns to the wartime literature available to Canadian children. The chapters in this second section are organized by genre, beginning with materials for younger readers: the cautionary tale, the 'little folks of other lands' story, the deathbed story, the didactic domestic tale. The next chapter deals with the animal story as it was adapted to the subject and setting of the war. Two subsequent chapters are devoted to boys' adventure tales and to girls' stories. This division reflects the commonplace view of the time that, after a certain age, boys and girls wanted different kinds of excitement in their books. As Adeline Cartwright, children's librarian at the Dovercourt branch of the Toronto City Library, wrote in 1915, '... the tastes of boys and girls divide – girls ask for tales of home and school life; boys demand books of school, sport, adventure and war' (*School*, Sept. 1915: 45). Cartwright's perception was certainly shared by the publishers of children's war books, who produced sharply different series for girls and for boys. The editors of the Canadian Sunday-school papers tried to serve all readers with news items, games, puzzles, scriptural instruction, and editorials, but they too felt that girls and boys had different tastes: the papers usually ran two serial stories at the same time, one for boys and another for girls.

I then turn from the literature of the war years to more recent books. Since 1990, Canadian publishers have issued more than thirty books for children that deal in some way with the First World War. The axiom that children's war literature is a distillation of broader social attitudes still seems to hold: the modern consensus of revulsion at the tragic waste and criminal slaughter of the war is vividly present in these children's books. Perhaps also in evidence is the brutalizing effect of the war itself. It has become a historical commonplace to assert that the industrial slaughter of trench warfare led to a brutalizing of society in general, to a greater acceptance of violence as a political and social instrument, and to the lessening of certain taboos about representing it.[11] Certainly many of the modern historical novels about the war present scenes of violence and sorrow that no writer or publisher would have deemed acceptable for young readers of an earlier time.

Also evident is a greatly altered sense of the relationship between the individual and the community. In the wartime children's literature produced in Canada, doing one's duty at home, at school, at church was presented as the highest virtue. The corollary to this, often made explicit, was that having been trained in these smaller contexts, the good child would naturally graduate to performing his or her duty to the state. The individual's preservation of liberty, life, and private conscience counted for nothing beside the honour and necessity of doing one's duty. In the wartime literature, the patriotic requirement to serve trumps all other concerns, yet in the modern books it is consistently challenged. These contrasts between wartime literature and modern books remind us that Canadian attitudes towards conflict, patriotism, and duty have changed.

Children's literature, with all that it suggests of escapism, fantasy, and optimism, may seem far removed from the adult business of war. Yet the children's books nonetheless contain what

Audoin-Rouzeau calls 'the hard kernel of national cultures of war' (12). This is as true of modern Canadian children's books as it is of wartime publications. Just as the children's literature of the war years presented the images and myths that were central to Canadian thinking about their nation's struggle, so too the modern books reveal the place that the war now occupies in the national imagination.

# PART ONE

## Patriotic Training

# 1 Doing Their Bit

Perhaps you think that you can't do anything to help with the war. When you see the boys in khaki going down the street, you get a queer little choky feeling inside you, and you say to yourself, 'When I grow up, I'll be a soldier too.'

But you don't have to wait until you grow up, you know, for you can be the most helpful little soldiers that ever lived, without going outside your own home or school.

You can fight the Germans by fighting the enemies inside your heart. Did you ever think of that?

*King's Own*, 3 Aug. 1918

The fundamental contribution children were expected to make to the war effort was to behave well, not only to lighten the cares of war-weary parents, but also to demonstrate that they were worthy of the sacrifices being made on the battlefields. Good behaviour at home was encouraged by analogy to military service: 'Mother is your commanding officer. Don't forget to salute her, to pay her every respect and to obey her orders, for obedience to orders is the first and the biggest and most necessary thing that a soldier has to learn' (*King's Own*, 3 Aug. 1918: 124). This application of military terminology to family relationships manages to elevate Mother to a new and powerful role as 'commanding officer' of the home front while simultaneously confining her to domestic duties.

But good behaviour was only the most basic requirement of children in wartime. It might be all that the littlest ones could do, but much more was expected of older, more capable children. Children, especially those in farm families or impoverished urban households, were expected to be useful. Chores that have disappeared from the lives of modern Canadian children – bringing in wood, minding a string of younger siblings, collecting eggs, milking cows, weeding the garden, and, for the urban poor, scavenging coal – were part of children's lives in the past. Many children of this period, or at least people whom we would consider children, were workers, as the 1911 census, with its inclusion of persons over the age of fourteen in the count of the 'gainfully occupied,' demonstrated. (The census that year also collected this data using the age of ten as the lower limit of the working population, as had been the practice in previous censuses.) Another indication of the expectation that children would work is the way the military determined who would get separation allowance: it was sent to the children of soldiers who were widowers 'but only if [they] were obviously too young for employment (initially under fourteen for boys and sixteen for girls, raised in 1915 to fifteen and seventeen, respectively)' (Morton, 'Supporting' 203). Thus it was not much of a stretch to expect that children who already were essential working members of their families would, like other Canadians, lend their hands to the war effort.

Most of the war work done by Canadian children followed the division of labour described by Neil Sutherland in his study of Canadian children: 'In one category was work done mostly by girls, and in the other work done by both girls and boys' (115). In the peacetime circumstances described by Sutherland, girls did the indoor chores: caring for siblings, preparing meals, cleaning the house. Outdoor chores like splitting and piling wood were boys' work, unless there was no boy to do them, in which case they became girls' work (115). When it came to war work, this meant that boys gardened and did extra farm chores to raise money for patriotic causes, while girls did needlework and, on occasion, gardened and did farm chores. But the breaking down of gender divisions so often cited as a consequence of the First World War, with women taking up jobs in factories and offices, can also be observed in children's war work. This change was not solely a matter of girls taking on 'male' jobs such as harvesting and ploughing; there was movement in the other direction too. Norah Lewis asserts that when it came to the war effort, 'where and when necessary, girls did "boys' work" and boys did "girls' work"' ('Isn't this,' 202). For example, boys participated in the patriotic entertainments and bazaars organized by churches and schools. Some boys even learned to knit. The junior fourth class at Brown Public School in Toronto raised money for wool by making candy and selling it at school; then the students got to work and in three months made a total of '120 pairs of socks, 85 from the girls, 21 from the boys, and 14 from friends of the class' (*School*, Jan. 1918: 357). In 'Don's Knitting,' a story that appeared in the *King's Own* in December of 1918, a boy with a broken leg is encouraged to use his enforced idleness to knit for the soldiers. When he rejects this suggestion as unmanly, his sister scolds him:

'Why, may I ask, is it so degrading to your budding manhood? You'd play the piano or the banjo by the hour with those same fingers that I'm imploring you to use in a manner befitting a patriot.' (206)

Abashed, Don does learn to knit. That this is indeed a manly activity is reinforced when he visits a hospital for returned soldiers and sees that they are knitting too.

Throughout the nation, at school and at church, Canadian boys and girls were called upon to 'do their bit' for the war. It is clear from children's own accounts that they were enthusiastic home-front soldiers, happy to participate in the exciting activities that were being organized in aid of war causes. They also were concerned about the victims of war, and their letters indicate that they wanted to do what they could to alleviate the suffering of the war refugees, the soldiers' families, and the men at the front.

Were all Canadian children happy to knit socks and give up their hard-earned pennies? There must have been occasional slackers and resentful foot-draggers. But such children could always have been called to task by the example of the soldiers. It would have been a hard case indeed who could still hold out when reminded of how men – even their own fathers, brothers, cousins, or uncles – were dying on the battlefields.

3 Students and teachers on the steps of Central School, Lethbridge, 1915. Courtesy Galt Museum and Archives, Lethbridge, Alberta, image 19760231218.

**Raising Money**

Across the country, Canadians threw themselves into fund-raising campaigns for the Patriotic Fund, the Red Cross, and Belgian relief. Advertisements, tag days, bazaars, and patriotic entertainments made frequent calls on Canadians to remember the victims of war. Considering how little money children had at their disposal and their low earning power, the amounts they contributed to these causes were significant. The *King's Own* noted in 1917 that 'the school children in Canada in their giving to Red Cross and other war funds have proved once more how quickly small sums mount to large totals. For example, at the end of January, 1917, the Patriotic Fund of the Schools of the Province of Saskatchewan amounted to $24,888.69; while for Belgian relief Saskatchewan children have given no less than $50,530.91' (3 Nov. 1917: 175). In his annual report, A.E. Miller, inspector of schools in Revelstoke, British Columbia, noted the children's contributions:

> During the early part of 1916 a Children's Self-denial Fund was opened in a number of city and rural schools. In each of these schools the pupils were asked to contribute for patriotic purposes not less than 5 cents and not more than 25 cents each month, the money thus contributed to have been either saved or earned by themselves. (Forty-fifth Annual Report 1915–16: 38)

In Victoria, schoolchildren raised nearly $4,000 by collecting waste paper: 'The first $1,318 of the money realized from the sale of paper was applied to general Red Cross purposes. Then came the demand for ambulances for service in France, and the schools undertook through the paper collection to raise $3,000 for this purpose' (*Victoria*, Jan. 1918: 25).

The war years coincided with the height of the school garden movement, which aimed to teach practical skills, nature study, and the value of manual work. School gardens also provided an ideal way to raise money for war causes. J.W. Gibson, the very active director of elementary agricultural education for the province of British Columbia, noted in his report for the academic year 1915–16 the conjunction of 'Patriotism and Production':

4 Girls collecting paper for the Red Cross in Earlscourt, Toronto, 1916. Detail of a photograph by John Boyd, Library and Archives Canada, accession number 19710120, item 13713, PA-069938.

The work of the teachers and the pupils throughout the Province during the past year in raising money for patriotic and relief purposes has excited the wonder and the admiration of everybody ... In many cases boys and girls who cultivated home and school gardens sold the produce and gave the proceeds towards some one of these most worthy causes. These patriotic deeds will never be forgotten, especially by the boys and girls themselves. (Forty-fifth Annual Report 1915–16: 71)

In 1917, the campaign on 'Patriotism and Production,' which involved some 170 schools in British Columbia, raised 'the handsome total of $9,359.22' for the Patriotic Fund and the Red Cross (Forty-seventh Annual Report 1917–18: 53). In Ontario, a special potato-growing scheme was launched in which the Department of Agriculture supplied seed potatoes to schoolchildren. The children earned enough from the potato crop to buy an ambulance for the Red Cross (*School,* June 1917: 666). The potato program was in place as early as 1915: an editorial in the May 8 edition of the *Young Soldier* announced that 'the children of Ontario are being urged to grow potatoes this summer in order to raise money for some patriotic cause' (8). A similar scheme for 'patriotic potato growing' was established in Manitoba (*Western School Journal,* June 1916: 219). In a letter to the *King's Own,* Ruby Patton of Margaret, Manitoba, described her school's patriotic work: 'In the spring each family brought one pail of potatoes and we cut them and planted them at school. We are going to sell them and give the money to the Red Cross Sewing circle.' The editor of the letters column, hailing Ruby as a 'Popatriot,' noted that 'the schools in the West certainly seem to be doing a pretty big "bit" and we wish their good efforts all success' (15 Dec. 1917: 198).

Another way that young Canadians earned money was by taking on the chores of fathers and brothers who had gone to war. In her letter, Ruby also reported that 'a lot of girls from our school were out harvesting and threshing, pitching sheaves or drawing grain.' Another correspondent to the *King's Own,* Ellen Ada McFadden, aged eleven, of Glenboro, Manitoba, was also doing a man's job and contributing her wages to the war effort:

I help my brother plough at summer holiday time, as men are very scarce and having three brothers in the army I have but two

5 Pupils ready to work in school garden, Lang, Saskatchewan, ca 1917. Courtesy of Glenbow Archives, image NA-3329-27.

brothers left. I got fifty cents a day and seventy-five the last few days I plowed. I put three dollars in the bank and gave two to the Red Cross. (10 Feb. 1917: 24)

Enterprising Aubrey L. Manley, thirteen, of South Maitland, Nova Scotia, wrote that 'there are so many ways to earn money for the Red Cross and other funds':

> I milk two cows twice a day and get in the wood and do a lot more things to help my mother out. And she gives me money. But I don't go and buy candy. I give it to the Red Cross to buy yarn to knit socks for the soldier boys who are fighting for us all. Mother knits socks and she is a member of the Red Cross here. (*King's Own*, 5 May 1917: 72)

The churches, as part of their function as social and recreational centres, became involved in wartime fundraising. Elsie Earle, aged eleven, of Sudbury, described with excited anticipation the 'Red Cross Sale' being organized by her Sunday-school class:

> We are going to fix the room like a tent and trim it with flags and banners. We will charge 15 cents admission, which will get you a cup of coffee, some sandwiches and a piece of cake. We will sell household articles, such as dusters, towels, etc., also candies. We will wear middies and skirts with nurses' caps and red crosses on sleeves and caps. (*King's Own*, 27 Nov. 1915: 192)

In the fundraising initiatives they organized themselves, young Canadians showed resourcefulness and energy. In Richibucto, New Brunswick, thirteen-year-old Annie Bell and her school friends 'made a quilt and sold tickets on it,' raising $15.16 for the Red Cross (*King's Own*, 20 Oct. 1917: 168). In Baildon, Saskatchewan, Orma Mundell and her Sunday-school chums formed 'The Baildon Girls' Belgian Society' and held a bake sale in a store in Moose Jaw, raising $33 for 'the Belgian children' (12 Jan. 1918: 8).

**Making Comforts**

What a delightful pleasure to tell you of the discovery I made this

summer in my holidays! It is not a discovery like the people used
to have in olden times, but just a simple thing. But it is a very useful thing to discover when every boy and girl is expected to do
their bit. It is knitting.

What a pleasure it is to be able to do something really worth
while for our country, and the boys that are fighting so bravely for
us. (Myrtle Lloyd, age fourteen, Bradford, Ontario, in *King's Own*,
24 Nov. 1917)

In addition to raising money, children also made comforts –
the small items such as socks, wristlets, washcloths, and pyja-
mas that eased the hardships of life at the front. In September
1915, the readers' club of the *King's Own*, TOKO or The Order
of the King's Own, invited letters on the special topic 'For the
Soldiers.' Several submissions printed in the November 27 issue showed that indeed, as the *King's Own* put it, 'thousands of
boys and girls, everywhere in Canada, are helping in the great
work being done for the brave soldiers and sailors now fighting for our Empire' (27 Nov. 1915: 192). This 'great work' was
composed of many small and humble efforts. For example, Jean
Gollan, aged ten, of Morewood, Ontario, described how her
'sister and another girl gave a Red Cross tea for the girls. Thirty-
four came. We made 800 mouth wipes, 300 face clothes [sic],
ten triangular bandages.' Katie McLeod, aged twelve, rolled
bandages:

> We are doing a lot of things in Cobalt to help the soldiers, but
> I think the most interesting of all is rolling bandages. One time
> my father took a girl friend and me to the Masonic Hall, and we
> with two men rolled one hundred and twenty-two bandages. It was
> great fun, only I got my finger cut while tearing the cloth. (192)

Lest boys feel excluded from this work, the *King's Own* suggested
a project in its craft column:

> Since the knitting of socks, sweaters, scarfs and other comforts
> for soldiers is so general a wartime occupation, the yarn winder
> in Figure 1 will not go amiss in any household. So here's another
> chance for you to do your bit. Make a winder for your mother or
> sister. (23 Feb. 1918: 32)

Making a wool winder (which would enable the knitters in the
household to convert skeins into more manageable balls) was
presumably a task more appealing to the boys than the actual
knitting. Another practical task engaged in by Canadian children was
the 'News from Home' scheme. Writing in the 6 January 1915
issue of the *Christian Guardian*, W.A. Craick observed that although the adults on the home front were contributing to the
war, there was 'no special service that the children, as children,
could render in the cause of patriotism' (9). His article announced a new 'movement ... specially adapted for the young':

> Boys may despise knitting, but they will not feel it beneath their
> dignity to undertake this scheme. Girls may weary of sewing, but
> they will not soon tire of the new way of showing their practical
> patriotism. It is a plan that has already caught on splendidly, and
> is spreading over Canada with great rapidity. (9)

The plan was to prepare scrapbooks or 'budgets' containing
items from hometown newspapers. 'News from Home' was also
promoted in the *School* as a practical lesson in patriotism and a
way for children to 'do their bit for the men behind the guns'
(Feb. 1916: 489).[1] The Salvation Army's *Young Soldier* reported
in November 1915 that 'thousands of these books have been
sent away since the work was first taken up, and the men in the
trenches appreciate them very much. Every week a big bale containing seventy-five books leaves Toronto en route for the front'
(13 Nov. 1915: 8).

**The 'Second Line of Defence': Soldiers of the Soil**

> The Ontario High School boy, not old enough, or not strong
> enough perhaps to don the khaki, can in this great food crisis
> play a man's part and do a work hardly less important than that
> of our gallant boys in France. (Ruth McKinnon, Chatsworth High
> School, Ontario, winner of 1917 Essay Contest; quoted in B. Wil-
> son, 148–9)

The most overt recruitment of Canadian children in the war
effort was the Soldiers of the Soil Scheme, initiated in 1917 by

the Canada Food Board to alleviate the farm labour shortage. Some twenty-five thousand urban boys, aged thirteen to eighteen, went to help on Canadian farms during the war (N. Lewis, 'Isn't this' 202). The older ones, aged fifteen to nineteen, were sent to farms where they were needed; younger boys could work only for relatives, to ensure that they would be supervised and cared for. The circular sent from the Canada Food Board to British Columbia schools in 1918 explicitly identifies the scheme as war work: 'Every manly boy wants to do his share in winning the War and while his older brother and father may be in the fighting line in France, he has his chance to do his share by helping Canada to produce the food without which the War cannot be won.' The accompanying assignment letter addressed to SOS volunteers warned that the work would be 'very hard,' but 'if you will "carry on" with the same spirit as that which actuates the boys at the front, you will be successful' (British Columbia). Girls could also volunteer as 'Farmerettes,' but they were expected to find employment through parents or teachers.

In Ontario, where the program was administered by the Department of Public Works, a vigorous campaign promoting it among teachers, principals, students, and farmers resulted in the participation of nearly 9,000 secondary pupils – 4,867 boys and 4,036 girls – in the summer of 1917 (B. Wilson 149–51). This high rate of participation may have owed something to the fact that students who completed three months of farm work were given credit for the school year, even though they left school in April (149–50).

The program also ran in 1918. An advertisement in the 14 March 1918 issue of the *Catholic Register* was headlined 'Listen, boys, listen,' and presented an 'SOS' from the 'Boys in the Trenches':

> For the sake of those who are fighting for Canada, for the sake of our Allies who stand steadfast in this ordeal of battle,
>
> For the sake of your mother, your sister, for everything that manly boys hold dear, join up with the Soldiers of the Soil, and help farmers to grow food for us.
>
> If you could see this ghastly battle line we know you would jump right in and aid us. But because you are too young to get in at this end of the fight, 'do your bit' by working on a farm.

By the end of June, the *Register* reported that in Ontario '15, 000 boys have been enrolled [and] many [of] them are now on the land'; across the rest of the country, some five thousand more had signed up (27 June 1918: 3).[2]

## The Thrift Campaign

The war was an extremely costly undertaking for Canada. In 1915, military expenditures alone accounted for more than all government spending in 1913. The crushing cost of war had led to taxes on tobacco, alcohol, and patent medicines; in 1917, corporate and personal income taxes were introduced. By 1918, the federal government's war expenditures were exceeding $2.5 million per day ('Key Economic'). Unable to raise sufficient revenues through taxation, the government appealed directly to citizens to save food and fuel, and to lend their savings to the nation.

*The Canada War Book* (or *Canada War Thrift Book*, as it was called in Ontario) was prepared by the National War Savings Committee and published by provincial departments of education for distribution to students and teachers throughout the country. It begins with a direct address to its audience:

BOYS AND GIRLS OF CANADA – this book has been written especially for you. You know a great deal about the world-war and you have often wished that you were old enough to go to the front as soldiers or as nurses ... What can boys and girls do? They can save time; every day at school must be used to the best advantage so that when the boys and girls become men and women, they will be fitted to take the places of those who will never return from the battlefield. They can save food and fuel; this book explains why such saving is necessary. They can save money; Canada needs money. (3)

Boys and girls are encouraged to 'go "over the top" in a very real sense by saving money and lending it to Canada' (4). The calculations of what children could contribute were impressive:

Suppose every schoolboy and girl in Canada saved a quarter a week all through 1919 and lent it to the Government. In a year the

Government would receive from them nearly twenty million dollars – enough to pay for all the rifles and ammunition our soldiers use, provide them with boots, and leave a million or two over for other purposes. (42)

Although the aim of *The Canada War Book* was clearly to convince children of the importance of thrift and to harness them as workers and savers, it was not just a throwaway publicity pamphlet, as the preface to the New Brunswick edition declared:

The War Book is a text-book, and instruction from it should be given for at least five minutes each day by the teacher. Questions based upon it may be given upon examination papers. (i)

This 'text-book' provided the official view of the war. The first chapter, 'Why Canada Entered the War,' explains that 'this young western nation forsook its peaceful ways' because 'Great Britain is her MOTHER COUNTRY' and because 'she had done all she could honourably do to prevent war' (6). The chapter entitled 'What Germany Stands For' is equally emphatic: 'Germany stands for what we call MILITARISM' and 'TYRANNY' (14), 'TREACHERY,' 'ORGANIZED CRUELTY AND MURDER,' 'SLAVERY' (15), and 'ROBBERY' (16). The chapter on Canada's part in the war describes the formation of the First Contingent – 'eager men besieged the recruiting depots' (18) – and Canada's 'baptism of fire' at Ypres in 1915, where 'the Germans carried on a fierce bombardment and sent gas across again and again but the Canadians "stuck it"' (20). The description of Vimy is short on detail but long on enthusiasm: 'Vimy! What Canadian boy or girl can read of Vimy without a thrill!' (21).

The point of reciting the achievements of the Canadian soldiers (the account covers up to autumn 1918 and the taking of Cambrai) is to emphasize that they 'have done their duty magnificently' and that it is therefore up to citizens to do theirs (22). An impressive chart lists the needs of the half-million Canadian soldiers, ranging from '4000 machine guns' to '1,000,000 pints of tea or coffee per day' (25). Children are told that their purchase of four Thrift Stamps (worth $1) 'will feed a soldier for two days or ... buy two pounds of high explosives, or a pair of soldiers' socks, or 28 rifle cartridges; or will provide vaccine to

inoculate 20 men against smallpox, ... or will pay Canada's war
bill for 13/450 of a second. Are not these things well worth doing, and well worth saving money to accomplish?' (26).
Children across the country seem to have taken seriously this
new demand on their savings. In the November and December
1919 issues of *School Days*, a magazine for pupils in the Vancouver school district, readers were encouraged to contribute 5
cents to the 'Children's Tribute Campaign'; the magazine confi-
dently predicted that $25,000 would be raised by BC schoolchil-
dren. Jean MacKenzie of Georgetown, Ontario, reported in the
*King's Own* that her 'Sunday School bought two hundred and
fifty dollars worth of Victory Bonds.' Jean earned her contribution by 'minding the baby, shovelling snow, and other odd jobs'
(31 May 1919: 88).
Another dimension of the thrift campaign was the emphasis
on frugality. Canadian children were enjoined not to waste any
precious food or materials. The *King's Own* published small advertisements reminding children of their duty:

A War Word for the Week

Eat less wheat
Eat less meat
Eat nothing just for fun;
Save all you can
For the fighting man
And help to beat the Hun. (3 Aug. 1918: 124)

Children were also admonished to give up sweets of all kinds
'because sugar must be saved for the brave fighters' (*King's Own*,
28 Dec. 1918: 208).

## The Mission Schools

The war effort reached aboriginal children too. To judge by reports in the Anglican *Letter Leaflet*, the children in the church-
run residential schools, like other young Canadians, participated
enthusiastically in raising funds and making comforts. At the
school in Wabasca, Alberta, 'the children did their "bit" for the
Belgium Fund':

A bottle was placed on the Schoolroom table, and the children brought their bits of money and put into it. We would give them extra work to do and paid them for it, and off they rushed to put it in. They got $4. Then a lantern lecture was given and collection taken, which amounted altogether to $11. (Jan 1918: 91)

A mission schoolteacher on the Gibson Reserve reported that 'the little Indian boys and girls of the school ... have been working hard for the soldiers, making them handkerchiefs which they marked "G.R."' (Nov 1914: 8). A letter accompanied the handkerchiefs when they were forwarded to the front:

Dear Soldiers, I am a little boy from Gibson School. We made some handkerchiefs for the soldiers and we are going to send them to you and so I hope that the British army will win the victory and I hope that our soldiers will all come back safe and we hear that so many are dead and suffering, so I am very sorry for this war is going on. So I hope that the drummer-boy will get my handkerchief. So good-bye from
Alec Decaire
I am a Canadian boy. I will stand for my flag.

Did aboriginal children participate willingly in these activities, or was participation forced upon them as part of the Anglo-conformist program of the mission schools? One possible answer lies in what is known about the response of aboriginal adults to the war. Although the exact number of aboriginal soldiers is not known, about 4,000 aboriginal men enlisted (Summerby 5). This number represented about one in three of the able-bodied aboriginal men of military age – 'one of the highest enlistment rates of any ethnic community in the country' and 'nearly twice the national average' (Vance, *Death* 246). Aboriginal women also showed their support by contributing to patriotic causes. In British Columbia, for example, they helped the IODE's 'Committee on Field Comforts':

Remarkable among the various groups of women united in this service are the Native Indian Women, descendants of the original inhabitants of the Province and Island, who have contributed the wool used, spinning and carding it themselves, and have sent large

6 This picture, which appeared in the June 1916 issue of the *Letter Leaflet,* was captioned 'Louisa Geddes, Gordon's School – Knitting for the Soldiers.' Gordon's Indian Boarding School was located in Saskatchewan. Courtesy of The General Synod Archives, Anglican Church of Canada.

genuine concern about the victims of the war – the Belgian refugees, the Canadian soldiers on the front lines, the soldiers' families at home, the wounded animals. And this compassion motivated them to do what they could. They were also motivated by a very understandable desire to be part of the great struggle that had engrossed the attention of the adults around them. Children did not perceive participation in the war effort as onerous or burdensome. On the contrary, the bazaars, auctions, patriotic entertainments, tag days, paper collections, and sewing bees associated with war work were exciting social occasions; they were recreational activities in an era when, for most children, there were few diversions at home. The patriotism taught in school and the hatred of the enemy cultivated by many forms of propaganda doubtless played a role in motivating children to do their bit, but children also did it because they wanted to.

# 2 Studying War

That first year of the war was the most wonderful in the history of our school, as, I daresay, of all Canadian schools. There never was, there never could be again, a year like it. We were all in a state of patriotic exaltation, and the relationship of teachers and pupils became a much closer and finer thing than could have been possible under any other circumstances.

Nellie Spence, *The Schoolboy in the War*

A state at war depends on young children being raised to believe that '*dulce et decorum est pro patria mori.*'

Suzanne Evans, *Mothers of Heroes, Mothers of Martyrs*

At the time of the war, there were approximately 1.4 million children enrolled in Canadian public day schools – more than 80 per cent of children between the ages of five and fourteen (Phillips 182). By 1910, Canadian children on average were spending a total of eighty months in school, roughly about eight years of schooling (185). Compulsory attendance laws, which by the end of the war existed in every province except Quebec, contributed to a doubling of enrolments between the 1891 and 1921 censuses; much of the growth in student numbers reflected the rapid expansion of secondary schools (Tomkins 111).

But enrolment and actual attendance were two different things. Across the country, weather and chores interfered with schooling. By 1911, average daily attendance in Canadian schools was 'just a little better than 64 per cent' (Phillips 186).

An editorial in the *School* noted that attendance in Ontario rural schools in 1916 was only 68 per cent (April 1918: 552). In towns and cities, some children were not attending school because they were at work. Still, by the time of the war, the majority of Canadians under the age of fourteen were attending school for a considerable part of the year, and it was an important influence in their lives.

In the first decade of the twentieth century, despite changes in pedagogy, 'patriotism and morality as the oldest goals of the Canadian curriculum remained central aims' (Tomkins 143). The old tie between religion and morality was weakening, and Christian virtues were gradually being turned into civic ones: as one historian of education has put it, 'It now was not God but the Union Jack that told pupils to be brave, pure and true' (Van Brummelen 10). This shift made patriotism and morality conjoined goals: the virtuous citizen was a patriotic one. Just how intent some Canadians were on instilling patriotism in children is evident in *Raise the Flag* (1891), an anthology of Canadian verse prepared especially 'as the most appropriate remembrance' for Toronto students who had written prize-winning essays on 'raising the flag' (iii). The poems treat such topics as 'the romantic and touching story of the foundation of this Province by the United Empire Loyalists' and the War of 1812 (iii). According to the preface, 'the triumphant martial spirit of a victorious people breaks out exultingly in the poems of this war – Queenston Heights, the Capture of Detroit, and the brave exploit of Laura Secord being described in stirring verse' (iv). As a reward book rather than a textbook, *Raise the Flag* had a limited audience, but it reflects the unabashed patriotism and military pride that were thought suitable, indeed necessary, in Canadian classrooms.

A conspicuous military element in Canadian public education was the cadet corps. According to George Tomkins, by 1913 there were 759 corps in schools across the country (124); Desmond Morton reckons that by 1914 some '44,680 youngsters had drilled with various cadet corps' (*When* 4). Even those who did not become cadets were exposed to military drill when, under the auspices of the Strathcona Trust, a uniform style of physical training was implemented in schools across the country.[1]

Militarism was also evident in textbooks. In literary anthologies, for example, tales of warrior heroes abounded. In the fifth book of the *Victorian Reader* (1898; authorized for Manitoba and British Columbia), about 20 per cent of the selections are martial, including Thomas Moore's 'The Minstrel Boy,' Bayard Taylor's 'Song of the Camp' (about the British in the Crimean War), and Robert Southey's description of the death of Nelson. The reader also includes Gerald Massey's 'Scarlett's Three Hundred,' a poem about Waterloo, the last stanza of which demonstrates the adulation of the warrior hero and the blithe treatment of death on the battlefield:

> One cheer for the living! One cheer for the dead!
> One cheer for the deed on that hill-side red!
> The glory is gathered for England's proud head!
> Old England for Ever, Hurrah! (57)

The third book of the *Ontario Reader* (1909) is similarly rich in material about war, including Moore's 'The Minstrel Boy,' Bayard's 'Song,' Tennyson's 'Charge of the Light Brigade,' David Garrick's 'Heart of Oak' (the official march of the British Navy), an account of the relief of Lucknow by 'an officer's wife,' and Henry Newbolt's 'The Fighting Téméraire.' This last contains the hearty affirmation '*For we're all in love with fighting / on the Fighting Téméraire*' (274; italics in original). The *New Canadian Readers: Book IV* (1900; prescribed for use in British Columbia, New Brunswick, and Prince Edward Island) includes such staples as 'The Charge of the Light Brigade' and Kipling's 'Recessional,' but it also honours some Canadian war heroes: there are items on Daulac at the Long Sault, General Brock, and Laura Secord. Included too is William Collins's 'The Patriotic Dead,' which begins, 'How sleep the brave who sink to rest / By all their country's wishes blest' (133). (This poem is also known as 'Ode Written in 1746.') Among the prose selections is 'The Duty of Canadians,' an address given by Lord Roberts in 1908 in which he stated that 'it is absolutely essential, even at the present day, for the safety and welfare of a nation, that the whole male population should be prepared to take their share in its defence in times of danger. The training should, I think, commence with the boys ...' (113).

The militarist tone of Canadian textbooks was so pronounced that, after the war, pacifist groups such as the Society of Friends

and the Women's International League for Peace and Freedom
campaigned for revision of all textbooks to ensure that children would no longer read of the glory of war; instead, as J.S.
Woodsworth put it, they should be taught 'the futility and sui-
cidal tendency of modern war' (quoted in Socknat, *Witness* 112).
Even before the war, there was criticism, particularly from the
Quakers, of the militarist tendencies in Canadian education. In
1904, Andrew Stevenson, a Quaker and teacher at Stratford Collegiate, decried the fact that 'in too many public schools and private academies some of the teaching, so far from inculcating the
principles of peace, is directly calculated to foster the spirit of
international hatred and war' (5). He maintained that 'it is the
business of the teacher of history to teach not patriotism, but the
truth' (10). Stevenson also objected to some literary selections
on the curriculum, especially Tennyson's 'Charge of the Light
Brigade,' with its lines 'Theirs not to reason why, / Theirs but to
do or die.' Stevenson claimed that 'it is this view that, more than
any other, is responsible for the continuance of the horrors of
war. It is blind obedience that makes these things possible' (28).
A Saskatchewan school inspector similarly 'deplored [the] war-
like spirit' that such materials cultivated (Tomkins 124). There
was some opposition to cadet training: the Women's Christian
Temperance Union in 1909 'had introduced resolutions against
such programmes in the schools' (Allen 334). But these were
isolated voices of protest, and not until the 1920s would there
be widespread and politically effective opposition to militarist
textbooks and to the cadet corps (Socknat, *Witness* 112–15).

Given that the pre-war curriculum was already suffused with
imperial nationalism and a reverence for military heroes, there
was no need for drastic change when war broke out. Canadian
schools quickly took on the task of teaching the war and of preparing their students to take their place in it. Like the French
schools described by Stéphane Audoin-Rouzeau, schools in English Canada became 'privileged vectors of the mobilization and
the organization of a war propaganda aimed at children' (24).[2]

In late 1914, the Department of Education of Ontario issued
a circular directing that the 'causes and the interests at stake, as
well as the relations thereto of the different nations directly or
indirectly concerned' in the war 'shall form part of the course
of study in History in every school of the Province so far as they

can be intelligently taken up in the different grades' (quoted in *School*, Jan. 1915: 302). The circular also 'intimates to all candidates concerned' that departmental examinations in English, Canadian, and European history 'will contain one or more questions' about the war. This directive was relatively limited and specific, but the war's place in the school soon began to spread out from history courses to affect other areas of the curriculum. How this happened can be observed in the wartime issues of *School: A Magazine Devoted to Elementary and Secondary Education.* Published by the Faculty of Education of the University of Toronto, the *School* served predominantly the teachers of Ontario. In its editorials, book reviews, and articles, the *School* not only argued for the moral and patriotic imperative to teach the war, but also supplied the information that would enable teachers to do so.[3]

## Teaching the War

In September 1914, the editors of the *School* were moderate, even ambivalent, in their discussion of the war. Although they displayed utter confidence in the righteousness of the Empire's cause, they were clearly reluctant to see the schools swept up in the fervour of war:

> We teachers stand in a complex relation to the war. As citizens we have the responsibilities of citizens who love their country. As instructors of youth it is our duty to shape the opinions and the future conduct of the citizens [of] to-morrow.
>
> Throughout the coming school year it is probable that we shall all be called upon daily to discuss the war, its cause, its course, and its events. Shall we not strive to lead our pupils to look upon this war without anger or hatred towards the German people? .... We begin this war not in exultation but in sorrow. (4)

As the war went on, the *School* moved inexorably towards a more bellicose view. This shift reflected a similar change in the larger society. Before the war, reformers of all kinds had embraced pacifism. In his study of Canadian pacifism, *Witness against War*, Thomas Socknat gives numerous examples of the support for general pacifist principles in pre-war Canada. The Women's Christian

Temperance Union had a Peace and Arbitration Department; so, too, did the Canadian National Council of Women (32). The Presbyterian Church of Canada endorsed the Canadian Peace and Arbitration Society, a secular organization founded in 1905 and supported by many political and religious leaders (29–30). But, according to Socknat, 'the pre-war peace movement more or less disintegrated with the shock of war,' and most peace advocates 'agreed with the majority of their fellow Canadians that the war was unfortunate but necessary to rid the world of European militarism' (45). This movement towards acceptance of the war as morally necessary is evident in the editorial in the January 1915 issue of the *School*, 'War and the Teacher,' written presumably in response to the news of German atrocities:

> Public feeling is intense. A war unjustly thrust upon us, atrocities that belong to the Middle Ages, an accursed espionage system have combined to develop passions that are well-nigh uncontrollable. These may at any time break out into excesses of thought and word, if not of physical action. What may they not do when the casualty lists contain the names of the Canadian soldiers who are soon to be in the firing line? We *must* be calm. Above all, we Canadian teachers, as sponsors for public security *must* 'keep our heads.' (302)

Two months later, in March of 1915, the *School* published a special issue devoted entirely to the war. The opening editorial exhorted teachers to participate wholeheartedly in the war effort: 'It is the Empire's war. It is Canada's war; Canadians must believe in it, pay for it, and help to win it! If this is to be done all Canadians, adults and children, must know the war and we schoolmasters must teach it' (442).

The articles in this special issue covered a variety of topics, ranging from 'The Causes of the War' to 'The Colonies and the War,' 'The Naval Campaign,' and 'The Canadian Militia.' Many of these articles were continued and updated in subsequent issues: 'Diary of the War,' 'War Maps and How to Use Them,' and 'Glossary of Military Terms' became regular features. So, too, did 'Questions on the War,' which over the months provided teachers with a bank of possible examination questions. Book reviews in the special issue covered items suitable for children:

*From the Trenches*, by Geoffrey W. Young, was praised as 'so clearly written, in such simple language, that children will enjoy it. It will give them a much more concrete idea of the effects of war than they can get from many other sources' (481). There were also reviews of items more suitable for high-school students and for teachers, such as General von Bernhardi's *Britain as Germany's Vassal* (493).

An article entitled 'Devices for Teaching War History' suggested that bulletin boards should display 'the pictures of the men of the hour' because 'every Canadian boy and girl should recognise, at sight, the pictures of King George, Premier Asquith, Sir Edward Grey, Winston Churchill, Lloyd George, Lord Kitchener, and General French' (506). The Library Table should offer 'copies of the important documents, famous speeches, etc., ... along with magazine articles, editorials clipped from our best English, American and Canadian papers ... [so that] any pupil whose work is finished and correct could be given the privilege of going to this table to read.' The author also suggested that a 'relief map of the western war area,' executed in Plasticine, with the armies marked by their respective flags, could add to the war information in the classroom.

Advertisements, too, emphasized the war. Copp, Clark's full-page ad was headed 'Notable War Books' (509). The Musson ad announced the publication of 'Important War Books' (511). The tag line in the McClelland, Goodchild and Stewart ad was 'Leading War Books' (513). Even the humorous filler was war-related, mostly borrowed from *Punch*:

> Little Girl (saying her prayers at her mother's knee) – 'and please God make me a good girl. Amen. How would it be, mother, to give the Germans cigarettes filled with gunpowder?' (462)

In 'The War and the Schools,' Professor W.E. MacPherson of the Faculty of Education at Queen's argued that history teachers should 'make clear at least to our older pupils something of the principles as well as the material interests at stake' and show 'the evidence that Great Britain exhausted all the resources of diplomacy to keep the peace' (498). But 'the main task' of the teacher 'will be to clarify and correct impressions, to organise materials, to explain historic backgrounds, and to imbue his discussions with the spirit of the love of truth and honour, and of a just and sane patriotism, strong to endure and willing to make fit sacrifice in a great cause' (499). This was the sort of history teaching that A. Stevenson, the Quaker teacher, had decried as more about patriotism than about truth.

In 1915, the *School* published four war numbers, and during 1916 it published six (Sept 1916: 58). This material 'proved so popular' that it was issued in book form. In the next month's 'Notes and News' column, the book was promoted as containing 'valuable material which has been tested by actual classroom use' (Oct. 1916: 128). While the *School* maintained its pre-war function – to supply news of interest to teachers and articles on pedagogy aimed at teachers of all levels and subjects – war remained a constant theme.

The editors of the *School* did not lose sight of the need to engage younger pupils in the study of war. A second bulletin issued by the Department of Education of Ontario, reproduced in the *School* in December 1915, suggested that in Forms I and II 'the teacher should content himself with stories ... of persons, places and peoples made prominent by the War' (348). For the next grade, 'he should add ... accounts of great events from the current history of the War and readings from "The Children's Story of the War."' In order to make this instruction 'concrete,' teachers were advised to include 'oral composition, with pictures and maps from journals and papers, with models of boats, airplanes, etc., from the manual training department, and with visits, where practicable, to training grounds, model camps, aircraft exhibitions, etc.' (348).

In February 1916, Helena V. Booker, a teacher in Hamilton, wrote about the problem of teaching the war to the youngest pupils:

What shall we say about the present war to our primary classes? We feel a great reluctance to bring so unhappy a subject before such young minds. But what do they hear at home? Many times only words of hatred, ignorant tirades, useless bragging, equally vain of purpose and harmful in their imprint on young minds. So if we speak of war let it be with the sole purpose of teaching patriotism, a love of our own country, not a hatred of our enemies – a positive, not a negative, thing. (562)

Booker recommended that all children recite the Empire
Pledge: 'I give my hand, my head, my heart to my country – One
King, One Empire, One Flag – I pledge myself to do my duty
always, and to love and serve my country forever' (562). She
also advised primary teachers to 'teach patriotic songs ... that
are pure, inspiring, uplifting, not those that brag of "mailed fist"
and revenge.' She recommended stories of heroism, but 'omit-
ting all horrors and details which are beyond the comprehen-
sion of primary pupils.'

The curricular focus of war instruction was clearly history and
geography, but the war was not to be confined to just those subjects: 'under the stimulus of the war, history, geography, the applied sciences, drawing, composition, and even literature have
taken on a new life as school subjects!' (March 1915: 442). For
'picture study' in art classes, the *School* advocated James Clark's
*The Great Sacrifice* (Jan. 1916: 428–9). This painting features a
fallen soldier in the foreground (with one neat bullet hole in
his left temple and no other visible wound), while above him
towers the crucified Christ. An editorial note advised teachers to
purchase a reproduction of this painting, in which 'by a wonderfully consoling conception the artist has linked the divine and
the human in the act of supreme sacrifice' (428). The equation
of the fallen soldier with the crucified Christ was, as Jonathan
Vance has pointed out, 'a solution to the problem of maintain-
ing the relevance of Christianity in the face of the war' (*Death*
36). It provided an analogy that made sense of the war, for 'just
as Jesus had given his life so humanity could survive, so too did
the soldiers offer their life for humanity' (36). One can only
speculate how children might have been affected by close study
of *The Great Sacrifice*, but, given that most would have believed in
the literal truth of Christ's crucifixion and its redemptive power,
it is hard to imagine a more powerful sanction for war. If death
on the Western Front could be equated with Christ at Calvary,
then surely the war was necessary and even good. As far as the
*School* was concerned, 'the lessons so powerfully portrayed by
this picture' were clear: 'At an inestimable cost of precious lives
the Empire is striving to pass on to the children a heritage of
unsullied national honour and of true British freedom, and,
moreover, by the sacrifices which the great war demands it is
bringing into closer intimacy the human with the divine' (428).[4]

It is difficult to gauge at this distance just how much of the war material provided by the *School* and by departments of education actually found its way into classrooms. But, given what Ramsay Cook has described as 'the conformist, nationalist mood which the war spirit stimulated in Canadian society' (198), it seems likely that most teachers taught the war dutifully, if not enthusiastically. Robert Stamp notes that in 1915, teachers in Hamilton were required to assert that they were 'pro-British' and 'Loyal British Subject[s], or else face dismissal' (Hamilton Board of Education Minutes, quoted in Stamp, *Schools* 95). In 1915, a teacher at the Annette Street School in Toronto was suspended when a trustee, acting on an anonymous letter from parents, accused him 'of uttering pro-German sentiments while discussing the war with his pupils' (quoted in B. Wilson xcviii).[5] One might also consider the case of Freda Held, a teacher at Carleton Street School, who resigned in early 1918 when she was accused of disloyalty. That Held could be hounded into resigning from her post – even though the parents of her students supported her – suggests that resisting pressures to be pro-war was a risky undertaking for educators (B. Wilson xcix, 155–7).[6]

In any case, because final examinations contained questions on the war, teachers could hardly endanger their students' results by avoiding talk of it. In British Columbia, a question on British history on the 1916 high-school entrance examination required students to identify the event associated with each of ten locations; the list included not only Agincourt, Bannockburn, and Lucknow, but also Gallipoli, Kut-el-Amara, and Ypres.[7] In the spelling exam, among the thirty-three words to be tested were 'Dardanelles,' 'Vosges,' and 'contingent.' Students writing the composition exam in 1917 were required to identify clauses, phrases, and adjectives in the following passage:

> Waddling over the scarred and pitted ground, which rendered Vimy Ridge the more difficult to cross, the uncouth tanks, like prehistoric monsters in appearance, steadily advanced to destroy the strongholds of the machine gun, while the brave Canadians, eager to close with the enemy, clambered over the tangled debris left by the ceaseless pounding of the British guns.

The presence of war in so many aspects of the curriculum sug-

gests that by at least the beginning of high school, children were
well informed about the conflict. Some of their knowledge had
come from home and from magazines and newspapers. But the
school was undoubtedly the most important source. The director of British Columbia's Free Textbook Branch observed that
schools needed to supplement what children were learning at
home: 'The little pitchers with big ears have been taking in a
good deal of war-talk, and public-school teachers have naturally
found a fresh interest in giving intelligent direction to these new
ideas. The older children, too, ought to have their ideas about
the war developed' (Forty-fourth Annual Report 1914–15: 94).
A school inspector in British Columbia applauded what the provincial ministry had done in making war materials available to
students:

> By its issue (to all the schools) of the 'Children's War History'
> and of suitable war pamphlets, in particular that dealing with
> the 'Scrap of Paper,' the Department has clearly indicated its at-
> titude in the matter. In this fourth year of the war its events are
> fast becoming history and as the children grow up in this war-time
> environment they should, according to their capacity, be led to
> understand the meaning of the mighty struggle, and to worthily
> appreciate that spirit of self-sacrifice which has prompted those
> noble deeds of heroism which are of daily occurrence, and which
> have too often involved the loss of loved ones. (Forty-sixth Annual
> Report 1916–17: 38)

To teach the war was not just a matter of instilling in students
some new facts of history or geography; it was a moral endeav-
our that would uplift the character of Canadian children and
young people. Perhaps the strongest demonstration for students
of the moral seriousness of the war was the departure of their
male teachers for the battlefields. An editorial in the January
1916 issue of the *School* noted that while teachers had 'special
duties' to teach the war and to 'aid all patriotic, Red Cross, and
recruiting organizations,' they also had 'the duties common to
the citizens of Canada' to 'fight in the trenches and nurse in the
hospitals' (393). There followed a 'Teachers' Honour Roll' listing the teachers from Alberta, Manitoba, New Brunswick, Nova
Scotia, Ontario, and Saskatchewan who had joined up (393–6).

In an article in the socialist *Canadian Forward* in 1918, the pacifist and suffragist Gertrude Richardson warned Canadian mothers about the 'unspeakable horror' of the 'militarisation' of schoolchildren (10 March 1918: 3). She cited a British teacher's manual that outlined military drill for cadets and suggested ways to direct every school subject towards topics of military value. Alarmed by this trend in British education, Richardson called on Canadian mothers to be vigilant: 'let us begin by watching carefully all that goes on in our schools,' so that militarists would not be able to place 'the bayonet and the rifle ... in the hands of children to whom we try to teach the ideals of humanity and brotherhood.' Richardson, perhaps because she lived in relative isolation in Swan River, Manitoba, seemed unaware of the extent to which the war had already become part of the Canadian curriculum.

**War Materials**

Teachers would have had no difficulty obtaining appropriate materials for the study of war. The special war numbers of the *School* and its regular features such as 'Diary of the War' provided extensive information. In Manitoba, the 1915 issue of the *Empire Day Annual,* published by the Ministry of Education and distributed to every school, provided in a question-and-answer format several pages of background material on the war. British Columbia schools were issued a copy of the 'Scrap of Paper,' which the Textbook Branch described as 'a translation and a facsimile of signatures from the original treaty of 1831 guaranteeing the independence and neutrality of Belgium, ... the breaking of which by Germany is responsible for the present war with Great Britain' (Forty-fifth Annual Report 1915–16: 78). The 'Scrap of Paper' was to 'be suitably framed and hung in a conspicuous place in every school-room.'

For their part, the commercial publishers were remarkably swift to provide war-related materials. The most important and certainly the most ambitious of these was Sir Edward Parrott's *The Children's Story of the War.* Aimed at British boys and girls, it was nonetheless considered appropriate for Canadian children, for they too were children of the Empire. The edition sold in Canada carried the imprint of Thomas Nelson and Sons,

Toronto.[8] Parrott had been an editor with Nelson since 1898 and was widely respected as the author of successful textbooks such as *Pageant of British History* and *Pageant of English Literature*, he was also the editor responsible for the Highroads series. He began the *Children's Story* in late 1914 and over the next five years produced ten volumes, running to more than three thousand pages in total.

There is no question that the *Children's Story* reached large numbers of Canadian children. In Ontario, a 1915 bulletin issued by the Department of Education prescribed it 'for use in Forms III, IV, and V of the Public and Separate Schools and in the Lower School of the High and Continuation Schools and Collegiate Institutes' (quoted in *School*, Dec. 1915: 349). Nelson's advertisements proclaimed it 'the most popular book in the schools.' In British Columbia, David Wilson, the head of the Textbook Branch, noted in his report for 1914–15 that the Education Department had ordered the first six numbers of the *Children's Story* for all the school libraries of the province and would continue to acquire it 'until the end of the war' (Forty-fourth Annual Report 1914–15: 94–5). The following year, Wilson reported that 'thus far all the schools of the Province have been supplied with Nos. 1 to 18 of "The Children's Story of the War"' (78). This represented a substantial quantity – some 1, 291 copies of numbers 1 to 6 and 1,749 copies of numbers 7 to 9 (76). Wilson's concern about the condition of the instalments – 'It is again urged that early steps be taken by School Boards to have the accumulated numbers of "The Story" suitably bound, as they will thus form not only a valuable but a permanent addition to the school library' (74) – suggests that the individual numbers were being well used in British Columbia schools. In Toronto, a survey on 'purely voluntary reading' conducted in a special reading room for high-school students in the Western branch of the public library found that, among the thirty-seven periodicals left on the reading table, eight were numbers of the *Children's Story* (*School*, April 1917: 469).

One wonders, however, whether anyone, short of Parrott himself, actually read the entire series. It deals in tremendous detail with campaigns ranging from the China Sea to South West Africa, from the capture of Trebizond in Turkey to the Isonzo front in Italy, from Kut-el-Amara to Ypres. Key battles on the Western

Front are reported as they unfolded hour by hour. Nor does Parrott neglect what happened on the seas. Naval engagements ranging from the Heligoland Bight and Jutland to the blocking of Zeebrugge Harbour are reported in detail, as is the sinking of the *Lusitania*. There are chapters on submarine warfare and on war in the air. Always mindful of his role as an educator, Parrott provides extensive background on every leader and nation involved in the war. This background undoubtedly was regarded as fulfilling the educational mission of the series, but perhaps it also served as convenient content in the absence of fresh or detailed information from the scenes of war.

As a publishing project in time of war when paper and labour were in short supply, the *Children's Story* is impressive, not merely for its length but also for the high editorial standards Parrott and his firm maintained. Attractive vignettes appear at the beginning of each number. Detailed sketch maps orient readers to battlefields on every front. The numbers are illustrated with photos or drawings from such publications as the *London Illustrated News* and the *Sphere* (sometimes as two-page spreads).

One has to admire Parrott's achievement, too, not merely for the apparently endless reserves of writing energy he possessed (his output over the five years of the war reached near-Dickensian proportions) but also for his mastery of a friendly tone, and his ability to range over the varied scenes of a vast and complex conflict. Moreover, month after month, year after year, he managed to extract a comprehensible narrative from what must have been very fragmentary reports. Nevertheless, the *Children's Story* is undiluted propaganda, coherent but tendentious. Parrott was an active member of the Liberal Party (he became the MP for an Edinburgh constituency in 1917) and, according to Michael Paris, was 'almost certainly known' to Charles Masterman (14). Masterman, the director of Britain's propaganda efforts during the war, recruited writers such as John Masefield, John Buchan, and Sir Gilbert Parker to produce literary materials that denounced pacifism and promoted Britain's cause (Buitenhuis 14-15). Paris concludes that 'it is likely that his history was written at [Masterman's] instigation' (14). As archivist Andrew Young points out, 'In all 56 issues, there is only one instance of the author gathering information first-hand, found in issue No. 54

... The other stories, we can surmise, came through government channels' (20).

Parrott begins the *Children's Story* in leisure: the entire first volume deals with the background to the war, including very long excursions into such matters as the history of Prussia, the Napoleonic Wars, the childhood and education of the Kaiser, and the life stories of Joffre and Kitchener. Parrott does not even get to the fighting until early in volume 2, when he discusses the Fall of Namur, which took place in August of 1914. At the end of volume 2, he is still on the events of 1914. At frequent junctures throughout the succeeding volumes, he stops to review the causes of the war and to bring newly arrived or forgetful readers up to the moment in their understanding. One can see that, as the war ground on, Parrott began shortening his accounts and losing his appetite for detailed digressions and descriptions. For example, by the time he reaches 1916 and the disastrous failure at the Dardanelles, he does not have much heart for recording it: 'The Gallipoli campaign was a diversion that did not succeed – a side-show that failed. I shall not, therefore, describe the progress of the fighting in full detail' (20: 266).[9] Similarly, the grim months on the Somme after the 'Big Push' in July of 1916 seem to have exhausted Parrott as they did the soldiers:

> I should weary you very much, and you would not be greatly enlightened, if I were to tell you of the little encounters which took place. The gains which resulted look very small on the map, but you must remember that they were only won by a courage and hardiness that was truly heroic. For weeks together men fought in slimy pits up to their waists in water, and frequently were very hungry, for the work of bringing up supplies was terribly difficult. (32: 253)

Despite the discouragement that Parrott must certainly have felt as the war and his task seemed to stretch into infinite distances, he managed to maintain throughout the fifty-six numbers of the *Children's Story* a remarkably consistent tone. The same messages about Britain and the conduct of the war are present throughout the entire series. If indeed the *Children's Story* was used in classrooms and consumed eagerly at the library table, it taught

Canadian children not just a set of facts about the war but also a
set of national and imperial values.

## Heroism

Certain words recur regularly throughout Parrott's work: 'hero,'
'gallant,' 'splendid,' 'nobly.' The frequency of these words does
not merely reflect the possibility that Parrott's imaginative energies occasionally flagged. It also indicates Parrott's unrelent-
ing focus on what he believed children wanted to know: that
the men who were fighting and dying were heroes. Much has
been written about the cult of the military hero in boys' adventure stories. Mark Moss describes it 'as a virtual industry in the
years leading up to the Great War' (54). The hero was not only
a narrative figure or a personal ideal: 'For a country as young as
Canada, the hero – Canadian, British, or American – became
the model of the supreme citizen' (55).

Once the war had begun, the notion that all Allied soldiers
were heroes became an indispensable theme. The very structure
of Parrott's series acknowledges the centrality of the hero in accounts of the war. With every description of a British engagement, whether on the Western Front or in one of the distant
campaigns in the Middle East or Africa or on the seas, Parrott
includes chapters on individual achievements. These chapters,
variously titled – for example, 'Soldiers' Stories of the Battle,'
'More Soldiers' Stories of the "Great Push,"' 'Sailors' Stories of
the Battle of Jutland,' 'Heroes of the Air' – recount the deeds
and impressions of individuals (often in first person), taken
from dispatches and newspaper accounts. As a Nelson's advertisement pointed out, Parrott's history 'dwell[s] mainly on those
incidents of heroism and self-sacrifice which specially appeal to
children' (*School*, Feb 1915: 433).

After each campaign or major battle there also appears a
chapter (or even chapters) devoted to those who won the Victoria Cross for their part in it, with such titles as 'The Beadroll of
Honour' or 'Valorous Deeds and Victoria Crosses.' In the first
of these, devoted to VCs won during the Retreat from Mons (23
August to 5 September 1914), Parrott's story of Lance-Corporal
Charles Alfred Jarvis, who fired the charges that broke down the
bridge at Jemappes, exhibits the reverent tone that will char-

acterize all his many subsequent VC stories: 'For this deed he was rightly enrolled in that glorious band of heroes who have wrought and fought and died to make us inheritors of deathless fame' (6: 42). When he comes to enumerating the VC winners in early 1917 (this time requiring three successive chapters), Parrott seems aware of the repetitiveness of his structure: 'Once more I return to the inspiring task of recording those outstanding deeds of heroism and self-sacrifice which glorify the work of war' (39: 307). Despite his celebration of VC winners, Parrott maintains the fiction that every soldier is a hero: 'Every battalion, nay, every company, in the British army, glories in its roll of heroes, all of whom, whether they received recognition or not, were worthy of a place on the highest roll of fame' (27: 325).

A special type of hero celebrated in the *Children's Story* is the child hero. Audoin-Rouzeau has described the 'typology' of the child hero in France: 'the child who goes off to war with a regiment, the child who has saved those who are older than he (either civilians or combatants), the child who refused to give information to the enemy or, taking an even greater risk, provided information to his compatriots' (131). Stories of such children, presented as 'absolutely authentic,' abounded in French war propaganda (130). Audoin-Rouzeau does not dismiss these accounts as pure invention: '... like everything related to heroism in time of war, the child-hero is obviously an artificial creation, but one which probably has its origin in some actual facts' (131). Once created, the child-heroes had a far-reaching existence. Some of those listed by Audoin-Rouzeau as the most frequent in French propaganda (135) also found their way into the *Children's Story*: for example, Louise Haumont, 'a little girl of twelve years of age' who goes to warn the commander of Fort Troyon that the Germans are coming (9: 228); and Emilienne Moreau, 'a pretty girl of eighteen,' who becomes 'the heroine of Loos' when she shoots two snipers (21: 355). Parrott also tells us about a boy who is 'probably the youngest sergeant in the world ... Prudent Marius, a French boy of fourteen, scarcely four feet in height,' who 'in spite of his youth ... was quite indifferent to shell and rifle fire' (10: 267–8). Parrott also includes examples of Russian children who go to war, including a group of girls who cut their hair and disguise themselves as boys (20: 308).

In contrast to the proliferation of child-heroes in French war propaganda, only one British child-hero acquired any degree of fame: Jack Cornwell, killed during the Battle of Jutland. The admiral's citation describes his brave action:

> Boy (First Class) John Travers Cornwell of 'Chester' was mortally wounded early in the action. He nevertheless remained standing alone at a most exposed post, quietly awaiting orders, until the end of the action, with the gun's crew dead and wounded all round him. His age was under 16½ years. (Quoted in Parrott 26: 294)

In his treatment of Cornwell's heroic death, Parrott emphasizes the moral lesson to be taken from his example: 'As a schoolboy he was in no way distinguished. His master described him as "an ordinary English boy." God grant that all British boys, wherever they might dwell, may be as "ordinary" as he!'

In his celebration of heroes, Parrott slips easily into the mode of the adventure tale. He introduces an anecdote about the capture and subsequent rescue of British sailors by suggesting that it 'sounds as if had been lifted bodily from the pages of a boy's book of adventure' (24: 132). A similar promise introduces another anecdote, this time about a British officer who was court-martialled for a 'mistake of judgment' during the Retreat from Mons, but who subsequently rehabilitated himself by enlisting in the French Foreign Legion: 'It sounds as though it were taken from a boy's book of adventures; but it is true – every word of it – and serves as another illustration of the old saying that truth is stranger than fiction' (31: 200). The protagonist of this story, as described by Parrott, is certainly the equal of any *Boy's Own* hero: 'Lieutenant-Colonel John Ford Elkington ... [was] a typical British officer – clean-cut, and lithe of limb, with frank, fearless, yet kindly eyes.'[10]

A further example involves a child-hero during the Easter Uprising in 1916. Parrott begins by describing how, on the Irish shore near Tralee, a man discovered an abandoned boat and some weapons. As he points out, 'Does not this sound like the opening of a detective story which promises to be most exciting?' (25: 215). Later in the account, 'a schoolboy named Martin Collins, a very smart lad of twelve and a half,' notices a man (who turns out to be Roger Casement) drop a piece of paper.

Martin retrieves the paper from a ditch and turns it over to the authorities. In true adventure-story fashion, Martin's quick thinking proves crucial in uncovering the rebels' plot:

> The paper was afterwards discovered to be a German code, which contained such messages as the following: 'Railway communications have stopped. Our men are out. Further men are needed. Further rifles are needed. How many rifles will you send us? Send another ship to ___' (216)

The line between such incidents and the exploits of a *Boy's Own* hero is very blurred indeed. The *Children's Story* was promoted and used as a textbook, a cross between reportage and history book; a reviewer in the *School* praised it as 'giv[ing] the pupils the narrative of the great struggle in language they can understand' (Dec. 1915: 333). But it was not just a question of language; it was also a matter of plot and tone. Children could understand the anecdotes in the *Children's Story* because they resembled adventure stories. Undoubtedly, this adventure-story element was appealing, but it also perpetuated the picture of war retailed in the boys' adventure books and serial stories. The excitement of the stories, the zest of the fighters, the triumph of the British hero because of his Britishness, the heroic opportunities in war for the quick-thinking lad – all these notions of warfare that were staples in the adventure tales pervaded Parrott's account.

**Service and Sacrifice**

One of the war's most important lessons for children was the value of doing one's bit and contributing in whatever fashion one could to the war effort. The *Children's Story* had its own initiatives for readers. Early in the war, the readers were asked to contribute to a fund to purchase an ambulance for the Belgians. Later in the war, the *Children's Story* started the Serbian Boys' Fund. In the second chapter of Number 22 – 'Dark Days in the Near East' – Parrott describes at length how, following the defeat of the Serbian army, 'the Serbian mothers, knowing that the hope of the nation lay in its children, sent their boys to follow the army to the sea' (20). He makes their story heart-rending:

It is said that some 18,000 of these poor lads began the journey, but that only half of them ever reached the sea. For months afterwards the wild hills of Serbia and Albania were strewn with the bones of the children who had perished. (20–1)

Some of the survivors were brought to Britain, and the fund was aimed at supporting and educating them. In number after number of the *Children's Story* there were advertisements for the fund, listing the names of contributors to date. Canadian children contributed about a third of the total amount collected by the fund.

**National Character**

In Parrott's version, every aspect of the war – its causes, its progress, its horrors, and its triumphs – could be explained in terms of national character. The British character, as revealed in the deeds of British soldiers and sailors, is consistently upheld as the model young readers should emulate. Britons were men of their word who fought according to the time-honoured rules of battle. They were also cheerful and cool in the face of danger. The most explicit description of British character appears in Parrott's account of the sinking of the *Tyndareus* in 1917 off the African coast southeast of Cape Town. When the *Tyndareus* hit a mine, it began to go down. (Fortunately, all the passengers were rescued because the ship's radio, undamaged by the explosion, was used to summon help.) On board was a battalion of the Middlesex Regiment, and its commander, Colonel John Ward, ordered his men to stay calm. Parrott uses this event as a moral lesson:

I want all boys and girls who read these pages to ponder deeply over this story, and to determine that, if ever they should find themselves in a similar situation, they will 'be British' in the same way. It is the glory of our race that the graver the danger grows, the cooler we become. Fluster and flurry, panic and frenzy, in the hour of peril are not only unworthy of Britons, but they hamper all efforts at rescue. 'In your patience possess ye your souls.' And if God wills that succour does not come, and that death must be our lot, let us call to mind the noble words of Colonel John Ward, and *'Finish like English gentlemen.'* (35: 59)

Staying 'cool' is indeed the highest expression of British courage. Parrott (extracting some positive message from an utter rout) commends the British soldiers at the Retreat of Mons for their display of this quality:

> The Germans believed that if they kept up a fierce artillery fire on our trenches our men would become so terrified that they would scuttle from their burrows like rabbits at the approach of a ferret. They did not then know of what stuff British soldiers are made. No fighters in the world are so cool and dogged; none can take such severe punishment without flinching, or wait so patiently for the right moment to advance. (6: 28)

In recounting the first part of the terrible siege of Kut, Parrott claims that 'there is always something in it to stir our hearts, and make us proud of our fellow-country-men' (23: 49). Even in this disastrous defeat, in which the starving British were forced first to slaughter their horses for food and then finally to surrender to the Turks, there is consolation in the thought that 'we Britons place at the head of all military virtues dogged endurance – the courage that "sticks it" to the bitter end.' And on the Western Front, despite the stalemate in the trenches, the British soldiers displayed their mettle in trench raids:

> This kind of warfare was especially to the liking of our men. It gave scope for gallantry, dash, and quickness of decision, and much skill and daring were displayed. As time went on, the Germans attempted to make similar raids on our line. Some of them succeeded, but more often they failed. (26: 304)

On the home front, too, the British showed that they were made of superior stuff: 'Those who know the British temper best will tell you that such naval raids and air attacks can only make our people more determined than ever to defeat the enemy' (15: 297).

The German national character, on the other hand, contains

obvious defects that have led to war. In the first number, Parrott
describes a fight between a German boy, on holiday at the English seaside, and an English boy, who objected when the young
German threw stones at the bathing machines. The German
boy, 'brought up to believe that he could do as he pleased,' refused to stop (1: 34). 'That German boy,' announces Parrott, 'is
now the Kaiser Wilhelm, the man who has plunged Europe into
this terrible war' (35). This anecdote renders nugatory Parrott's
exhaustive treatment of the causes of war, in which he reaches
back into the Prussian past and covers all the complex terrain
of the Balkans, for from it emerges one simple point, eminently
comprehensible to schoolchildren: the Germans are bullies.

   As the war goes on, Parrott's rhetoric becomes more in-
flamed, his denunciations of the Germans more vehement:

   The German nation has never known the meaning of the word
   'chivalry.' From the first moment of war the Germans showed that
   they were ready to perpetrate every kind of baseness and cruelty
   in order to win. They sank to their lowest depths when they mur-
   dered Nurse Edith Cavell. The civilized world shrank with horror
   at the deed. But the Germans showed no shame; on the contrary
   they applauded the crime. (29: 109)[11]

If there is a message for Canadian children here, it is that Germans simply do not understand the British virtues and are inca-
pable of exercising them. But Canadian children, because they
belong to the Empire, do understand fair play. If exposed to the
hazards and trials of war, they will exhibit the pluck, resource,
gallantry, and cool daring that are the natural inheritance of the
true Britisher.

   Although Canadians are subsumed in the Empire as 'Britishers,' they also possess national characteristics of their own. In
'The Rally of the Empire,' Parrott describes how Canada re-
sponded to the declaration of war:

   From all parts of the Dominion they came – French Canadians
   from Lower Canada; farmers, and artisans, and clerks from Ontario; the hardest riders and the best shots of the prairies; the miners, trappers, and pioneers of the west and north. (5: 275)

Desmond Morton has noted how this stereotype of Canadian soldiers as 'robust, free-spirited pioneers' was at odds with the facts: by 1918 more than a third of the CEF 'listed their occupations as "industrial,"' and only 22.4 per cent were farmers, hunters, fishermen, or loggers (*When*, 278). In Parrott's summary of the Canadians who enlisted, only two of the six occupational terms refer to urban employment. But Parrott's picture fits perfectly with the view of Canadians promoted in British children's literature: as R.G. Moyles and Doug Owram have pointed out, '... no setting was more desirable than the "wild and woolly west" of Canada' (37). The Royal North-West Mounted Police officer, the Hudson's Bay Company trader, the French trapper, the laconic 'redskin,' the indomitable settler – thanks to writers such as R.M. Ballantyne, Macdonald Oxley, and F.S. Brereton, these Canadian types became 'icons of heroic adventure in juvenile literature' (Paris 105). Parrott draws on this tradition to portray the Canadians at war. In his account of the Second Battle of Ypres, entitled 'The Battle Glory of Canada,' he praises the Canadians who held the line in the first German gas attack:

> Every Briton may thank God that the Canadians were where they were when the cloud of poison gas sent the Turcos fleeing in panic to the rear. These sons of the eldest daughter of the Empire, who prior to the war knew little or nothing of the art and discipline of warfare, were now called upon to save the situation when all seemed lost. (19: 193)

Parrott's comments emphasize that the Canadians are neither professional soldiers nor conscripts, but citizen soldiers doing their duty.

Several anecdotes in the *Children's Story* reveal the high-spirited, boyish side of the Canadian soldiers (as befits 'these sons of the eldest daughter of the Empire'). This, it should be noted, was not merely prejudice on the part of a Britisher like Parrott: English Canadians themselves saw their country as 'the rambunctious youngster' and Britain as 'the stern older brother' (Thompson 97). Parrott recounts, for example, how some Canadians terrified a group of German soldiers 'by shouting Red Indian war cries.' When the Germans 'heard these bloodcurdling sounds, ... [they] turned and got back to their own lines with more haste than dignity' (31: 231). On another occasion, in order to carry out a winter raid, Canadians donned ladies' white night-dresses. which were 'to be stained red before the end of the adventure' (35: 98):

> ... when the moon was shining and the ground was white with snow, the Canadians in their night-dresses pushed across No Man's Land, and fell upon the German trenches. After quick bouts of bayonet work and bomb-throwing, the raiders returned with prisoners. The news of this extraordinary raid flashed along the telephone wires, and staff officers laughed as they held the receivers to their ears. (98)

This account of bravado in the snow draws on the pre-existing image of Canadians as heroic adventurers of the frozen north, and it reinforces Parrott's implicit argument that all Canadian lads, simply by virtue of being Canadian, will behave in a similarly high-spirited, indomitable fashion on the battlefields.

Parrott's portrait of the Canadians reflected the commonplace view of the day. Another information book of the war years, Richard Wilson's *The Post of Honour: Stories of Daring Deeds Done by Men of the British Empire in the Great War* (1917), describes the 'Canadian spirit' in the same manner:

> When the Canadian troops arrived at the Western Front Sir John French wrote of them, 'The soldierly bearing and the steadiness with which the men stay in the ranks on a bleak, cold, and snowy day are most remarkable.' Other leaders spoke of their high spirits and love of fun; others again of their cleverness in finding new ways of doing things, and, later, of tricking the enemy.
> ... The Canadians, after their custom, treated their officers in a free-and-easy manner which seemed at first somewhat strange to the ordinary British soldier ... But there was always a standing dispute among Canadian officers and men in the heat of action as to who should go first into the stiffest part of the fight. (52–3)

**A Rational War**

Perhaps the most important function of the *Children's Story* was to instill confidence that the Allies would win. Parrott's seemingly omniscient command of history, geography, and strategy, his bird's-eye views of the battlefield, his moral certainty about Britain's part in the war – all these contribute to the impression, never articulated but everywhere present, that he understands the war and knows how it will conclude. Fundamental to this reassuring picture is the premise that the war is an orderly, purposeful conflict. Even after the terrible losses at the Somme, Parrott insists that there is reason behind it:

> I want you particularly to remember that our main object in making this huge offensive was not simply to win ground, but to put out of action as many Germans as we possibly could. A wise general keeps always in his mind's eye the main business of war – namely, to destroy the forces of the enemy. (29: 64)

In Parrott's version of the war, everything is organized to ensure the comfort and safety of the troops and maintain their high morale. He specifically asserts, for example, that the Canadian volunteers departing from Valcartier in 1914 were 'fitted out with the best of everything. Their clothes and weapons were as good as money could buy, and their horses were especially fine' (5: 278). But the Canadians were later to curse their Ross rifles and the Canadian-made boots that fell apart in the mud. No matter how bad things get, Parrott manages to find some positive message. After describing the hellish conditions at Passchendaele, he concludes by noting that 'a correspondent tells us that a padre who watched the troops struggling through the mud exclaimed, "How the Germans must admire and fear those men!"' (43: 209).

The emphasis on technology and planning in the *Children's Story* also reinforces the impression that the war is being conducted in a rational, even scientific, manner. There are frequent illustrations of the machinery of war, ranging from machine guns to tanks. This emphasis no doubt was intended to capitalize on the fascination that 'the mechanics of guns and charts, of locomotive engines and explosives,' had for young readers of the period (Lerer 151–2). But the charts and diagrams in the text suggest that waging war is, in essence, a technical matter.

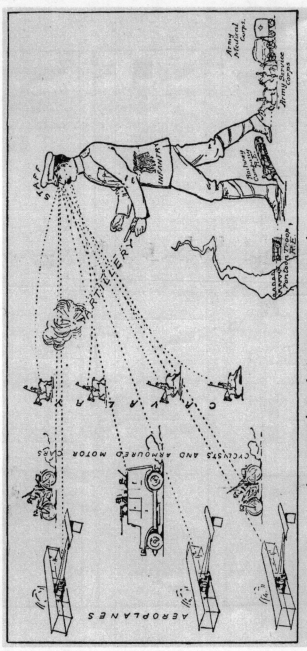

A comparison between a man and an army.

7 An illustration from *The Children's Story of the War* (no. 4: 208). Library and Archives Canada.

It is not until the very end of his account that Parrott abandons this tone. The final pages are sombre, and his young readers (if any were still reading after 3,552 pages) must have found Parrott's conclusion a surprising volte-face:

> ... I have recorded countless heroisms and have related numberless stories which stir the heart like the sound of a trumpet. But there is another side to war which no tales of valour and self-sacrifice must make us forget, even in the hour of our triumph. We must think of the awful bloodshed; the horrible waste of human life; the agony and tears of those who have lost their dearest and best; the tens of thousands of ruined homes, each one the centre of a family life, and the dearly-loved roof-tree of parents and children; the carefully-tilled fields, carved out of the waste by generations of toiling men and women, and now turned into waste once more; the sufferings of those who have fallen into the hands of a pitiless enemy; the loads of debt which will cripple the nations for generations to come. If we realize all this, we cannot fail but come to the conclusion that war is the most terrible disease that afflicts mankind and that the greatest and most blessed work in which we can engage is to strive, heart and soul, for the perpetual peace of the world. (56: 270–1)

The rhetoric of this passage suggests the profound exhaustion of a war-weary world. The third sentence, running to nearly a hundred words, suggests how immeasurable the costs of war are, ranging from the intimate tears of the bereaved and the destruction of homes, to the larger-scale tragedies of devastated lands and economies. The long catalogue of war's costs reaches an apex with the description of ruined homes and fields; it ends with what still lies ahead – the burden of debt that 'will cripple the nations.' Each of the eight phrases contains some reference to people, reminding us that, ultimately, individual human beings bear the costs of war. 'Dearly-loved roof-tree' and 'carefully-tilled fields' – the tenderness of these metonyms for home and culture indicate how Parrott lamented what the war had done. Yet, throughout the many instalments of the *Children's Story*, he had insisted on the glorious side of war, not its human cost.

## Lessons of War

Textbooks, lectures, and exams represent only the outer forms of education. The inner, invisible process of learning takes place according to a syllabus and timetable of its own. Just as enrolment figures during this period do not reflect actual attendance, so too the official directives and prescribed materials for teaching the war cannot be assumed to represent what children actually learned. Of course, they acquired some of the facts and terms associated with the war; otherwise, they could not have passed examinations. They learned the patriotic songs and memorized the poems. But how much of this information they actually retained and how it affected their outlook are matters now impossible to gauge. Still, given that so much of the curriculum was infused with war-related facts and notions, every Canadian child who was attending school must have been exposed to a certain amount of teaching about the war.

In addition to overt instruction about the war in history, geography, English, and other subjects, schools also engaged in more subtle forms of indoctrination. The next chapter examines what children learned about war in school, not from textbooks or lessons, but from physical activity, music, and drama.

# 3 Children of the Empire

The greatest sentiment, as well as the most stirring, which we could put into the minds and hearts of our children, in my opinion, is 'Civis Britannicus sum.'

George Ross, Minister of Education for Ontario,
'Memorandum with Respect to a Patriotic Day for
the Schools of Canada, 1898'[1]

It is indeed a strange irony that the war now described as the birth of our nation and Canada's coming of age was taught to Canadian children as a war for the defence of the Empire.[2] In wartime patriotic training, it was the Empire, not Canada, that children were enjoined to love, protect, and serve.

In Canada, imperial loyalty as a special cause had its roots in the late 1880s when, as a result of a prolonged economic depression, Imperial Federation began to seem like an appealing solution to the country's economic woes. Within an economic union of the Empire, preferential tariffs could secure markets for Canada's goods. Imperial loyalty was also a reaction against the seductive danger of continental union: reciprocity with the United States might bring economic benefits, but it was sure to diminish – perhaps even eradicate – the qualities that made Canada distinct. Opponents of reciprocity turned to the imperial connection as the best way to improve trade while protecting Canadian traditions and institutions. What began as a commercial idea gradually became a set of political, racial, and cultural notions about Canada's relations with the Empire and the Motherland.

This metamorphosis was doubtless aided by the rising tide of the new imperial sentiment in Britain. John MacKenzie has described the 'ideological cluster' that characterized this sentiment: 'renewed militarism, a devotion to royalty, an identification and worship of national heroes, together with a contemporary cult of personality, and racial ideas associated with Social Darwinism' (2). The enormously successful propaganda associated with what MacKenzie calls this 'new type of patriotism,' as manifested in books, illustrated weeklies, music-hall shows, popular songs, and advertisements, certainly reached Canada; moreover, the many British immigrants of this period brought to their new country attitudes that had been shaped at home by the imperial message.

In Canada, the power of the new imperial loyalty reached its height during the South African War, which Carl Berger has called 'the decisive event in the history of Canadian imperialism' ('Introduction' 3). Canada had refused to aid Britain in previous struggles such as the Sudan, but in 1899 public pressure forced Prime Minister Wilfrid Laurier to send Canadian troops to South Africa. This decision was not an unmitigated triumph for Canadian advocates of imperial loyalty, as Carman Miller points out in *Painting the Map Red*. In Quebec there was 'virtually unanimous opposition and indifference' (16); many French Canadians actually sympathized with the Boers, seeing them as a similar minority 'trying to preserve their national identity against the corroding influences of an alien culture' (28). In English Canada too, some people were reluctant to fight an imperial war. German and Irish Canadians were against it, as were the Women's Christian Temperance Union, farm groups, and radical elements in the labour movement (22–3). But the imperial loyalists who welcomed the war had many allies. Progressives, even many social gospellers, supported the war as a moral crusade against the backward, slave-owning Boers (17). Others accepted the war, not on moral or ideological grounds, but on practical ones: it was a chance to find new markets for Canadian goods, 'forge a mature relationship with Britain,' and 'purchase British protection of Canada's territorial interests' (19). Certainly once Canada had entered the war, patriotic sentiment became the order of the day, and even the Quebec press came to support it (441). The South African War provided a spur to Canadian nationalism, perhaps best symbolized by pride in the Canadian soldier, who was seen as stronger and tougher and more self-reliant than the British Tommy. At the same time, the war was an occasion to 'feed the fires of imperialism' (436). In 'Our Bit of "The Thin Red Line,"' a poem that appeared in *Poems and Songs of the South African War: An Anthology from England, Africa, Australia, United States, but Chiefly Canada* (1901), W. Wilfred Campbell expressed the curious mixture of national pride and imperial loyalty that became so potent in Canada:

> And stand or fall, though we go to the wall,
> Canadian hearts are true,
> Not only to stand for our own birth land,
> But to die for the Empire too. (Borthwick 36)

This dual loyalty, which amounted to a condition in which 'imperialism was one form of Canadian nationalism,' was of course not felt by all Canadians (Berger, *Sense* 259). But among Canadian educators, it had forceful adherents.

In his study of the development of Canadian curricula, George Tomkins provides several examples of how English-Canadian educators conceived of the teaching of patriotism, both Canadian and imperial. Sir William Dawson, the geologist, educator, and first president of the Royal Society of Canada, emphasized the teaching of patriotism in his speech to the first meeting of the Dominion Educational Association in 1892: Dawson spoke of the need for young Canadians 'to grow up as members of one common country with a sentiment for Canada common to all' (quoted in Tomkins 108). This national sentiment would be cultivated 'by the training of our children not as sectionalists but as Canadians and beyond this as integral parts of the great empire to which we belong.' Dawson's remarks represented implicit support for the 1890 Manitoba Schools Act, which, in removing French as an official language and ending public support for Catholic schools, had ignited a national controversy about the place that French-speaking Catholics had in Confederation. Part and parcel of the uniform Protestant, English-language identity that Dawson evidently believed Canadian schools should foster was loyalty to the British Empire. Another late-nineteenth-century educator, Alexander MacKay, who served as president of the Dominion Educational Association from 1895 to 1898, advocated the establishment of Empire Day in order to develop 'the larger British sentiment' and also to promote the 'cultivation of feelings of loyalty and attachment to our country and to its institutions' (quoted in Tomkins 144). In other words, these educators preached imperial loyalty as an overarching faith that could unite Canadians of many different backgrounds.

Perhaps the most vocal and effective of the educators who embraced imperial nationalism was George Ross, a teacher, author, and politician, first appointed minister of education in Ontario in 1883. (He later served as premier from 1899 to 1905.) Ross's greatest contribution to imperial sentiment was the creation of Empire Day, a special school holiday to celebrate Canada's ties to Britain. Empire Day originated when Mrs Clementina Fessenden of Dundas, Ontario, wrote to various newspapers and to Ross, proposing that 'the schools devote a day each year to patriotic exercises' (Stamp, 'Empire' 33). Ross took up the idea and decided to call this new holiday Empire Day, which, he wrote, 'suggests that larger British sentiment which I think now prevails throughout the empire' (quoted in Stamp, 'Empire' 34).

The first Empire Day celebrations took place on 23 May 1899 in Ontario, where, according to Robert Stamp, the new holiday was adopted enthusiastically because of 'its compatibility with concepts of loyalty and patriotism prevalent in turn-of-the-century Ontario' ('Empire' 35). Soon it became 'an approved day in all provinces' (Sheehan 34), and by 1913 it was being celebrated in Britain, Australia, and other parts of the Empire as well (Bloomfield 75–6). In his 1910 pamphlet 'The Origin and History of Empire Day,' the journalist and editor J. Castell Hopkins proudly noted that 'to Canada belongs the honour' (4) of initiating 'this important Imperial celebration,' which in 1909 was observed 'throughout the British world ... by 55,000 schools' (3).

At the core of Empire Day celebrations was the message that belonging to the Empire was a privilege. Because of the imperial tie, Canadian children could see themselves as proud inheritors of British character and culture. In his Empire Day pamphlet, Hopkins quoted in full the 'talk with teachers' that George Ross had written for his 1893 volume *Patriotic Recitations*. (This volume was an early attempt on Ross's part, prior to the establishment of Empire Day, to encourage in Ontario children 'a more intelligent conception ... of the greatness of the Empire' [quoted in Hopkins 5].) While acknowledging that Canadians differed 'in our habits, laws and modes of thought from our kinsmen in the British Isles,' Ross affirmed that 'we are of the same race, and equally interested in the prosperity and honour of the Empire' (5). Ross exhorted teachers to stress 'the essential unity of the Empire' (5). This indeed was what Empire Day did in Canadian schools. Among the 'Mottoes for Banners or to adorn school walls or Blackboards' provided on the inside cover of a 1915 Empire Day program was the stirring if confusing slogan, 'The Empire is my country; Canada is my Home' (Women's Canadian). As Stamp points out, Empire Day also was viewed as a way to 'indoctrinate Central and Eastern immigrant children in appropriate national and imperial outlooks' (*Schools* 94).

Imperial loyalty was not just a once-a-year message on Empire Day. In school textbooks, which consistently presented the symbols, legends, and rituals of British identity as Canadian, 'loyalty to and love of Britain were vigorously encouraged ... from Confederation to the 1920s' (Van Brummelen 18). For example, the frontispiece of the *Ontario Readers: Third Book* (1909) presented a message from Earl Grey, governor general from 1904 to 1911, encouraging pupils to 'remember what Empire Day means' and 'by your own conduct and example to make Canada not only the most powerful, but the noblest of all the self-governing nations that are proud to owe allegiance to the King.' On the final page of *A Beginner's Reader* in the British Columbia Readers series (1915) was the Union Jack and an accompanying dialogue for children to read aloud; the game suggested for this page was to 'let the class play soldiers, carrying the flag' (64). A penmanship exercise in the first book of the New Canadian Readers series (1901) consisted of 'God Save the King' (90). As Timothy Stanley puts it, textbooks 'did not differentiate between Canadian nationalism and British imperialism' (117). The physical environment of the classroom communicated the same values: according to C.E. Phillips, 'the characteristic school [of 1910] exhibited on its walls scenes of military heroism and portraits of royalty' (467). These 'national and patriotic pictures' were intended 'to exert a silent but constant influence on the pupils.' The superiority of the British race, the supremacy of British industry, the invincibility of the British navy, the benevolence and power of the British Empire – these imperial myths were taught to Canadian children too.

By the time of the First World War, Empire Day was already a well-established school occasion, one that could readily be employed for war propaganda. Propaganda may seem a heavy-handed term for instructional materials, but I use it deliberately. In *Propaganda and Empire*, John MacKenzie offers the following definition of propaganda:

> the transmission of ideas and values from one person, or groups of persons, to another, with the specific intention of influencing the recipients' attitudes in such a way that the interests of its authors will be enhanced. Although it may be veiled, seeking to influence thoughts, beliefs and actions by suggestion, it must be conscious and deliberate. (3)

MacKenzie acknowledges that much of the material disseminated in Victorian Britain by groups such as church organizations and publishers was not overt propaganda of this 'conscious and deliberate' sort but rather a form of 'self-generating ethos reinforcement, [that is,] a constant repetition of the central ideas and concerns of the age' (3). Materials produced by Canadian ministries of education in support of Empire Day display elements of both types of persuasion. They constitute propaganda inasmuch as they were prepared by government officials, presented the official view of the war, and undoubtedly were designed to cultivate patriotism with the long-term goal of ensuring recruits. Many of the adolescents who were exposed to these materials would soon be old enough to enlist. On the other hand, the principals and teachers who presented this material to students were engaged less in 'conscious and deliberate' influence than in the sort of 'ethos reinforcement' described by MacKenzie.

Perhaps the most ambitious Empire Day publications were produced in Manitoba, where the Department of Education had since 1908 distributed Empire Day annuals to all the province's schools ('Victoria Day'). During the war years, the Manitoba annuals promoted a militant, imperial patriotism. For example, the 1915 Manitoba *Empire Day Annual* begins with a letter from the minister of education, G.R. Coldwell, addressing the students not as Canadians but as citizens of the Empire:

> The Empire is at war. The Motherland is in danger. And the thrill of our response to her call for aid is felt around the world ...
>
> ... while our soldier heroes guard the lines, and our brave sailors keep their ceaseless vigil on the seas, it behooves the boys and girls of Manitoba to take heed that our race is making history, to shirk no effort nor sacrifice whereby they may do their part in bringing this war to a successful issue, and by their greater diligence and greater faithfulness to lay solid and enduring foundations for the peace that is to be. (5)

Coldwell's exhortation brings the war into each child's everyday life. Through individual choices about behaviour, study, and money, the child must help to win the war. Coldwell holds up before his young readers the example of 'our soldier heroes' and 'our brave sailors'; if this is the standard by which sacrifice and effort are to be measured, no child at home can ever feel he or she has done enough. It is noteworthy too that Coldwell extends civic responsibility into the future, calling on children to prepare themselves in order to build a better post-war world.

Included in the 1915 annual are full-page photos of King George V and of the late Field Marshal Earl Roberts. (Roberts was regarded as a special friend of the children of the Empire: an address by Lord Roberts was reprinted in full in the *Children's Story of the War*.) Another page is devoted to photos of 'Our Leaders in War': Earl Kitchener, Sir John Jellicoe, Field Marshal Sir John French, and Major General E.A.H. Alderson (then in command of the Canadian Corps) – Englishmen all. Much of the text consists of a catechism-like series of thirty-nine questions and answers about the war, for all Manitoba pupils were to be 'made acquainted with the essential facts in connection with the outbreak of the War' (7).[3] The questions and answers comprise a very detailed account of the events leading to the war, aimed at demonstrating Britain's blameless and honourable part. Here, for example, are two questions (complete with page references to the Blue Book that had been issued to all schools):

*26. Did Germany ask Britain to enter into a conspiracy in regard to Belgium?*
Yes, Germany asked Britain to stand aside and allow Germany to march her troops through Belgium. (29th July, Goschen to Grey, page 53).
*27. Why could not Britain agree?*
Because she had given her word of honour to protect the neutrality of Belgium. (9)

In addition, there are four pages of excerpts from speeches by British prime minister Herbert Asquith, Lord Rosebery (former prime minister), and David Lloyd George (then chancellor of the exchequer), prefaced with the suggestion that 'pupils be encouraged to memorize some or all of the following extracts' (15). In one of these extracts, Asquith declares: 'From Canada, from Australia, from New Zealand, from South Africa and from Newfoundland, the children of the Empire assert, not as an obligation, but as a privilege, their right, and their willingness to contribute money, material and what is better than all, the strength and sinews, the fortunes and lives of their best manhood' (15). 'Children' here means the colonies, the 'whelps' or 'cubs' of the Motherland, but the Manitoban pupils who had to memorize this passage might well have taken it more literally.

In the final section appear patriotic poems and songs that teachers could incorporate in Empire Day celebrations. Teachers devised their own program for the day from the materials in the annuals; they were invited to submit their program along with 'photographs and a brief account of the day's proceedings' to the *Western School Journal* (1917: 6). Most of the poems in the 1915 annual are by Harold Begbie, the author of biographies of Baden-Powell and William Booth, and a popular patriotic and religious writer of the day. Typical of the Begbie poems in the annual is 'The Old Man's Share,' a reworking of the Abraham and Isaac story, narrated by a father who sends his beloved son off to war:

I used to dream of days to be,
You working here beside of me!
But old men, too, must pay War's price:
So here's your father's sacrifice. (21)

The annual also includes songs for Empire Day celebrations. 'Stand by the Union Jack,' a Canadian song composed by W.E. Delaney and dedicated to the Imperial Order Daughters of the Empire, contains a rousing chorus: 'Stand by the Union Jack, the flag of liberty! / And fight for the Empire which allows no tyranny. / All forward! By land and sea, press on to the attack! / Hip, hip hurrah! for Britain's flag, the grand old Union Jack!' (24).

In 1917, on the fiftieth anniversary of Confederation, the theme of the Manitoba *Empire Day Annual* was 'the great Imperial project of Confederation' (6). Throughout, the annual emphasizes the British heritage that has shaped Canada: 'We are Canadians and British. We inherit from those who have gone before us the great privilege of freedom and self-government for which our forefathers fought and died just as our fathers, brothers, and friends are fighting to-day for the same principle' (3). Along with images of the Fathers of Confederation and Old Fort Garry, the 1917 annual contains pictures of Canadians at Ypres (28) and at Langemarck (34). These victories in the British cause would be counted among the signal and defining moments in Canadian history.

The theme of the 1918 Manitoba *Empire Day Annual* was the Union Jack, 'the flag of the British Empire, the outward and visible symbol of its being, strength and purpose' (3). Among the selections for memorization is Frederick George Scott's 'The Colours of the Flag' (20). In Scott's patriotic tribute to the Union Jack, blue 'is for the waves of the boundless sea, / Where our vessels ride in their tameless pride,' white is for 'the honour of our land,' and red for 'the blood of our heroes slain.'

The 1919 annual was devoted to the eleven men from Manitoba who had won the Victoria Cross, for their 'story should be an inspiration to every boy and girl in Manitoba' (3). The war was over, but children were expected to continue to cultivate the 'right spirit' of service to the nation and the Empire, as exhibited by the VC-winners who 'when duty called, ... were not found wanting' (3).

In other provinces, too, Empire Day publications were used as vehicles for war propaganda. In Ontario, the Department of Education issued for Empire Day in 1918 *Canada's Part in the Present War,* a book-length compendium of war information.

The 1919 annual, entitled *Annals of Valour*, provided nearly two hundred pages of war information for Ontario teachers and students, focused chiefly on 'the part played by Canada's soldiers in the campaign of the last year' and on 'the valorous deeds of individual soldiers' (6). These publications were intended to serve as enduring textbooks on the war: subsequent examination questions in Ontario were based on their contents (*School*, Jan. 1920: 271).

Empire Day was not the only national occasion on which Canadian children celebrated the connection with Britain. The Methodist Church designated the Sunday nearest July 1st 'Patriotic Day,' and during the war, special services were held on this Sunday. The Methodist Book and Publishing House advertised its special Patriotic Day products in the *Sunday School Banner*:

> It is in these days, if ever, that we need to stir every ounce of patriotism that we possess into life. Be glad of the opportunity to dwell on the part we have in the life of this great Christian Empire, and help the scholars realize their duty to the country. (June 1916: 44)

Along with a 'specially prepared service' on the theme of heroes, the firm offered celluloid Union Jacks or Canadian flags. In June 1918, the advertisement for Patriotic Day encouraged Sunday-school teachers to 'get the "Service" idea into the boys and girls,' asserting that there was 'no better place to instill patriotism than right in your own Sunday School.'

### Drills and Patriotic Entertainments

On the very first Empire Day in Ontario in 1899, the Toronto Normal and Model School was 'the centre of Ontario's public celebrations'; the boys of the School gave a rifle drill and, as the report in the *Globe* put it, 'the young ladies went through some graceful evolutions' to the tune of 'The British Grenadiers' (quoted in Stamp, 'Empire' 36). Drills and other forms of choreographed movement would remain an important part of Empire Day celebrations. For example, *Canada's Part in the Present War* set out a model program for Ontario school observances of Empire Day in 1918, including, along with scripture reading, prayer, singing of the national anthem, and lessons on the war, a flag drill: 'The Assembling and Saluting of the Flags of Great Britain and her Allies' (5). Drills were not reserved just for Empire Day. On the programs of the many 'patriotic entertainments' sponsored by schools and churches, drills had an honoured place.

Since the early nineteenth century, drill had been used in British classrooms to 'teach obedience and discipline [and] inculcate respect for law and order,' but gradually it became a more 'overtly martial' activity (Heathorn 110). When the physical deficiencies of British volunteers became apparent during the South African War, drill in elementary schools was seen as the remedy, at once improving the physical strength of the nation's youth and imparting to them military discipline and skills. Lord Meath, the popularizer of Empire Day throughout Britain and the Empire, started the Lads' Drill Association in 1899 to bring to British children military and patriotic training of the kind that young Germans were given; Meath was an early proponent of preparedness for war with Germany (Bloomfield 81). While drill was intended to build children up physically, improved health and increased strength were viewed not so much as good ends in themselves but as the foundation on which to build (in Lord Meath's words) 'the principles that make for good citizenship – discipline, duty, mutual service, and patriotism' (quoted in Bloomfield 75).

The relationship between physical movement and patriotism derives from the nature of organized group movement. Anne Bloomfield notes that 'the physical repetition and conformity of design' imposed by the drills were intended to cultivate an equally conforming 'frame of mind, since it was believed that as the pupils learned the drill so their faithfulness towards the Empire would develop' (82). The drills required the child to operate not as an individual but as part of a group – good preparation for becoming a loyal citizen and a reliable soldier.

In Canada, physical training had become compulsory in most provinces by the early 1890s. It consisted primarily of 'military drill and gymnastics for boys and calisthenics for girls' (Tomkins 123). As Tomkins points out, in Canada as in Britain, drill was concerned not just with physical well-being:

The major goals of physical training encompassed discipline,

moral and social self-control, military preparedness and patriotism, this last including the Canadianization of immigrant children. As with manly games, therapeutic values were ascribed to
calisthenics and military drill as a means of combatting physical,
mental and moral decline resulting from urban life and the de-
bilitating influences of materialism. (123)

In school physical training, drill became an ever more important element. By 1907, the federal government intervened to
'assist provincial departments of education by providing some
drill instruction in schools and courses for interested teachers'
(123–4). Tomkins notes that this federal incursion into the provincial realm of education was justified 'by referring to Section
91 of the B.N.A. Act which gave Parliament the right to make
laws necessary for the maintenance of peace' (124). Teachers
in every province had to obtain a certificate in drill in order to
qualify for their licence.

The greatest impetus to the teaching of drill in Canadian
schools occurred in 1909, when the federal minister of militia persuaded Lord Strathcona, Canada's high commissioner
to Britain, to fund military and physical training in Canadian
schools. The Strathcona Trust, established with an endowment
of $500,000, provided funds to schools across the country: 35
per cent was to be used for cadet training, 15 per cent for rifle
shooting, and 50 per cent for physical education. By 1911, the
syllabus developed by the Strathcona Trust had been adopted in
every province, and it remained the basic guide for physical education until the 1930s (Dunae, 'Strathcona'). The introduction
to the *Syllabus* stresses the 'mental and moral influence' of physical training: 'The child unconsciously acquires habits of discipline and order, and learns to respond cheerfully and promptly
to the word of command' (5). The syllabus lays out a program of
progressively more challenging calisthenic moves. While it does
not prescribe formal military drills, it does use such commands
as 'attention' and 'at ease' (26), and marching manoeuvres of
various sorts – turning about on the march, wheeling, changing step on the march, numbering, opening and closing ranks –
figure largely in the syllabus's recommendations.

The military value of this kind of training was very evident to
its proponents. Tomkins quotes Alexander MacKay's advocacy

8 Boys learning to shoot in physical drill class in Lang, Saskatchewan, ca 1918–19. Courtesy of Glenbow Archives, image NA-3229-31.

of the Strathcona system at the 1909 meeting of the Dominion
Education Association:

> [It is] a uniform language of movement which will prove to be
> enormously valuable when it is the language of every school, of
> every boy and girl in the provinces, in the dominion, within the
> Empire, as the basis for the orderly management of any crowds for
> any purpose, as a preparation for the cadet instruction in the High
> Schools and as a fundamental training for the defenders of our
> Empire and our homes should the contingency ever arise. (124)

By the coming of the war, drill was being practised in schools
across the country. Even the residential schools had cadet corps
that drilled: in 1916, the local Indian agent reported that at
the Coqualeetza Institute near Chilliwack 'the cadet corps, 50
strong, organized at this school, receives drill instruction once a
week. This is very beneficial as it teaches the boys discipline, and
provides them with healthy exercise' (Department of Indian Affairs Annual Report 1916: 428). Drill seems also to have been a
popular recreational activity: many organizations, ranging from
the Boy Scouts to St John's Ambulance, incorporated it into
their training.[4] For virtually every 'demonstration' (similar to a
term-end concert or performance) described in the Salvation
Army *Young Soldier*, a drill is mentioned as part of the program.
For the many patriotic entertainments sponsored by schools and
voluntary organizations during the war, drills were ideal group
performances to round out the program.

Expressly for this purpose, a Toronto educator named Edith
Lelean Groves wrote a series of Canadian drills during the war
years. Groves had first written drills during the South African
War; more than a decade later, the outbreak of another war
provided renewed stimulus to her deeply patriotic imagination.
Between 1916 and 1918, Groves produced twenty works, pub-
lished as the All Canadian Entertainment series by McClelland,
Goodchild and Stewart.[5]

The biographical sketch written to introduce *Everyday Children*, a posthumously published collection of Groves's poems,
recounts numerous examples of her great popularity with pupils
and colleagues. She was a pioneer in establishing special education programs (MacMurchy 17); she was elected thirteen times

to the Toronto Board of Education and became its first woman chair (16). Groves had direct experience of the war's cost, for one of her stepsons was killed at Passchendaele, and the other was wounded at Hill 70 (14–15), yet there is nothing dark in the jaunty patriotic drills she wrote for Canadian children. Her view of what was appropriate for school readers – 'No melancholy tales of death and disorder'(14) – evidently also governed the content of her wartime drills.

Groves's drills were exceptionally effective instruments for infusing children with loyalty to nation and empire. The work of preparing an All Canadian Entertainment, which included making costumes, rehearsing movements, and memorizing recitations and songs, would ensure, as no lesson or textbook could, that children absorbed the patriotic message of these works.[6] Groves was fully aware of this effect. In the introduction to *Saluting the Canadian Flag* (1917), she encourages teachers to 'make this a real live Canadian Patriotic Exercise': 'Don't let the children merely speak the parts, but let it be your business as teacher to see that each child who takes part in the Exercise realizes to the full extent what he or she is saying. As Canadians we have done far too little of this ...' (3).

Groves started with the limited form of the military drill, but to it she added ingredients from the music-hall traditions of Victorian England. (As a teacher and the wife of a school principal, Groves might seem entirely too middle-class to have had any contact with the working-class milieu of the music hall, but the music hall 'appeal[ed] to all social classes' [J. MacKenzie 40].) The result was a hybrid of song, dialogue, and movement with incomparably more emotional power than a mere drill. It was not accidental, according to the economist J.A. Hobson, that the term 'jingoism' derived from a music-hall song, for the music hall was, he thought, 'a more potent educator than the church, the school, the political meeting, or even than the press' (3). While 'in ordinary times politics plays no important part in these feasts of sensationalism, ... the glorification of brute force and an ignorant contempt for foreigners are ever-present factors which at great political crises make the music-hall a very serviceable engine for generating military passion' (3). Certainly the war was a 'great political crisis' that called forth the particular powers of music-hall entertainments to stimulate patriotism.

An important element from the music-hall tradition that Groves incorporated was the use of 'topical and chauvinistic songs' (J. MacKenzie 40). For *The War on the Western Front*, she recommends 'The Maple Leaf Forever,' 'Keep the Home Fires Burning,' and 'We'll Never Let the Old Flag Fall' (6).[7] 'Keep the Home Fires Burning' also appears in *Canada Calls* (12) and in *A Patriotic Auction* (22). There were two versions of Groves's *Fancy Flag Drill*, one based on 'Rule Britannia' and the other on 'We'll Fight for the Grand Old Flag' (this latter an updated version of a South African War song). 'Young Citizens in the Making,' a scene in Groves's *Primary Pieces*, ends with the children 'wav[ing] their flags in unison and sing[ing] a verse of some Patriotic song' (4). As George Mosse has observed, patriotic songs are 'a potent weapon' in the war of propaganda because they have 'no need for argument, reason, or logic' (21).

Another device that MacKenzie identifies as central to the music hall's political effect, the patriotic tableau, has a similarly prominent place in Groves's drills (40). In a tableau, 'actors strike an expressive stance in a legible symbolic configuration that crystallizes a stage of the narrative as a situation, or summarizes and punctuates it' (Meisel 45). The tableau tradition, with its many variations from music hall to school nativity plays, nudie shows, and aristocratic divertissements, is an ideal model for amateurs. It makes few dramatic demands on participants, relying for its effect not on the skill of the actors but on the audience's familiarity with archetypal images and mythological figures. It was, for this reason, a popular element in the 'demonstrations' given by children in the Salvation Army. A report from the *Brockville Times* (reprinted in the *Young Soldier* [23 Jan. 1915:10]) gave an enthusiastic description of the Army Christmas concert:

> Three tableaux were shown very effectively, entitled 'The Soldier's Farewell,' 'A Red Cross Scene,' and 'The Wondrous Cross,' respectively, the latter being especially good, eight young ladies, dressed in white, building up a white cross singing at the close 'Nearer, My God, to Thee,' and taking up various positions, one with her arms around the cross and the others kneeling or reclining at the foot.

Whether or not Groves was familiar with the Salvation Army's adoption of secular drama for religious purposes, she seems to have done something similar in transposing the techniques of the music hall to a pedagogical context. Whereas the tableaux presented in Salvation Army demonstrations tended to rely on familiar hymns for their iconography, Groves used the national symbols Britannia and Miss Canada. The drill *Britannia*, for example, ends with the title figure on a pedestal surrounded by children representing the provinces of Canada and select colonies of the Empire, a tableau that draws on popular images of Queen Victoria receiving tribute from her subjects. The fact that each child has placed a gift 'at the feet of Britannia' (5) – wheat sheaves from Saskatchewan, shawls from India, spices and jewels from Ceylon – intensifies the pagan symbolism of Victoria/ Britannia as a goddess to whom tribute and loyalty are due.

For the close of *Canada Calls*, Groves recommends a curtain tableau centred on Miss Canada: 'Have the children group themselves prettily around Canada while the curtain is down, then have it slowly rise upon the tableau' (5). This arrangement signals the patriotic message that the nation can count on her children. Miss Canada, as the symbol of the nation, appeared in many nineteenth- and early twentieth-century political cartoons, sometimes as a maiden in contemporary dress, and sometimes as a goddess in garments resembling the warrior garb of Britannia. A *Montreal Daily Star* cartoon showed her this way, crowned by a wreath of maple leaves, carrying a cornucopia of grains and wheat, and with a maple-leaf-emblazoned shield at her feet (Hou 24). In *Canada, Our Homeland*, Groves gives specific directions for her appearance:

> A tall girl with light hair should be chosen to represent Miss Canada. She should be dressed in a long white gown, with a row of maple leaves around the bottom, a girdle of maple leaves, and sprays of the leaves daintily arranged in her hair. (1)

A similar form of Miss Canada served as the generic cover image for the All Canada Entertainment series, with the addition of a Union Jack draped over her, in imitation perhaps of Britannia's classical aegis or cloak.

The tableau that ends *Saluting the Canadian Flag* relies on a different sort of visual message:

9 Cover from the All Canadian Entertainment series. Library and Archives Canada.

When the word is formed, the pianist plays a chord on the piano and at the signal the children drop upon their knees. Another chord is played and the head of each child is bent forward until it is resting on the back of the child in front ... It will take a good deal of practice to make the letters well, but ... the effect of the human 'CANADA' will be quite worth while. (6–7)

In this symbolic configuration spelling out CANADA, disciplined children quite literally embody the nation.

Another element of the music hall adopted by Groves is its miscellaneous character. The music-hall entertainment 'created a digest of other theatrical material: jingoistic and satirical songs and sketches, tableaux of battle scenes ...; miniature melodramas, spectacular acts, and wildly patriotic concluding extravaganzas' (J. MacKenzie 55). Groves's *The Soldiers of the Soil and the Farmerettes*, for example, begins with a drill of girls and boys dressed in rustic costumes and carrying rakes; they perform first in a 'miniature melodrama,' to use MacKenzie's phrase, based on John Greenleaf Whittier's poem 'Maud Muller.' Then they sing a patriotic song of Groves's own devising, set to the tune of 'My Old Kentucky Home':

> We're young Farmerettes and we're Soldiers of the Soil,
> We're working so busy and bright;
> For we know if the Hun were to win the fight in France,
> Then, our own Canadian home, Good-Night! (14)

The final drill, in which all the children join hands and declare that 'we can all do our best to keep up the food supplies for the Allied armies and our own dear boys overseas' (160), is not exactly a 'concluding extravaganza,' but it is certainly patriotic.

MacKenzie's examples of music-hall and concert titles from late Victorian Britain – 'War Songs of the Day' (56), 'Britannia,' and 'New Patriotic Entertainment entitled "Albion's Nationalist"' (60) – sound very much like the titles of Groves's playlets. The same ideology that 'underpinned' such music-hall productions, which consisted of 'pride in race, brotherhood of the white Dominions of settlement, the justice of British rule in India, and the need to defend the Empire against aggressive rivals' (60), permeates Groves's playlets too. Racial pride, for example, so central both to the New Imperialism in Britain of the late nineteenth century and to imperial nationalism in Canada, is unmistakably part of Groves's patriotism. In the epilogue to *The Wooing of Miss Canada*, Groves includes the stern warning that 'we must be ever on the alert to guard well [Canada's] interests, to watch the immigration and see that undesirables do not enter and to ever remember our watchword, "Canada for Canadians"' (32).[8] One of the dollies to be auctioned off in *A Patriotic Auction* bears the label 'Made in Germany'; when the auctioneer asks whether it should be offered for sale, the children in the play respond, 'Why, she's an Alien Enemy. No one would buy her!' (21).[9] Even Groves's specification that the role of Miss Canada be played by 'a tall girl with light hair' suggests that only a Euro-Canadian can represent the nation.

One ideological element in Groves's playlets that is not part of the boisterous jingoism of the music-hall tradition is her emphasis on sacrifice. *A Patriotic Auction* presents this idea in terms immediately understandable by children: four 'little mothers' offer their dollies to be auctioned off in order to raise money for an unspecified patriotic cause.[10] By giving up their dollies for the auction, the 'little mothers' are acquiring practice in sacrifice, learning to become women who will give their sons to the war. As the girl who gives up her Beauty Doll (a popular Eaton's product of the period) mournfully says, 'We all have to do our very best for the cause – the cause of Patriotism. Here take her (sadly); she is all I have' (17).

That girls, too, should be prepared to do their part seems a special concern of Groves. Perhaps she felt that there was already plenty of material designed to shape young boys into soldiers, but girls were not receiving similar guidance and inspiration about their wartime duty. In any case, Groves's playlets seem noteworthy for their focus on what girls and women can do. In *The War on the Western Front*, four phalanxes of knitting girls represent Belgium, France, Britain, and Canada. Canadian women did indeed knit tremendous numbers of socks, wristlets, and other items for the soldiers; some became so proficient that they could produce a pair of socks a day (Read 185). But this image's effectiveness is based on more than its accurate representation of women's war work; it is strengthened by its literary and mythological connections.

The immediate literary context for Groves and her readers was surely Katherine Hale's poem 'Grey Knitting.' Hale (Amelia Warnock), the wife of poet and anthologist John Garvin, was a literary critic, lecturer, and singer, and 'one of the most influential figures on the Canadian literary scene' (Blenkhorn). 'Grey Knitting' was enormously successful. Published in pamphlet form by William Briggs in 1914, it was advertised in the *Christian Guardian* as 'The Newest Patriotic Booklet' and 'a dainty, timely book of poems dedicated to the women who knit' (2 Dec. 1914: 22). It was evidently for girls too: an advertisement headed 'Books for the Children' in the *Christian Guardian* describes *Grey Knitting and Other Poems* as the 'ideal Christmas gift' – 'delightful verse, gotten up in unique, illuminated cover and tied with the yarn your mother or sister is using' (8 Dec. 1915: 24). Under the influence of this poem, knitting became the highest form of feminine war service, an act of devotion as much as a practical craft. In Hale's poem, and by extension Groves's *The War on the Western Front*, knitting derives this special aura from the image of Penelope at her loom:

> Whispers of women, tireless and patient –
> 'Foolish, inadequate!' we hear you say;
> 'Grey wool on fields of hell is out of fashion,'
> And yet we weave the web from day to day.[11]

The idea that a woman whose man is away at war should occupy her hands and hours with the feminine arts seems to run from Penelope down through the centuries to the wives, sisters, and daughters of home-front Canada. The cover illustration for Hale's *Grey Knitting* suggests another antecedent for wartime Canadian knitters: the Fates who spin and cut the thread of life. In the upper left hand corner sits a soldier, drying his socks over a fire. From the socks trails a thread, twining through the title, and arriving, in the lower right-hand corner, on the needles of a woman in a rocking chair with a child at her feet. The thread connects the woman to her loved one at the front; if she does not continue to work her needles, the thread of life will be cut.

Athena provides another link between Penelope and the home-front women of Canada. Athena is the ancestress of Britannia, at least in her post-Napoleonic incarnation (Warner 48), and thus of Miss Canada. She is also the martial goddess who guided Odysseus at war and finally led him home, and the patroness of women's work and thus the special protector of Penelope (Warner 94–5). So perhaps Groves's troops of knitting girls, marching as their needles click, succeed as symbols of women in wartime because of their deep mythological antecedents, especially the way they incarnate both the female and the male aspects of Athena. They are warrior knitters, at once domestic and martial.

The particular role for children, both boys and girls, in the war effort is another recurrent theme in Groves's playlets. A recitation entitled 'What can we do for our country' appears both in *The War on the Western Front* and, with minor variations, in *The Soldiers of the Soil and the Farmerettes* (16):

> What can we do for our country,
> British or Belgian or French?
> We cannot help over in Flanders,
> We cannot fight in a trench.
> Canadian children can't handle
> Bayonet, musket or gun.
> What can we do in this struggle
> To conquer the savage Hun?
> Those things are out of the question,
> But each can be doing a bit;
> And we are helping our soldiers
> When a warm grey sock we knit. (22) [12]

*Canada Calls* similarly emphasizes what children can contribute. It begins with various categories of adult citizens, such soldiers, sailors, miners, farmers, and foresters, describing what they are doing for the war. The last of these is a representative of Canada's housewives: 'Our Battlefield – is the kitchen; our ammunition – food; our watchword – conserve; our faithful friend and true ally – Good Fairy Thrift' (17). The housewife declares that 'we have also marshalled our children' for patriotic service; in come 'two tiny little tots' (5) to deliver lisping recitations about how they have learned to eat up all their crusts and to 'beware of Bad Fairy Waste' (18). They are followed by a group of older children carrying banners who explain how they too are serving: 'When Canada called for greater production, the children replied by planting war gardens. They have learned that even children can help' (20). The children read aloud the slogans on their banners: 'LETTUCE BEET THE KAISER,' 'GIVE YOUR KALE TO BEET THE HUN,' 'LET ARTICHOKE HIM,' and 'WE'LL TURNIP AND PLANT HIM' (20). The final group consists of Farmerettes and Soldiers of the Soil, who declare that 'we cannot go overseas to fight, so we are fighting the enemy at home' (21). The sequence of these examples of national service, starting out with adults and culminating with children and young people, draws attention to the importance of children's contributions: just like sailors, soldiers, miners, and housewives, children 'should be traitors indeed were [they] to fail to respond to Canada when CANADA CALLS' (22).

Groves's contemporaries embraced her works as eminently suitable for school and church concerts. In a 1916 review of three All Canadian Entertaiments, the *School* declared them 'brimful of Canadian patriotism' and 'just what teachers have been asking for' (Oct. 1916: 96). A later omnibus review praised them as 'good, patriotic entertainment adapted to the abilities of Public School children' and noted that 'even the smallest rural school can undertake an evening function based on one of these drills or plays' (Dec. 1917: 310). The *Ontario Library Review and Book Selection Guide* recommended eight of Groves's drills in its August 1917 issue (47). An advertisement from the school supply company Russell-Lang's of Winnipeg in the February 1918 issue of the *Western School Journal* includes seven titles by Groves, indicating that the market for her drills extended beyond Ontario. Several items in the *Letter Leaflet* mention drills performed at concerts in Anglican mission schools: Deaconess Stapleton at Lac La Ronge Mission described the Christmas eve concert in which 'some of the Senior children showed how they could drill, and ... 16 of the biggest girls gave a most pleasing red, white and blue "Scarf March"' (April 1915: 194). This may have been Groves's *Patriotic Scarf Drill*. Methodist Sunday schools also used them: an advertisement from the Methodist Book and Publishing House in *Sunday School Banner* promotes four of her drills for use in Patriotic Day entertainments (June 1916: 44). The wartime popularity of drills is also evident in L.M. Montgomery's *Rilla of Ingleside*: the concert that Rilla and the Junior

THE YOUNG SOLDIER.                                    Oct. 2, 1915

## THE YOUNG SOLDIER

Printed for The Salvation Army in Canada, Newfoundland, Bermuda, and Alaska, by The Salvation Army Printing House, 18 Albert St., Toronto

### Young Soldier Office, Toronto.

There is a beautiful story told of old Jewish times. It is as follows: There had been a great drought —no rain for many months. The fields were parched, and the springs were dry, and there was distress everywhere. The people came together to pray for rain to come. Rabbis and great men prayed, but no rain came. Prophets and rulers prayed, but the sky remained cloudless. At last came a quiet, plain, unknown man, and he offered prayer. At once clouds began to gather, and soon the rain was falling. The people asked him who he was, and he answered: "I am a teacher of little children." This man was heard in Heaven when rabbis and prophets had pleaded in vain.

### AN INTERNATIONAL PARTY

#### Given by Juniors of Woodstock, Ontario.

On Monday, August 23rd, the Woodstock Juniors gave a unique and spectacular demonstration, entitled "John Bull's International Party." The Juniors were dressed in twenty-four different costumes, and a very pretty picture they made, as they sat on the platform, each one holding either the flag of the country they represented, or an Army Flag.

Treasurer George Cleaver represented John Bull. He was arrayed in a long black coat and high silk hat, and wearing a Union Jack across his manly bosom. Young People's Sergeant-Major Joliffe sang a solo, in which every Junior was introduced to John Bull and the audience. Afterwards each Junior came forward and gave a short reading, describing the work of The Salvation Army, the number of the

Officers, Cadets, employees, and Institutions of the respective countries. Throughout the entertainment the Juniors sang songs that had a bearing upon The Salvation Army work in other lands.

Everything went off successfully, while John Bull declared himself to have been well entertained by his party. Ensign Tutte, our Commanding Officer, was chairman. We were very glad to see a large audience. Sergeant-Major Joliffe and the Juniors deserve much credit, as they have worked hard at the practices. We regret to have to report the resignation of our Young People's Sergeant-Major. Since her command of the Young People's Work the Band of Love has been commenced. Brother Greene and his daughter, Sister Ruth Greene, are endeavouring to fill Mrs. Joliffe's place.—E. R.

Faith gives us living joy and dying rest.

John Bull's International Party at Woodstock, Ontario

Names are as follows: Back Row (left to right): Young People's Sergt.-Major Mrs. Joliffe, Ensign Tutte, C. O. Third Row: Willie Stanbridge, representing S. A. Military Work; Ruth Ferris, Australia; Violet King, Denmark; Charlie Shrimpton, Korea; Annie Maltby, Norway. Second Row: Clara Maltby, Japan; Charles Ransom, America; Wilfred Manning, France; Faith Greene, Britannia; Anna Greene, Wales; Alice Deadman, Ireland; Edna Pilfrey, Scotland; Harold West, South Africa. First Row: Grace Cochrane, Holland; Gertrude Ransom, Italy; Elsie Deadman, Slum Work; Emma Stanbridge, India; Hilda Atkinson, Sweden; Eva Pilfrey, Switzerland. Front: Violet Curson, Finland; Florrie Maltby, England; Arthur Hurse, S. A. Naval Work. Unable to be present: Bramwell Greene, Canada; Calvin Greene, New Zealand; Gordon Pilfrey, S. A. Military Work; Milton Pilfrey, Children's Work.

10  A Salvation Army demonstration on a patriotic theme, 'John Bull's International Party,' performed by children in Woodstock, Ontario, in 1915. From the *Young Soldier*, 2 Oct. 1915: 8. With permission The Salvation Army Archives, Canada and Bermuda Territory.

Reds organize 'in aid of Belgian children who are starving to death' (112) includes 'the cutest flag drill' for 'three small girls' (102).

In a time when virtually 'no Canadian-authored popular fiction series appeared that was *not* published in the United States,' Groves's playlets were 'the only known series published in Canada and not issued simultaneously elsewhere' (Gerson 146, 157n16). Perhaps, in light of their imperial and nationalist sentiment, they did not interest the American publishers who handled the work of other Canadian authors of the day. However, the very fact that McClelland, Goodchild and Stewart found it worthwhile not only to reissue Groves's earlier playlets but also to publish several new ones without any co-publishing agreements with British or American firms suggests that there was a very good domestic market for them. As Paul Litt has noted, 'the war gave ... domestic productions a comparative advantage over American cultural products,' and Canadian publishers did very well with their war-related titles (335).

Groves's works were certainly pro-war and pro-Empire, but were they propaganda? To call them that implies Groves sat down with politicians and recruiting officers to figure out the best way to brainwash Canadian youth. But, of course, that is not what happened, nor would such a deliberate campaign have been necessary. Like many of her fellow educators (at least to judge from the pages of the *School*), Groves believed in the moral rightness of the war. The corollary of this belief was the conviction that children's participation in the war effort was not merely a matter of political or practical necessity; it was a moral imperative. Contributing to the great struggle would strengthen and ennoble them. In *The Soldiers of the Soil and the Farmerettes*, the children declaim, 'The war has brought us in its train / New viewpoints, thoughts and new ideals: / True SERVICE now is what appeals' (16). When earnest and energetic people believe these things, there is no need for official propaganda. As Niall Ferguson has observed about popular culture in Britain during the First World War, '... war propaganda did not have to be produced by governments; it produced itself' (229).

# PART TWO

**Stories of War**

# 4 Brave Little Soldiers: Stories for Younger Readers

'A boy can be a hero at home, just as well as at the front.'

'How?' Ted eagerly asked, twisting around so he could look up into Uncle Harry's face. Ted just longed for the time when he would be old enough to enlist and wear a uniform like Uncle Harry, and do something hard and brave.

Uncle Harry smiled into Ted's eager face as he replied, 'By doing faithfully and well the tiresome every-day duties, like a soldier. Do you suppose a boy who neglects to keep the wood-box full for mother, and runs off to play instead of filling the water pail, will make a good soldier?'

Playmate, 11 August 1917

A boy thumbing through the Eaton's catalogue in the fall of 1915 could have found some exciting new items for his Christmas list. There was the Soldier's Cut-out Puzzle set with four puzzles, 'each of which represents a war scene,' and the Game of Soldiers with '13 soldiers, one officer, Two Cannon, plenty of ammunition' for just 49 cents. The Soldier's Set with 'breast plate, hat, cuffs and revolver, belt and holster' was 'a big value' at $1. Parents were advised to order this item early 'so as not to disappoint the boy' because 'every boy will want to play soldier this year.' There were tin soldiers – the Royal Dublin Fusiliers or the Scots Guards – and the Soldiers on Parade set, with twelve soldiers mounted on horses, plus a pop-gun that 'shoots corks strong enough to knock over the soldiers and also makes plenty of noise.' There also was a new mechanical toy: an armoured motor car with a 'soldier in khaki seated at a quick-firing gun.' To go with all this, a boy might want a Regulation Officer's Uniform in Khaki Serge, sizes 3 to 10 years, at $4.95.

Better things were yet to come: by 1917, a boy could find the Big Dick Machine Gun in the catalogue: 'The very latest in toy machine guns will fire shots as quickly as you care to turn the handle.' The Soldier's set – 'the delight of every boy' – was still available, but now it could be supplemented with the Sword and Sheath; 'no boy would consider himself a soldier without this outfit.' Girls might be attracted to the doll set, to be sewn and stuffed at home, consisting of a Red Cross nurse and a Highlander for just 10 cents. There was also the foot-high Red Cross Nurse doll, made in Canada, at 50 cents.

These war games and props seem to have excited very little concern among parents or educators. The Sunday-school papers contained no injunctions against them. Even the Salvation Army's *Young Soldier* presented war games as a perfectly normal pastime for little children. In 'Our Red Cross,' a story that appeared in the 17 October 1914 issue, the boys are 'playing soldiers' with 'tins tied on with a bit of string for drums and sticks for guns' (5). They won't let the girls join in: '"No, you silly, girls can't be soldiers. They have to stay home and make shirts." And then they all marched off. We did feel bad.' The problem is resolved when one of the girls thinks of playing Red Cross, and it is 'such a lovely game that we forgot all about the boys.'

Such a story and the 'lovely game' it depicts domesticate war, as if it were just another grown-up pursuit children could play at. On the one hand, this acting-out of war may have enabled children to manage their fears and to reassure themselves that enemies could be defeated and wounds healed. On the other, playing at war and reading about it also laid the groundwork for children to accept war as a natural activity and thus to 'take one step closer to becoming active combatants' themselves (E. Johnson 75). In France and Germany, some war toys were even regarded as explicitly educational, preparing boys for what they would encounter on the battlefield (Mosse 141–2); perhaps the same kinds of toys – tin soldiers and realistic war machinery – were similarly regarded in Canada.

While few Canadians saw any dangers in the apparently uni-

Oct. 17, 1914.                    THE YOUNG SOLDIER.                    5

# OUR RED CROSS

### (SEE FRONT PAGE PICTURE.)

[England, as you know, is at war, and many of the Public Schools have been taken over as barracks for the soldiers. Many children, therefore, are enjoying extra holidays, and the following article shows how some of them employ their time.]

We can't get into our school. The soldiers came to live in it during the holidays, and when we went back there they were, lots and lots of them, looking out of the windows and laughing at us. So we went home again, and mother was a little cross. She said, "Well, I can't have you all round here among the washing. Go along out and play." Ella and Dot and Alice and I said their mothers felt just the same!

The boys were playing soldiers, they had tins tied on with a bit of string for drums, and stick for guns, and they were making an awful noise.

"Hi, Ted; Teddy Brown," cried a, "can we play?"

"Left, left, left," said Ted, who was the captain; he did not take a bit of notice. But Bobbie Eaves called out rudely, "No, you silly, girls can't be soldiers. They have to stay home and make shirts." And then they all marched off. We did feel bad.

"Aren't boys mean?" Alice said. "Fink yemselves ev'ybody," put in ?.

But then Ella thought of the Red Cross, and it was such a lovely game that we forgot all about the boys. We had papers for aprons and handkerchiefs for caps (some of us), and El-

la's baby's ???? for a flag, and Ella's baby's barrow for an ambulance cart (the baby was asleep and her mother let us have it), and then we went out for a march.

Of course all the folks made room for us when they saw the Red Cross on our arms (we made it with two long tram tickets). Besides, Ella had put on the flag. Nurses off out to the Front, so they knew who we were. The policeman at the crossing stopped all the horses and buses to let us pass. "OH.M.S.!" he said. We did not know what that meant, but we did feel proud!

And just a little way further down the street if we didn't come across those boys again!

Bob and Ted were fighting, because Bob wanted to say "Left, left!" as well as Ted, and Ted wouldn't let him. There they were, rolling about in the dust. It was dreadful.

"Do you give in?" Bob said.

"Ye-s-s," groaned Ted. "Oh, my head."

"Red Cross to the front," called out Ella, and we all marched up. Those boys were surprised.

We tied up Ted's head, and Bob lifted him into the ambulance. He made out he was very badly wounded, but he wasn't really. Only he likes to be made a fuss of.

And what do you think? Those boys all want to play Red Cross now. We let them come in and we don't say anything. (That is what teacher calls doing good for evil.) But Ella is the leader all the same!

## ONLY JUST STARTED,

### But Work Is Prospering.

The children's work in Fort Frances is very good. Although only started a few weeks, our average attendance is thirty, both the Young People's meeting on Tuesday and on Sunday afternoon. About twenty children have been converted and are doing well. On Labour Day we had a picnic, when everyone enjoyed themselves.

**Early Fall of Snow.**

On the morning of Sept. 28th a light fall of snow occurred at Quebec. This is very early for snow to appear, and it has not been known to fall before the end of September for many years.

Kitty, aged three years, while playing in the garden one day, fell and twisted her ankle. She came crying to her mother, and said: "O mamma, I hurt the wrist of my leg!"

"Ted made out he was very badly wounded, but he wasn't really!"

11  Illustration from the 17 October 1914 issue of the Salvation Army's *Young Soldier* (5). With permission The Salvation Army Archives, Canada and Bermuda Territory.

versal pastime of 'playing soldier,' one farm wife, writing to the *Saturday Press and Prairie Farmer* in 1916, did express concern:

> What in the world are mothers thinking of that they make soldiers of their boys from the time they are babies. I refer to the uniforms being sold for boys of all ages. Wherever I go, I see small boys wearing them. Now I firmly believe in teaching children to be good citizens, to love their country and to be loyal to it; but I do not believe that a military uniform has any place in such teaching. They are only learning to love the uniform. Are we mothers to go on and teach our boys love of war instead of peace? Do we see our children, now infants, as soldiers of the future and engaged in another awful carnage such as we have at present? It seems inconceivable that women should go on making soldiers of their children, instead of teaching them to hate war. (Quoted in Roberts 20)

To judge from the numerous photos of children in uniforms that have survived from the war years, many Canadian mothers did indeed make 'soldiers of their children.' Even Salvation Army members dressed their little boys in military, not Salvationist, uniforms. A report in the 24 July 1915 issue of the *Young Soldier* describes two-year-old Eric Hamilton in his military uniform: 'His father had him dressed thus for the purpose of collecting funds for the Red Cross. At a recent lawn social little Eric sold flags, and gravely saluted every purchaser. On occasions such as these, Eric is always in great demand, and attracts quite a deal of attention. He is the most snap-shotted baby in town' (95).

In allowing and even encouraging their children to play at war, Canadian parents seem not to have feared that they were cultivating 'love of war'; they were simply going along with the tide, acknowledging their children's undoubted fascination with the war and incorporating them into the great cause of the moment. Yet this attitude, which the farm wife quoted by Roberts argued would lead only to 'another awful carnage,' perhaps reflected an adult need to make the war seem less disturbing and alien. As George Mosse claims about toys and games designed to involve children in war, '… children served to mask the reality of war through their chivalry and romanticism, treating it as a happy and joyous game' (142).

Just as toys and games rendered the war less threatening, so

12 This advertisement for soldier suits appeared in the Fall-Winter 1916/17 issue of the Eaton's catalogue (281). From the Collection of the Archives of Ontario; used with the permission of Sears Canada Inc.

too did books and stories. They did this by subsuming the war within familiar genres of children's literature. Eric J. Johnson has noted that propagandists 'recognized the utility of appropriating preexisting genres and forms of children's literature to package their ideologically charged messages' (59–60). In his study of illustrated war propaganda for children, Johnson examines war alphabet books for children (among other types of picture books), including a First World War example from Britain: *The Royal Navy: An ABC for Little Britons*. I have found no evidence that war alphabet books were available in Canada, although the *Little Folks Alphabet*, published in Toronto in 1919, did include a Red Cross nurse for 'N' and the Union Jack for 'U.' But war stories in other genres for small children – the cautionary tale, the evangelical deathbed story, the quest narrative, and even the fairy tale – were definitely read by Canadian children.

The domestication of war within familiar didactic story patterns distinguishes materials for young children from the adventure-oriented materials for older children. While the war adventure tales and girls' stories of war were also adaptations of familiar genres, they did not, to the same extent, contain the chaos of war within highly predictable and domestic story forms. I mean domestic here quite literally: many stories for younger readers focus on the child in war, not as an independent agent, but as part of a family. Restoring order at the familial level resolves the problems caused by war. Another dimension of the stories for younger readers is the explicit scriptural content. Not surprisingly, this is very evident in the Sunday-school stories, but it is also present in works published by secular presses. This religious dimension seems related to the didacticism of the war stories for younger readers and to their reassuring plot patterns. Despite the war, such stories seem to say, the world is a predictable place in which good grown-ups and a benevolent God will sort things out.

## Cautionary Tales

One of the first war books available in Canada was a parody of Heinrich Hoffmann's famous *Struwwelpeter*. In *Swollen-headed William: Painful Stories and Funny Pictures after the German!* E.V. Lucas transfers all the mischief done by Hoffmann's child characters and their consequent punishments to Kaiser Wilhelm, that naughty boy who has brought on himself and Europe all the troubles of war. Lucas, an editor of *Punch* and the author of numerous books of travel and satire, was among the authors summoned by Charles Masterman in September 1914 to aid the government in producing war propaganda (Buitenhuis 14). Whether *Swollen-headed William* was written in response to Masterman's request or whether it was Lucas's own idea, it certainly delivers effective anti-German sentiment. Published in England in the fall of 1914 by Methuen, *Swollen-headed William* was brought out in Canada by Musson in the same year.

Lucas's parody follows closely Hoffmann's original. The illustrations by George Morrow look as if they were traced from Hoffmann's drawings, with only slight variations to introduce the parodic political content. In transposing this book from the peacetime nursery to the war, Lucas makes some very interesting changes. For example, in the original tale of Harriet, the girl who plays with matches, there are two pussycats warning her of the dangers. In the Lucas/Morrow version, those cats are labelled Bismarck and William I – guardians, as it were, of Germany's Empire who weep when William reduces it and himself to 'smoking ruins' (6). In Hoffmann's *Struwwelpeter,* three white boys who mock a blackamoor are punished by being dipped in an inkpot by Agrippa; then they are as black as the boy whom they have mistreated. In *Swollen-headed William,* this story turns into a triumphalist parable about the British Empire and Germany's doomed attempts to acquire it. The blackamoor is transformed into a 'wealthy English Colonist … beneath whose skilful, kindly sway / Our vast dominions smile each day' (7). The mocking boys are Kaiser Wilhelm, Bethmann Hollweg (chancellor of Germany), and Bernhardi (the chief proponent of German militarism, whose 1911 book *Germany and the Next War* was widely read in Britain). It is Agrippa, labelled 'Destiny,' who rebukes the three: 'Boys leave the Englishman alone; / For though you fight till all is blue / He'll never give his sun to you' (8).[1] When they persist in tormenting the colonist, Agrippa plunges them into his inkpot and they come out black. Now 'the Englishman enjoys the fun' (10). Perhaps the nastiest story in the original *Struwwelpeter* is that of poor Conrad who sucks his thumb. His mother warns him that the tailor will cut off his thumbs if he persists in this bad habit. In *Swollen-headed William*, the Kaiser sucks his thumb as soon as his mother (Europa) goes out, and it is Lord Kitchener who administers the punishment.

*Struwwelpeter*, according to Barbara Smith Chalou, 'has long been regarded as an example of hideous Germanic cruelty toward children in its glorification of arbitrary obedience to authority' (2). But it was also regarded as a 'funny manual of good sense, eminently reasonable and straightforward' (Zipes 131), and it was a popular and much-translated book in Britain before the war; indeed, Lucas's parody could hardly have succeeded if his readers had not been well acquainted with the Hoffmann original. In *Swollen-headed William*, Lucas turns perceived 'German' cruelty against the German emperor himself. By presenting the European conflict as a cautionary tale, *Swollen-headed William* is ruthless but reassuring: just as bad little children are punished for their sins, so too bad rulers will get their just deserts.

A cautionary tale of quite a different sort appeared in the *Young Soldier*, prefaced by the editorialist's announcement that 'what the Salvation Army thinks about war is very plainly put in the story you will find in this issue of "The Young Soldier," entitled "The Golden-Mist Giant"' (29 Aug. 1914: 8). In this story, part fairy tale, part cautionary tale, a young boy named Jack is visited by the Giant, who has 'the face and figure of a hero, a Viking, a leader of men' (10). The Giant is a fluid, ghostly figure: '... though his uniform changed (he was always in uniform) and was sometimes that of a poor man and then trappings and armour of a mighty prince, the golden glow and the deep golden mist that were about and over him were ever the same, making his shabby clothes seem glorious and his splendid ones positively dazzling.' The Giant insinuates his way into Jack's thoughts, encouraging him to value 'courage and great deeds.' Inspired by the persuasive Giant, Jack gets into a fight with a classmate, hitting him so hard that Jack fears he has killed him. Mother is very disappointed in Jack's behaviour and, in a rare touch of irony for a mother in a Sunday-school story, notes, 'How brave and courageous to show how badly you can hurt another boy's body' (11). Jack tries to justify his actions: '"Brave men fight," said Jack getting red and speaking low.' But Mother's response is strong and unequivocal:

When all the world believes fighting, battering, killing, and bringing untold misery on everybody is brave, do you mean to tell me
the boy or man who starts to show that peace is best and right has
no pluck? Where does our blessed Lord give us orders to fight with
our fists or weapons, or make war on each other?
... Is bloodshed and murder any the less bloodshed and murder
under their other names of fighting and war? (11)

The Giant tries to keep Jack on his side. With Satanic sophistry,
he disputes Mother's position:

'This is woman's nonsense,' said the Giant. 'Where is the glory in
peace on earth?' He lifted his cloak of golden mist, but through its
shining Jack thought he saw a vision of burning houses, homeless,
starving, weeping women and children, and the wounded and
dead bodies of men. THAT is why the Giant covers himself with a
mist of gold glory to hide the horrors he brings. (12)

Now that Jack can see the true nature of the Giant, he is able
to resist him and to turn towards God. Lest any reader miss the
point of this story, it concludes with the declaration that 'the
name of the Golden-Mist Giant is WAR.'
     The fairy-tale elements – the shape-shifting Giant, the power
bestowed on the weak child, the glimpse the story gives into
dark realms of violence – blend with an evangelical type of cautionary tale in which the erring protagonist is saved by an avowal
of faith. 'The Golden-Mist Giant' does not end with the fairy-tale
convention of happily-ever-after in a prosperous kingdom. But it
does end with a utopian fantasy: Jack's father affirms that 'a big-
ger, brighter day [is] dawning' and in this new world, Jack will be
'a Peace Man': 'No more fighting for you, Jack, in the bloodshed
and war way' (12). In the schema of Salvationist thinking, faith
was the route to a better and more peaceful world.
     The Salvation Army's *Young Soldier* published considerable
numbers of war-related articles in 1914 and 1915: tales of child
heroes, accounts of the suffering of the Belgian refugees, and
animal stories appeared in its pages. But in its editorials, the
paper condemned war and the cruel spirit it had awakened. It
urged young people not to yield to 'that foolish mob passion
which manifests itself by ill-treatment of foreigners in our midst'

and reiterated the Army's position that 'our mission is to help all in need, no matter what nation they belong to or whether their soldiers are fighting ours or not' (29 Aug. 1914: 8). As the editorialist asserted, 'War only comes because of greediness and anger, and it leaves behind it tears and sore places and hunger and sickness, and death.' This is indeed the message of 'The Golden-Mist Giant' – an unusual example of writing for children that condemns war as an unchristian activity.

## Piety and Patriotism

In each issue of the Anglican children's periodical, *New Young Soldier*, there was a Scripture Lesson, consisting of a scripture passage, then a 'Golden Text,' 'Daily Home Readings,' and 'The Lesson Explained' (this last being a short essay, usually signed by a clergyman). A lesson on Isaiah 9:2–7, a text which announces the future coming of the Messiah, compares it with Canadians' desire for the end of the war:

> When peace is declared how glad we shall be. How good it will be to have our loved ones and friends home again. We shall not have to be reading about Zeppelin raids and submarines. That is just how the Jews felt when they heard this message from Isaiah which is today's lesson. (23 Dec. 1917: 1)

In the March 31 issue, Mary Magdalene's visit to the tomb of Christ, described in John 20:1–10, is likened to a dawn raid. Blind Bartimaeus, who 'received his sight' from Christ in Mark 10:46–52, is compared to the many soldiers who return home 'wounded and unfit to take up their former occupations' (16 June 1918: 1). Judas's betrayal of Christ (Mark 14:32–50) is made more vivid by discussing 'the German spy system' (21 July 1918: 1).

If the ministers who wrote these explanations felt that a war analogy was the best way to bring home the meaning of a scripture passage, then one can only assume that war was a topic uppermost in children's minds. Moreover, the war analogies in the Scripture Lessons imply that war and Christian faith are compatible. Adults might have pondered the moral complexities of several Christian nations killing each other's young men, but children were unlikely to do so. They must have accepted, more or less uncritically, the merging of the Christian struggle against Evil with the British Empire's war against the Hun. The close coincidence of 'King' and 'king' no doubt aided this conflation. In a story in the *King's Own*, a Presbyterian paper, a young woman is wearing the badge of the magazine's TOKO club, The Order of the King's Own. When a wounded soldier enquires about it, the confusion about kings becomes evident:

' – it doesn't mean King George – at least – '

'I understand,' interrupted the man saluting reverently, soldier fashion; 'it means the King of kings; what's your marching orders?'

'"Live pure, speak true, right wrong, follow the King,"' Edith repeated promptly.

Young Edith herself can scarcely distinguish between the 'kings' whom she must serve. A short item on military and civilian uniforms similarly uses military terms to describe religious duty: it reminds children to 'see to it that you are wearing the right uniform of love, truth, sobriety, and purity, and that you are real and trustworthy soldiers of the King of Kings' (21 Aug. 1915: 135).

A book published in 1916, *A Soldier of the King: A True Story of a Young Canadian Hero*, by Helen Stirling, demonstrates this intertwining of the war with spiritual matters.[2] The soldier of the title is Charlie Russell, a boy with an unnamed fatal illness; his final, noble act is to raise money for Toronto's Hospital for Sick Children. Charlie takes courage from his heroes, the soldiers. A military funeral with a procession of soldiers down the city streets 'fill[s] Charlie's little soul with noblest pride, but a new, strange sorrow' (13).[3] His favourite song is 'The Little Soldier.' Its chorus – 'When I'm big, I'll be a soldier, / That is what I'll be' – becomes Charlie's own motto. After an especially painful treatment, the doctor reminds Charlie of his 'grand song' about becoming a soldier: 'You could not sing it for us to-day, could you Charlie? But some day you will, as you come marching back from the war, with the Victoria Cross on your breast. Just now this is your battlefield ... and there are very few braver soldiers on any field' (29–30).Charlie's favourite tales are imperial and martial: 'He seemed never to tire of the brave doings of his soldier boys, and Piper Findlater, who, sorely wounded, piped his Highlanders up Dargai Heights and inspired them to make the charge which meant so much to England, in the struggle in India, became one of his best beloved heroes' (23–4).[4] When the pain is particularly intense, Charlie encourages himself by whistling 'Cock of the North' – the very tune played by Piper Findlater (32). Other images of the Empire at war bolster Charlie's courage: '... he sang his little song, and ... for him the room broadened out into a South African veldt, and he led his khaki-clad men across the open, rushed them up the kopje ... till the great movement came, when he led them on to victory' (39–40). Charlie's doctor is impressed by the boy's bravery: 'I am as proud of this little soldier as I am of our big Canadians who are fighting so nobly for our Empire, and so is your General. He fought with pain, too, Charlie, and gained the victory, and so will you' (35).[5]

Charlie's final effort is to make things that he can sell in order to raise funds for the children's hospital. But even as his 'wonderful work' is being praised, the little soldier is fading away. His father tries to encourage Charlie: 'You'll win all right, Piper – you must, you know, you can't help it – you're British.' But the little boy dies, and 'another brave soldier passed out of the trenches to his new and wonderful billet' (55).

Charlie is a descendant of the pious, doomed child so common in nineteenth-century evangelical literature. Even the epithet 'little' (as in 'the little soldier') ties him to this tradition: as Maria Tatar has noted, citing the examples of Little Nell, Little Eva, and the Little Match Girl, 'the term *little* functions as a death sentence' for nineteenth-century fictional children (246). The 'pattern of infant piety and happy death,' which was a central narrative in evangelical tracts for children, derived from a late seventeenth-century Puritan tale, *A Token for Children, Being an Exact Account of the Conversion, Holy and Exemplary Lives and Joyful Deaths of Several Young Children* (Bratton, *Impact* 36). Charlie does not go through a conversion – he is pious already – but his 'exemplary' life and 'joyful death' link him to this type of didactic literature. The adaptation of the dying child conversion story to the context of war demonstrates how genres can be 'kidnapped' to serve new moral purposes. 'Kidnapped' is Jacqueline Bratton's word; she uses it to describe how such genres as popular romance were Christianized by the evangelical writers (68).

In the case of *Soldier of the King*, an explicitly Christian genre is adapted to serve patriotic ends. By connecting Charlie with the soldiers, Stirling invests them with the exemplary virtue of Charlie. If Charlie, the soldier of the heavenly king, has a happy death and goes to that 'new and wonderful billet,' then so too will the soldiers of the temporal king.

This fusion of war and religious themes in children's stories seems part of the larger effort to incorporate the war into the fundamental Christian 'rhythm of death and resurrection, suffering and redemption,' that was at the heart of so much war rhetoric and imagery (Mosse 77). If the war could be understood as a part of this pattern, then to die on the battlefields was not really death at all but a sacrifice, sure to win for the fallen eternal life and for the survivors a redeemed and better world.

**The Child's Mite**

It was expected that children in Sunday schools, like the widow with her mite in the biblical parable, would give their humble pennies to such church-related charities as mission funds. When the war came along, causes like the Belgian refugees and the Red Cross took their place alongside the traditional calls on children's charity. In the Sunday-school magazines, many stories depict children who work hard or give up something precious in order to donate to a war cause. These stories provide models of the 'exercise of ceaseless self-denial' which the Presbyterian Commission's 1917 report, 'The War and the Christian Church,' called for as the appropriate Christian response to war (Kilpatrick 15).

In 'The Patriotic Twins,' a story in the *King's Own*, 'Busy Twin' Roger and 'Dreamy Twin' Frank want to give to the Patriotic Fund. Like Martha and Mary, each finds his own way to be of service: Roger earns money by doing chores, while Frank sells his toy boat. Their mother is proud: 'When one is willing to spend his play hours in work, and the other ready to give up his dearest toy, then I'm sure that when you grow to be men you'll be good soldiers' (13 March 1915: 44).

Jim, the protagonist of 'Bobs and the Red Cross,' faces a harder choice. When he hears about 'the splendid Red Cross work' and sees his Aunt Martha knitting 'for the brave soldiers in the trenches across the sea,' Jim's 'boyish heart burn[s] with desire to help.' Jim is very attached to his pet Bobs, a Manx kitten, but when two ladies offer him $10 for the kitten, he gives up Bobs in order to earn the money for the Red Cross.[6] Jim's generous impulse is rewarded, for at the end of the story the new owners return Bobs to him. From this story, the author draws a message that is both Christian and patriotic: 'Who shall say that there was not One who had seen and directed it all – even as of old He accepted the spirit of submission to His will and gave back to a father, unharmed, that which He had asked as a test of love?' By 'the offering up of his best loved possession,' Jim has done as Abraham did, and, like the patriarch, he is given back the sacrifice he freely offered.

Another biblical motif of sacrifice is employed in Lilian Leveridge's 'Spikenard Very Costly,' about a family who decide at Thanksgiving to '*prove* our thankfulness by *giving up* something – something for the Belgians or the soldiers' (*King's Own*, 16 Oct. 1915: 167). Instead of buying herself a new hat, Mother buys 'an armful of grey wool' to knit into socks. Little Joe is going to send his 'big white Teddy bear, his last gift from Santa Claus ... to some little Belgian boy.' Another son, Douglas, gives thirty-five cents, the price of a box of cartridges. Hazel gives 'a ten-dollar gold piece' that she got for selling a precious gold locket. Mother is so touched by Hazel's gift that she sells her heirloom china 'for a very substantial check, which eventually travelled across the sea to a certain hospital, built and endowed by Canadian women for wounded soldiers in France.' Leveridge concludes her story by making explicit the parallel with Mary's gift to Jesus: 'And the sweet savor that went up to heaven from the Thanksgiving sacrifices was the odor of "spikenard, very costly" – which means *love*.'[7]

## Little Children of Belgium and France

The American author and illustrator Lucy Fitch Perkins (1865–1937) is remembered for her 'twin' series. Beginning in 1911 with *The Dutch Twins*, Perkins produced more than twenty books, including a 'geographical' series about twins in other countries and a 'historical' series featuring stories of twins in societies of the past. The books were aimed at a variety of reading levels: there is a primer version, for example, of *The Dutch Twins*, and also a version for older children. Her two books set in countries at war – *The Belgian Twins* (1917) and *The French Twins* (1918) – were intended for children in Grades 4 and 5. Several of Perkins's books appear on Lillian Smith's 1917 list of recommended books for children's divisions of Ontario's public libraries. Both *The Belgian Twins* and *The French Twins* were favourably reviewed in the *Ontario Library Review and Book Selection Guide*, the review of *The French Twins* describing it as 'probably the best book that has yet appeared in this delightful series and [a book that] presents a pathetic picture of child life in the war zone' (Nov. 1918: 51).

The first of Perkins's war books, *The Belgian Twins*, begins with the predictable pre-war idyll of August 1914, as the family Van Hove work together in the fields to bring in an abundant harvest. The first sign of war is the sound of hoofbeats in the night, when a messenger comes to warn the villagers that the Germans are coming. Father Van Hove goes off to fight, leaving Mother to finish the harvest. The children earnestly do their part: Jan tries to feed all the pigs, but ends up spilling the slops and nearly falling into the sty himself; Marie tries to make breakfast but lets the kettle boil over, putting out the fire. Fearing that they might have to flee, Mother Van Hove gives Marie a locket with her own picture in it and drills the children on their full name and home so that if they become separated, they will be able to identify themselves. She reassures them that she will find them 'even if I have to swim across the sea' (68). When the German army advances on the village, Mother hides the children in the root cellar with their dog Fidel. Hours pass, and when the children finally venture out, the house is empty. Like the good little children they are, Marie and Jan pack up their clothes and some remaining bits of food in a bundle on a stick; they leave a note for their mother in case she returns, and, along with their dog, start walking.

The children make their way to Antwerp, to Rotterdam, then to England, and ultimately America. While Perkins does not dwell on the German atrocities in Belgium, she does make it clear that homes were destroyed and civilians were killed. Marie and Jan encounter German violence: they are nearly shot by a soldier who is maddened by their protective dog. Yet, throughout their perilous journey, the brave little children persevere with the help of kind adults. An especial benefactor is an old woman, an eel catcher, who cares for them when they get left behind by the crowd of refugees on the road. The story she tells Jan and Marie about 'the King of the Eels who lived in a crystal palace at the bottom of the river' serves the little children as an allegory of hope: 'Lots of folks can't see a thing in the river but the mud, [but] if you look at it the right way, there is a whole lovely world in it' (114–15).

Certainly, for Jan and Marie, the world does turn out lovely. When they arrive in America, their new foster mother, Madame Dujardin, sees Marie's locket and realizes that the twins' mother is no other than her own sister Leonie, from whom she has been estranged since she and her husband came to America.[8] When a cable finally arrives from the twins' mother, Madame Dujardin tells her the miraculous news, and soon Mother Van Hove and their father, who has been convalescing from the loss of a leg, come to America. The wealthy uncle gives them his country estate to live on and look after, and all ends well in America, far from the battlefields.

*The Belgian Twins* seems to unfold in the real world: it describes historical events such as the siege of Antwerp, mentions real places, and employs convincing material detail about life in Belgium. But it is not just a 'little folk of other lands' story designed to teach geography and comparative culture. It is also a fairy tale, in which Belgium at war stands in for the timeless Mittel-Europa of the traditional fairy tale. Jan and Marie are Hansel and Gretel – two children abandoned in a dark wood. The witch of 'Hansel and Gretel' is mirrored by the eel woman, who feeds the twins instead of fattening them for the table. It is not a duck that takes them over the river, but a kindly bargeman. And while Jan and Marie do not arrive home with pearls and gems, they do bring wealth to their parents by miraculously ending up with their rich aunt and uncle in America, a land of peace and prosperity which serves as the fairy-tale kingdom where the brave little children are finally safe.

When Perkins wrote her second war book, *The French Twins*, the United States was engaged in the war, and she could no longer treat it as a quasi-mythical horror happening on the other side of the world. But realism about war was equally impossible. As a consequence, *The French Twins* seems to veer unhappily from discussions of the morality of war to spy-catching adventures, and even to a patriotic allegory in which cheery Americans rescue the beleaguered French. Perkins still uses a conventional form, the quest narrative, to shape her story: the protagonists are forced to flee from their home but, after various adventures, enjoy the 'redemptive reestablishment of home, family, and friendship' essential to such narratives (Myers 328). (Another way to categorize Perkins's plot is as a home-away-home narrative, a type that Perry Nodelman and Mavis Reimer have identified as central to many works of children's literature [189–90].)

The twins of this story, Pierre and Pierrette Meraut, live in Rheims, and the town's famous cathedral functions as a symbol of Christian virtue under fire. When in catechism Pierre is reciting the Ten Commandments, he gets stuck after 'Thou shalt not kill,' and he tries to cover his forgetfulness by asking a question:

> Aloud he said: 'If you please, your reverence, I don't understand about that commandment. It says, "Thou shalt not kill," and yet our soldiers have gone to war on purpose to kill Germans, and the priests blessed them as they marched away!' (16–17)

The fact that Pierre's question arises, not out of some precocious philosophical concern, but out of embarrassment makes it more plausible. The Abbé responds in a way that attempts to make sense of the obvious contradiction of Christians at war:

> God sees our hearts. He knows that the soldiers of France go forth not to kill Germans but to save France! Not wantonly to take life, but because it is the only way to save lives for which they themselves are ready to die. Ah, my children, it is one thing to kill as a murderer kills; it is quite another to be willing to die that others may live! (18)

This response clearly sanctions killing, and it elevates the soldier to the status of a martyr. Yet, short of outright pacifism, which is not Perkins's message, it is hard to imagine a better answer – better, that is, in the sense that it reassures both Pierre and the readers that adults understand what they are doing and have made a reasoned decision to engage in war. Perkins depicts Christian compassion as a force that can triumph over the ugliness of war. When bombs land on the cathedral, which has been turned into a hospital for both German and French wounded, the patients must be evacuated. Angered by the sight of French doctors and nurses helping the wounded Germans, the townspeople shout, 'It is the Germans who burn our Cathedral. Let them die with it' (85). But the Abbé and the Archbishop resist the mob, declaring, 'If you kill them, you must first kill us' (86).

It is impressive that in this formulaic book for children, Perkins broaches the very difficult question of how to reconcile compassion with patriotism. Moreover, with discretion she manages to indicate the physical horrors of war. When their wounded father returns from the Battle of the Marne and is kept in the cathedral-turned-hospital, the children visit him, but Mother will not let them stay: '"No," answered his Mother firmly, "the sights here are not for young eyes"' (72). And though proud Pierre – he has boasted of his father to all the other children – wants to get from his father more details of battle, his father is reluctant: '"Well, my boy," he said after a pause, "there is much I should not wish you to know"' (74–5). Still, what he does tell Pierre fills the little boy with patriotic zeal. Pierre's response seems a very realistic expression of an impotent child's desire for spectacular revenge:

'France can have all of my legs!' he cried in a burst of patriotism. 'And when I'm big enough, I'm going to dig a hole in the ground and put in millions of tons of dynamite and blow up the whole of Germany! That's what I'm going to do!' (76)

Unfortunately, combined with this even-handedness is an intrusive championing of American virtue. As the family flees from Rheims to the village of the twins' grandparents, they come across a camp for Foreign Legionnaires, among whom are two Americans. These two Americans, known as Uncle Sam and Jim, become friends and protectors of the twins. And then two American women arrive in the devastated village where the family has taken refuge. The younger of the two, 'in excellent French,' explains their mission:

'We are Americans,' she said, and at that name every face smiled
back at her. 'We have come to help you restore your homes. America loves and admires the French people, and since we women
cannot fight with you, we wish at least to help in the reconstruc-
tion of your beautiful France. Your government has given us permission to start our work here, and has promised help from the
soldiers whose camp is near. The money we bring from America
will help purchase materials, and with your labor and the help of
the soldiers we shall soon see what can be done.' (142)

The truck the girls have arrived with contains 'the very things
for which [the villagers] had been longing so eagerly,' ranging from garden tools and seeds to cloth, knitting needles, and
food (143–4). Several more American girls arrive to rebuild the
health and homes of the French villagers.

For a time, the focus shifts to the doings of the Americans,
and *The French Twins* threatens to turn into an instalment of the
Campfire Girls. But Perkins returns the twins to the spotlight by
having them discover an informer talking to a German spy. For
their good work in spy-catching, Pierre and Pierrette are made
'honorary members of the regiment' of the Foreign Legion
and receive a reward (199). Perkins, at her best when depicting
domestic detail and the little dramas of a child's life, stumbles
when the spy-catching is introduced, for it seems a far-fetched
plot device for such young protagonists.

*The French Twins* and *The Belgian Twins* impose upon the story
of the war and its child victims a profoundly reassuring frame-
work: after adventures and dangers, both sets of twins escape
the war zone and find a new and safer home. In both cases, this
restoration of domestic order is accomplished by the interven-
tion of American wealth and resources.

## Her Nearest Duty

Little Canadian girls, like their mothers, could contribute to the
war effort by knitting for the soldiers. But even knitting might be
too much of a distraction from a girl's real duties in the home.
In 'A Brave Little Soldier,' which appeared in the boys and girls
section of the *Christian Guardian*, Marjory is 'so pleased' when
she finally learns to knit (8 Dec. 1915: 14). Marjory is just five

and must ask her mother to write a letter for her: 'Dear soldier. My dear little girl Marjory knit this all herself. If you want another wash-cloth or socks, or anything, just write and let her know, and she will knit them for you.' Absorbed in her exciting war work, Marjory neglects to go to the baby when she cries. Mother chides Marjory, but she replies, 'Mother, don't you know that I'm knitting for the soldiers?' (15). Mother does not want 'to spoil Marjory's joy in her knitting,' so she lets the matter drop. But grandma intervenes and manages to persuade Marjory to help mother by looking after the baby. How she does this is not made clear, but 'somehow when grandma was around you knew that God was very kind and very near.' When father comes home, mother tells him 'how brave Marjory had been to leave her knitting to attend to the baby.' Father praises his little daughter: 'I guess Marjory was doing her nearest duty, just like the brave soldier who will receive the wash-cloth.' His words remind girls that the best way to help is not to do something showy or public but rather to attend to domestic responsibilities – to one's 'nearest duty.' This rather discouraging lesson is glamorized by the analogy to the 'brave soldier.'

The example of the soldiers was also invoked to remind girls to be diligent in their work. In 'A Soldier's Sock,' which appeared in *Playmate*, the Methodist weekly for 'juniors,' Rosabel and her twin sister, Isabel, are knitting socks when Rosabel discovers an error:

> What was one dropped stitch, anyhow? She kept right on knitting stubbornly. Isabel's sock was an inch longer than hers already. She couldn't afford to ravel any out. (6 April 1918: 55)

Both girls are 'very proud of being able to do something to help their country in time of need,' but Rosabel's pride is shadowed by the knowledge of her error. After father reads to them 'about the sufferings of the soldiers, of the cold, wet trenches, and of the long, frozen marches when their feet left bloody stains upon the snow,' Rosabel realizes she cannot send an imperfect sock. She lies awake that night until finally her conscience forces her to get up, unravel the sock, and redo it. As the twins' grandmother points out, '… that sock was worth more to Rosabel than it would be to the soldier who was to wear it, for it gave her the opportunity to prove that she had the courage to acknowledge her mistakes and to rectify them, too.' The soldiers provide a Christ-like model that Rosabel cannot ignore. If they are giving so much, then Rosabel must make her best effort too. This story uses the soldiers' suffering in order to make even girls' domestic duties seem a quasi-sacred vocation and a duty to the state.

**Home-Front Soldiers**

A story in the *King's Own* in November 1914, 'A Sixth of a Shoulder,' by U.N. Macdonnell, initiated a plot type that would appear innumerable times throughout the war years: the boy who is too young to enlist redirects his patriotic energies to service on the home front. Instead of engaging in war games or playing with toy weapons, the boys of the Sunday-school papers find more constructive, less overtly violent, outlets for their war enthusiasm. In Macdonnell's story, two envious boys watch a troop train leaving town:

> 'How long do you suppose the war'll last?' asked Fred suddenly.
> 'Oh, a good long time, my father says,' replied George hopefully. 'We're fourteen. They say they had boys of sixteen fighting in the civil war in the States.' (28 Nov. 1914: 191)

George and Fred lament the fact that the girls 'have the start of us these days': 'Your Sue's knitting socks for the soldiers, and our May's got a nightshirt on the go, and even the little kids are cutting handkerchiefs. Seems as if there wasn't anything a fellow could do to help.' Their male pride stung by this recognition, the two boys find a way to be just as useful as the girls: they do garden chores for a widow whose eldest son has gone to war.

In 'Doing His Bit,' ten-year-old Gordon feels useless: 'Daddy's away in France, and Aunt Mary's a nurse in Salonika, and Mother knits socks, and I've got to do something' (*King's Own*, 1 Sept. 1917: 137). The minister advises Gordon to 'try to be a generally useful boy. Do all the things you can to save your mother steps, and then she'll have time to knit more socks, don't you see?' (138). In this spirit of helpfulness, Gordon volunteers to take a meal to a worker at the local munitions factory. He spots a fire at the factory and manages to warn the workers in time to save them.

In 'How Four Boys Served Their Country,' an Empire Day fishing trip is cancelled when young Robert persuades his friends to weed the garden of a woman 'whose husband had been among the first to enlist when the war began nine months before' (20 May 1916: 83). But they get their fishing trip too: Rob's mother sees the good work the boys have done, so she arranges for them to be driven to the creek at the end of the day. Rob's Aunt Mamie praises him when she tucks him into bed that night: 'My soldier boy, you have served two Kings loyally this day.'

Sometimes boys do not willingly take on their duties. In 'Their War Work,' brothers Fred and Ned resent having to run errands for their neighbour, Mrs Campbell, whose son has joined up. They decide to show how tired they are of doing chores by leaving her wood basket only half-full. But then a letter for them comes from Bernard Campbell:

> Dear Boys, wrote Bernard, 'Our regiment has been ordered to entrain for the front to-night, but before I go, I want to thank you both for all your kindness to my mother. It means a great deal to me, since I had had to leave her, to know that you two fellows could be relied on to help her in any emergency and I'm proud and happy that two fine chaps like you are just as earnest in doing *your* war work, as I am in doing mine. You'll surely grow up to be fine soldiers, and I wish you were old enough to be in my company now. Good-by and God bless you.' (15 Dec. 1917: 197)

The boys are guilt-stricken, especially when they discover a shiny new bicycle for them in the Campbells' woodshed. Fred and Ned fill the basket properly and then confess to their mother what they did. She scolds them: 'It would have broken the dear old lady's heart to know that you thought it a burden to help her when her *own* boy has gone off so bravely to risk his life for all of us who stay at home' (198). This seems a perfect example of the 'Change-of-Heart' story, a narrative and moral pattern that R. Gordon Kelly has identified as one of the dominant formulas in nineteenth-century American children's magazines (38). 'Their War Work,' like the change-of-heart story type discussed by Kelly, 'combines a conscious recognition of the erroneous nature of ... former behavior with a conscious resolution to do better' (43).

The most cynical propagandist could hardly have contrived material more likely to create a reserve of willing recruits. In these stories every soldier is virtuous; every boy worth his salt wants to be one. Again and again, children are rewarded spiritually and materially when they do their little bit for the war. The virtues cultivated in the Sunday-school papers – obedience, industry, self-denial, idealism – were the qualities of a good Christian child, but they were also the attributes of a good soldier. Obedience especially is identified as a virtue both at home and in war. As a grown-up in one of the Sunday-school stories explains to three little boys dressed up as Highland soldiers, 'The boy who is obedient now is the one who will serve his country best when he grows up. Those who learn to obey best make the best leaders' (*Playmate*, 5 June 1915: 92).

Despite all the enthusiasm for soldiering, the Sunday-school stories never look in much detail at what soldiers actually do. The exception, not surprisingly, appeared in the Salvation Army's *Young Soldier*. Little Frank, holding forth on his military ambitions, announces: 'You'll see me coming home some day, Bob, wearing ever such a lot of medals' (15 Sept. 1915: 8). His friend Bob has no illusions about war:

'Well, I s'pose I can't be a hero, then,' said Bob sadly, "cause I don't want to be a soldier. I shouldn't like to kill people.'

# 5 Dogs of War and Other Animals

The Soldier's Kiss

Only a dying horse! He swiftly kneels,
Lifts the limp head and hears the shivering sigh;
Kisses his friend while down his cheek there steals
Sweet Pity's tear; 'Good-bye, old man; good-bye!'

No honours wait him, medal, badge, or star;
Though scarce could war a kindlier deed unfold;
He bears within his breast, more precious far
Beyond the gift of kings, a heart of gold.

*Young Soldier,* 4 November 1916[1]

According to Peter Shaw Baker, author of *Animal War Heroes,* the British forces had over one million animals in service in 1917; the total number used by all the belligerents during the war was more than sixteen million (vii). Animals of many kinds – horses, mules, donkeys, birds, dogs – played a vital role in the war effort. The consequence of this was, of course, huge numbers of animal casualties. Some twenty thousand pigeons were killed in the line of duty (Gardiner 99). An estimated eight million horses died (including those of all belligerents). On the Western Front the horses 'perished not from enemy fire but from cold, disease or starvation, so famished that they chewed other horses hairless or ate each other's rugs and choked on buckles' (Cooper 7).

Throughout the war, publications for children regularly carried 'news stories' or 'reports from the Front' describing regimental mascots, animal heroes, or pets in the trenches. There were also several works of fiction that represented the war from the perspective of an animal. Part of the reason for the popularity of the animal war story must be the fact that in the pre-war period the animal story was an absolute staple of children's reading. Moreover, in an age when more children lived in the country than in the city, and when horses were still a major means of transportation, working animals were part of everyday life. Just as they played a vital role in the peacetime economy, so too they were essential to the enterprise of war. Any story that represented the battlefields would inevitably have to include some reference to the animals who carried soldiers, pulled guns, hauled supplies, and transmitted messages.

But the numerous animal stories of war were not simply a reflection of the practical truth that animal strength and talents were needed in the war. Two other factors contributed to the rise of this distinctive sub-genre of war literature. The first is the didactic tradition of the animal story, reaching back to the fables of Aesop. The second is the special vulnerability and moral immunity that animals – and children – possess in wartime.

The decades preceding the war had been a golden age for the didactic animal story. Novels such as Anna Sewell's *Black Beauty* (1877) and Margaret Marshall Saunders's *Beautiful Joe* (1893) had been tremendously popular. Saunders's *Beautiful Joe*, written in deliberate imitation of *Black Beauty*, became an enormous success: it was 'the first Canadian book to become a world bestseller, the first to sell over a million copies and the first to achieve multiple translation' (Waterston 137). In both these animal autobiographies, the narrators display a human-like range of thought and emotion. This fullness of character is, of course, in sharp contrast with the protagonist of the animal fable, who is neither a realistic animal nor a fully realized character, just a cipher for a particular human attribute. Yet both *Black Beauty* and *Beautiful Joe* retain the didactic spirit of the animal fable, for their intent was to teach children compassion towards animals and towards their fellow humans.

The same decade in which *Beautiful Joe* became so popular saw the emergence of another type of animal literature: the wild animal story, that Canadian innovation usually attributed to Charles G.D. Roberts and Ernest Thompson Seton. This type of animal story did for the wild animal what *Black Beauty* and *Beautiful Joe* had done for the domesticated one: it introduced a new understanding of the animal as a sentient, even rational creature, not a mere bundle of instincts. And although there are no wild animal stories about the war, the new realism that this type of fiction brought to the depiction of animals can be seen in some wartime animal stories.

James Turner has attributed the late-Victorian concern for animal welfare to a displaced guilt among the middle classes. Unable or unwilling to ameliorate conditions for the lower orders of humans, they directed their sympathies and reform efforts towards animals: '... alleviation of animal suffering may possibly have provided a cathartic outlet for consciences uneasy about the sufferings of their own species' (54). This phenomenon of displacement is also at work in animal stories about the war. If readers in Canada or the United States felt some guilt about their inability to stop the suffering of soldiers and civilians in Europe, then reading about animals who are rescued from war or pass through battle unharmed (as virtually all the protagonists of the animal war stories do) might well have provided a 'cathartic outlet' of the same kind suggested by Turner.

In discussing the animal stories of Marshall Saunders, Gwendolyn Davies notes that they appealed to not only 'Victorian society's moral conscience but also its residual confusion over the separation of human and animal pain' (181). If animals suffered, then it was surely as wrong to hurt them as to hurt human beings – and vice versa. Davies quotes Turner's view that an '"instinctive" revulsion from the physical suffering even of others' was 'uniquely characteristic of the modern era' (Turner xii; quoted in Davies 181). If so, then this modern sensibility, newly attuned to the suffering of others, was about to confront another phenomenon of the modern age: the huge scale of suffering inflicted by industrialized trench warfare. This encounter between heightened sensibility and mass suffering may help to explain the power of many literary responses to the war, ranging from the rhetoric of heroism and sacrifice to the passion of anti-war poetry. It might also explain the smaller phenomenon of the animal war story. Reformers like Saunders believed that 'humane treatment of animals is indivisible from the moral treatment of human beings' (Davies 178). From this perspective, animal war stories are not allegories: their animal protagonists are not stand-ins for human victims but fellow beings suffering equally from the evils of displacement and grief, injury and death. Nonetheless, even for those whose intent was to show the moral equivalence of harming humans and harming animals, it was more acceptable to depict violence against animals. Describing a Belgian child losing its hands to a German sabre would have been excessively gruesome, but in *Me'ow Jones, Belgian Refugee Cat*, a book I discuss later in this chapter, a parallel act of violence against an animal is described plainly: a German picks up a Belgian cat by its ears and slices off its head. Here cruelty to animals is depicted not just for its own sake – that is, to acknowledge that there were animal victims of the German invasion of Belgium – but also to represent crimes against human beings.

Peter Webb's discussion of animals in Timothy Findley's *The Wars* suggests another type of human-to-animal displacement in war fiction. Webb argues that Findley transferred some human suffering to animals in order to make the horror of war fresh to us. Webb argues that so much has been written about the fate of the ordinary soldier on the Western Front that we are inured to it, but 'when we see animals suffering in *The Wars*, the representation reawakens the sympathy and outrage that ought always to be a part of emotional responses to tragedy – human or otherwise' (235). This may explain how animals function in modern war literature, but the prominence of animals in wartime children's literature cannot be explained as a technique to counter desensitization. Young readers during the war years, even those well informed about the fighting on the Western Front through letters, newspapers, films, and schoolbooks, cannot have succumbed to any sort of complacency about trench warfare, for they did not understand enough about its horrors to be indifferent to them.

Reinforcing the didactic value of the animal war story was the belief that animals, like children, possess a special vulnerability and moral immunity. Neither animals nor children choose to go to war; they are swept up in conflicts that are not of their making. To quote the inscription on the Animals in War Memorial in London, 'They had no choice.' One could argue that the same is true of the ordinary soldier, but even in wartime, adults have choices and powers that animals and children do not. Thus, one way to represent the child's helplessness during wartime is to focus on what happens to animals. Here, too, one can see both allegory and realism: the animals may be stand-ins for the human victims of war, especially its child victims, but they are also, in themselves, beings who suffer. Moreover, because animals lack voice and weaponry, they are not tainted by the evils of the battlefield. *War Horse*, British writer Michael Morpurgo's 1982 children's book about the First World War, is narrated by a horse who goes to the Western Front with a British cavalry unit. As critic Jean Webb observes, Morpurgo's decision to have the horse, Joey, tell the story means that it is told 'from the position of an innocent consciousness caught up in the conflict, yet powerless to alter his condition.' This association of innocence and powerlessness in animal victims of war has obvious parallels with the situation of child victims of war.

In her introduction to *The Animals' War: Animals in Wartime from the First World War to the Present Day*, historian Juliet Gardiner sums up the moral and even ontological problems raised by the use of animals in warfare:

> The various movements in recognition of animal rights have caused us to think deeply about animals being used in situations that are as dangerous to them as they are to the fighting men alongside them. Animals do not give their consent for war, but then throughout history men have been forced ... into wars whose objectives were decided by politicians and by generals and not by those who fought and died. Recent work on animal sentience has shown us how near at least a number of animal – and bird and insect – species are to human consciousness. So how far is the 'bravery' of animals simply an evolutionary instinct, and how far and in what ways is it a conscious and selfless conquering of fear for a perceived objective?
>
> At this stage in our knowledge it is not possible ... to answer such questions definitively. But the range of ways, the variety of situations, in which animals go to war and the contributions they have made ... should remind us that our understanding of war is diminished and impoverished if we fail to consider the role that animals play alongside that of the fighting men and women, and the civilians of all ages, in times of conflict. (11)

Gardiner's perspective is a modern one, informed as it is by recent scientific understanding of our genetic similarities to other species and of animals' capacity for communication and rational choice; it also reflects the perspective of the modern animal rights movement. Nonetheless, one can see that in the war years, there was a similar belief that the animals so central to the prosecution of the war could not be forgotten. They, too, were part of the story of war.

**Animal Soldiers**

Many articles in the children's magazines described hard-working animals in military service.[2] These articles were presented as news reports about actual animals and their human comrades. In 'Dogs in the War,' the Rev. M. MacGillivray describes the dogs used by French sentinels at listening posts: '... the dog hears things and smells things to which the human ear and nose are dead, and so often detects danger unsuspected by the human sentinel' (*King's Own*, 13 July 1918: 111). Rev. MacGillivray reserves his highest praise for the Red Cross dogs used by the French army to locate and even bring back the wounded in no man's land: '[Their] feats of sagacity, courage and endurance border on the miraculous.' An item in the Anglican *New Young Soldier* entitled 'Dogs in War Time' describes dogs in the Army Medical Corps: in the field, 'each dog carries a complete "first aid" field dressing under the Red Cross saddle which he wears' (16 Oct. 1916: 5). The author's comment on the dogs resembles what in hero stories was asserted about the ordinary soldier's invaluable but unsung contribution: 'When the stories of the war are told, many lives will be credited to the faithful work of these well-trained dogs.'

Like other participants in war, animals could get injured, but the articles always reassured readers that wounded animals were well looked after. Readers of the *New Young Soldier* would have been relieved, for example, to learn that 'a hospital has been opened in Paris to treat the wounded dogs which have played so large a part on the French side in the present war. The official Red Cross dogs, the messenger dogs, and even those kept by the troops as mascots are being cared for there when sick or injured' (17 March 1918: 7). Horses, too, were well cared for: '... a corps of expert veterinary surgeons and attendants are at hand to look after any animal that may be wounded or otherwise disabled' (*King's Own*, 5 June 1915: 91). A picture accompanying this article 'shows one of the devices for keeping healthy horses healthy. British cavalrymen are filling long, shallow canvas tanks in order to water the horses about to be brought up by their comrades.' The neat paddock in the photo, set midst pleasant fields, seems impossibly Arcadian for the Western Front. Perhaps such places existed behind the front lines, but it seems unlikely that the millions of war horses were cared for in such surroundings. A short item on training cavalry horses asserts that 'soldiers who have the management of war-horses know how needful it is for them to be gentle and obedient ... and this is so thoroughly understood now-a-days in training army horses that only kindness is allowed to be used' (*King's Own*, 18 Nov. 1916: 186). An article in the Salvation Army's *Young Soldier* reported that animals, like the soldiers, were susceptible to 'nerve-shock' caused by exploding shells: 'Horses occasionally fall down and give every appearance of having been shot, though actually unhurt. Dogs suddenly and unaccountably go lame, though untouched' (3 June 1916: 14). It took the animals 'as long as three weeks to recuperate.' These descriptions of the care provided for war animals affirmed that the moral and behavioural standards preached at home still held on the battlefields. The treatment of animals becomes, in effect, a synecdoche for moral quality. The Allies, since they are kind and decent to their animals, must be in the right; they could not be guilty of the sort of atrocities attributed to the Germans.

In 'Animals That Help,' an article in *Victoria* magazine, Donald A. Fraser describes working animals on the home front. For example, 'Peter, a fine Boston Bull, ... has collected several thousands of dollars for the Blue and Red Cross societies, and besides supports a wounded soldier in one of the hospitals' (Feb. 1918: 31). In a similar article in the *King's Own*, Fraser describes another stalwart Victoria dog, Muggins, who stood faithfully at the Empress Hotel, where 'for hours he will patiently wait for the coin to drop in to his jingling money-boxes, and often he has quite a load to carry home' (17 Aug. 1918: 132). As in the Aesopian fable, these patriotic animals serve as moral exemplars: 'If little dumb animals can work hard like this to help along the good cause of winning the war, how much more ought we, who have friends and relations bleeding and dying in the midst of the struggle, do to help them in their hours of suffering, or to help our country to become so efficient that the day of victory may be hastened?' (*Victoria*, Feb. 1918: 32).

A topic deemed of special interest to young readers was the work of the Blue Cross.[3] An article in the *King's Own* explained this organization's mandate: '[It] cares for the horses that are so very necessary on every battle field, and on the lines of communication, and that are in constant danger from shell fire and exposure' (13 March 1915: 43). In the *New Young Soldier* appeared a profile of Prince, a Newfoundland dog that was 'a very successful collector for the Blue Cross fund for horses disabled in the war' and had thus 'served his King and Country as faithfully and as true as any subject of George V' (24 Feb. 1918: 6). A letter from an eleven-year-old boy in the *King's Own* describes how he and his younger brother raised money for the Blue Cross by dressing up their pony for the July 1st parade 'with bandages on all her legs and one on her head to represent a wounded horse':

> When we got to the exhibition grounds we took off all her bandages and when our time came, we again dressed her up to let the people see what is being done by First Aid for wounded horses on the battlefield. We then made a collection and in all got over $40.00, and gave it to the secretary, who sent it to London, England.
>
> .... I forgot to tell you that after I put the bandages on I gave out the report: 'Maybelle troop horse, 5th Canadians, barbed wire wounds on legs, flesh wounds on head.' (12 Oct. 1918: 164)

Another favourite topic in information pieces was the special fidelity of 'our dumb friends.' An account of the sinking of the British battleship *Formidable* on New Year's Day, 1917, in which only 201 were saved out of a crew of 800, notes that the Captain's dog was 'faithful to the end,' going down with the ship beside his master (*King's Own*, 17 April 1915: 64). A story from France, 'A Hero of the Marne,' describes how a French soldier is saved by Léon, the regimental pet. Léon finds the man when he is wounded on the battlefield; he goes back to the French lines and gets some soldiers to return with him to where the man lies wounded (29 May 1915: 86). A similar anecdote concerns 'a brown-and-white setter, named *Fend l'air* (through the air), who is a real hero of the war' (*King's Own*, 21 Aug. 1915: 136). *Fend l'air* dug out his wounded master, a sergeant of the Zouaves. A very similar story entitled 'The Dog That Saved a Soldier' describes the rescue of Henri by a French dog (12 May 1917: 76). In yet another version, 'A Soldier's Dog Story,' the heroic dog tells the story himself (25 May 1918: 82). The proliferation of these stories suggests that the faithful dog became one of the myths of war, exemplifying in animal form the most important virtues of human combatants: loyalty and comradeship. The sameness of the dog stories (identical anecdotes appeared in several publications) suggests that, like child hero stories, tales of faithful dogs, even if based on some actual occurrences, were elaborated and disseminated as semi-official propaganda.

Many regiments and ships' crews adopted mascots because they were 'supposed to bring good luck' (*King's Own*, 10 July 1915: 112). The Australians were said to have a kangaroo at the front. One French regiment had Chanticleer as its mascot; although 'his destination [was] the cookery pot,' the regiment decided to keep him because he crowed at the sound of the guns (*King's Own*, 7 Aug. 1915: 131). A British soldier in Mesopotamia had adopted a pet gazelle, and 'more than one regiment from Western Canada are said to have brought young bear cubs to England with them' (10 July 1915: 112.) The most famous of these was 'Winnipeg,' an orphaned black bear cub brought to England in 1915 by an army surgeon with Princess Patricia's Canadian Light Infantry. 'Winnipeg' served as the regiment's mascot, but when the PPCLI went to France, the bear was left in the care of the London Zoo, where he in fact remained until his death in 1934. It was at the London Zoo that A.A. Milne's son Christopher Robin saw 'Winnie,' and his affection for the bear inspired the books that made his father famous ('Winnie-the-Pooh').

The mascots are invariably depicted as amusing and contented creatures; one article in the *King's Own* goes so far as to assert that of all the animals at the front, 'regimental mascots appear to have the best time, for they stay in billets, live on the fat of the land, and are made much of by the local inhabitants' (19 Feb. 1916: 32). Even animals in the thick of the fighting are depicted

13 This appeared on the cover of the 27 February 1915 issue of the Salvation Army's *Young Soldier*. With permission The Salvation Army Archives, Canada and Bermuda Territory.

as curiously invulnerable. 'Puppies in the Fire Zone' describes how a fox terrier, the pet of a regiment of Spahis (Arab soldiers), gives birth to a litter on the front lines. The soldiers make a cave deeper than their own dugouts so that the dog and her puppies will be safe (*King's Own*, 23 Dec. 1916: 206). A rather more artful story of this kind is Marshall Saunders's 'A Cat of the Trenches' (reprinted in the *King's Own* [4 Aug. 1917: 124] from *Our Dumb Animals*, the journal of the Massachusetts Society for the Prevention of Cruelty to Animals). It describes a cat that carries her kittens from the German trenches to the British lines. After an initial tour of inspection, she makes three more journeys to bring her kittens to safety: 'Finally she had three kittens safe in the English lines, and speculation as to her reason for the removal of the kittens was in vain. She never told why she deserted the Germans.' In 'Pete of the Fifth,' a Canadian version of the mascot story, on the day of Vimy Ridge a unit of Canadian Engineers adopts a French dog that has 'a dozen cute tricks, such as jumping over a stick, or through your arms, standing and walking on his hindlegs, and begging for bully beef' (*King's Own*, 27 July 1918: 120). Pete is also 'a war-seasoned veteran' who 'never seemed to understand how anyone in his right sense would ever go into that land of mud and shell-fire.' Some animals are represented as distinctly partisan. One article describes an Italian officer's pet monkey that so dislikes the Austrian flag that it goes over the top and wriggles through barbed wire and over the parapet of an Austrian trench in order to capture it (*King's Own*, 26 Jan. 1918: 15).

Perhaps the attention given to animals is an instance of the deployment of natural imagery in representations of war. George Mosse has described how the 'verdant natural setting' in many war postcards and the natural elements included in the design of war cemeteries worked 'not only to symbolize hope, but also to induce tranquility, to calm anxiety and fear' (129). Although from a certain point of view, animals were not separate from the troubles of the human world, they were, from another point of view, representatives of uncorrupted and incorruptible nature. The sprightly innocence of the trench mascots and their faithfulness to their human masters were tokens of hope that even the mass death of industrialized war had not permanently scarred the world.

**Animal Refugees**

Two children's novels published during the war depict the invasion of Belgium from the perspective of an animal. *Pierrot, Dog of Belgium* (1915), by Walter Alden Dyer, and Edward Branch Lyman's *Me'ow Jones, Belgian Refugee Cat: His Own True Tale* (1917) were written to encourage children to give to Belgian relief. While both Dyer and Lyman were Americans, these books were available to Canadian children.[4]

Dyer dedicated *Pierrot, Dog of Belgium* 'to the Commission for Relief in Belgium waging a bloodless battle against famine and the ravages of war.' The Commission, created in October 1914 by Herbert Hoover, was astonishingly successful in mobilizing the American public: by the end of the war, it had 'distributed over 2.8 billion dollars worth of necessities of life in Belgium and Northern France' and still had thirty million dollars in reserve ('Hoover's Legacy in Belgium'). Early in the war, American newspapers were full of reports on the suffering of the Belgians, so it is not surprising that Dyer became interested in using a Belgian setting for a dog story. Or perhaps it is more accurate to suggest that he became interested in using a dog story in order to write about the plight of the Belgians.[5] The first words of Dyer's preface – 'Belgium lies bleeding' – suggest his purpose is to evoke sympathy not just for the dogs but also for the people of Belgium.

Pierrot in peacetime is a working dog, a *chien de trait*, who hauls farm produce to market. In the same spirit as those authors who assured children that the Allies were kind to their horses, Dyer is quick to point out that in general the working dogs of Belgium are not maltreated: 'A Society for the Prevention of Cruelty to Animals has been active, and in some of the cities one may occasionally observe placards reading, *"Traitez les animaux avec douceur"*' (32). This information, of course, signals that the Belgians are a virtuous people.

When war breaks out, Pierrot is taken away by Belgian soldiers and taught to haul a machine-gun cart. As combat transforms him from an 'exceedingly devoted and affectionate' farm dog into a soldier (36), Pierrot realizes what he has lost:

If a dog cannot fully reason, he can at least remember, and Pierrot

felt that he had lost what was best in life and he could not understand why. He saw it all again – the peaceful dairy farm ...; the busy
city and the laughing newsgirls; ... the gentle hands and voices and
the joy of being loved ... But of course Pierrot was only a dog and
war is war. One cannot be bothered with such trivial matters when
the fate of dynasties is at stake. (64–5)

Dyer's irony here seems a sophisticated touch for young readers, especially when in other war stories, children were reading
about heroes who gladly forsook all the comforts of home in
order to defend the Empire.

Despite Pierrot's appealing gentleness, he also possesses a
credible degree of dog-like ferocity. When the Germans kill his
handler and then his cart-mate, Pierrot retaliates, just as nor-
mally peaceable men did on the battlefield: 'Unreasoning rage
seized Pierrot, and with what remained of his once agile strength
he leaped at the man's throat and sank his fangs into the flesh'
(72). After his one act of battlefield savagery, Pierrot reverts to
the faithful dog stereotype. Following 'the homing instinct,' he
eludes the Germans and makes the long walk eastward towards
his farm (79). After many days of 'plod[ding] doggedly along'
with one injured hind foot (83), Pierrot finally returns to his
original masters. This happy ending, with dog and family reunited, reflects a pattern seen in many war stories for young children, in which the restoration of domestic order symbolizes the
end of war.

A second refugee animal story, Lyman's *Me'ow Jones,* is narrated by a cat who, when 'the War Man' invades Belgium, flees
with his master and mistress to America. In the 'Foreword to
Grown-Ups,' Lyman identifies himself as the manager of the Belgian Relief Fund (which indeed he was) and claims that there is
a real Me'ow Jones: 'ME'OW did his full share, through the sale
of his photographs, in helping the Author to raise during the
first few months of the war, more than two million dollars for the
starving Belgian women and children' (x).[6]

As an animal autobiography, *Me'ow Jones* belongs to what Tess
Cosslett identifies as one of the 'most persistent and popular
genres of animal story' in the long nineteenth century (63).
Cosslett describes a number of works from this period narrated
by dogs, donkeys, rats, horses, and kittens. The purpose of the

animal autobiography was 'to argue for the better treatment of animals by humans.' While this 'education in moral sympathy' is cultivated by the animal-narrator's description of his suffering (and that of other animals he encounters), the object is not merely to make children kinder to animals. As one of the wise and benevolent adults in *Beautiful Joe* asserts, 'Children who are taught to love and protect dumb creatures, will be kind to their fellow-men when they grow up' (145).

The immediate precedent for Lyman's book was likely S. Louise Patteson's *Pussy Meow: The Autobiography of a Cat* (1901). Written in order to do for the cat what *Black Beauty* had done for the horse and *Beautiful Joe* for the dog, *Pussy Meow* contains an episode in which Meow attempts to foil a thief (modelled on a similar scene in *Beautiful Joe*). She calls the thief 'the Burglar Man' (228); Me'ow Jones's use of 'the War Man' to refer to German soldiers may be an echo of this.

Throughout *Me'ow Jones*, Lyman paints the Germans as thorough villains whose brutishness is revealed in their treatment of animals. As the German army approaches, a neighbour reveals that he is in fact a spy; this man's first act upon revealing his German identity is to cut off the head of his own pet cat (43). This, as I observed earlier, is an obvious reference to the widely believed story that the Germans had mutilated Belgian children. Later, Me'ow Jones recounts how two young Belgian war refugees who befriend him got separated from their mother: 'The War Man had tied her to a tree because she tried to stop his beating of a Belgian War Dog he had caught' (85). In contrast to this cruelty displayed by the Germans, the Belgians are animal lovers. During the escape from Antwerp, Me'ow Jones meets some Belgian soldiers who rescue a kitten trapped in a ruined house (56).

When, after many adventures during the German siege of Antwerp, Me'ow and his owners arrive safely in America, they set about preparing boxes of clothing to send back to Belgium. Inside the boxes they tuck 'catnip balls, with letters asking those in Belgium to give them to the kitties of the kiddies who need the things. So few people think of the homeless Belgian cats!' (85). While the overt focus here is on the 'kitties' of Belgium, its 'kiddies' are the major objects of American charity and of Lyman's concern. Me'ow Jones stands in for the Belgian child, that central symbol of the evil of war. He is in fact quasi-human,

## CHAPTER ONE

### Me'ow's 4 "Me'ows"

*I'm the refugee Belgian cat;*
*I'm silky and purry and fat;*
*ME'OW is my name*
*And I'm glad that I came;*
*But I wish the bad War Man would Scat!*

14 Illustration from *Me'ow Jones, Belgian Refugee Cat: His Own True Tale*, by Edward Branch Lyman, illustrated by Julia Daniels. In the public domain; reproduced from author's collection.

for he not only talks and writes books but also has his meals sitting up at the table in a high chair.

*Me'ow Jones* was clearly intended to recruit boys and girls as contributors to the Refugee Fund. In the conclusion, Me'ow, 'the only refugee cat in Big America where there are so many millions of boys and girls and grown-ups to be told of their unhappy Belgian brothers and sisters across the sea who need help and love,' addresses his readers directly:

> ... I send out this Little Book, as my greeting and as my plea. I ask
> you to think often of the home country that I love; of the dear,

brave King and Queen ...; and all the people and cats so dear to
them. (89–90)

The plight of the Belgians was glorified as a sacred martyrdom,
sacred because it was the justification for so many deaths; yet
in Lyman's book the German invasion of Belgium is trivialized
by being presented from the perspective of a kitten. This seem-
ing paradox illustrates what George Mosse sees as a necessary
dynamic in the representation of war, for both glorification and
trivialization are needed in order to make it tolerable (143).

## Animal Pacifists

Another wartime book narrated by an animal, Marshall Saunders's *The Wandering Dog: Adventures of a Fox-Terrier* (1916), does
not deal explicitly with the conflict.[7] The novel's main plot concerns a dog's adventures in New York as he climbs the social
ladder: it begins with Boy arriving in the Bowery, unknown and
friendless, and follows his ascent to the country retreat of a well-
to-do New York family. Along the way, Boy encounters echoes
of the war across the sea, and in all of these is an unmistakable
note of pacifism. For example, the son of a black washerwoman
who takes in Boy entertains the dog with his banjo, singing the
famous Arthur Bryan song 'I Didn't Raise My Boy to Be a Soldier' (41). Lady Serena, an English suffragette whom Boy helps
to rescue when she falls into an icy pond, is described as 'an
ultra who wouldn't stop her militant work on account of the
war' (62). Lady Serena has come 'to America to wait for the
fighting to be over in Europe,' and her view of the conflict is
that 'she can see lots of reasons for smashing windows, but none
for smashing men's ribs.'

The most pointed reference to the war occurs when Boy
breaks up a fight in a Riverside Drive park. News of a German
victory has made a Dachshund insufferably proud, and the other
dogs – a French bulldog, a Belgian griffon, an Irish wolfhound, a
Scotch terrier, a Welsh terrier, and an English bulldog – are itching to 'have the pleasure of licking that hyphenated-American
dog' (110). When Boy counsels neutrality, the other dogs back
off, and the Dachshund is full of gratitude. But Boy doesn't want
the German dog's thanks. He scolds him for his foolishness in

provoking the other dogs. The Dachshund replies with a familiar piece of German propaganda:

> 'It was for the Fatherland,' he exclaimed, 'and the sacred domestic hearth prized by dogs as well as men.'
>     'You say that like a little parrot,' I remarked, 'and I don't believe you bullied that griffon on your own responsibility. You've always been a good dog up to within a week. Who's been coaching you?'
> (112)

It turns out that the little 'hyphenated' dog has been listening to 'that new German police dog that has come to the Drive.' Boy advises the Dachshund to ignore the subversive talk of the German police dog, and warns that a new English mastiff is arriving soon: 'You're probably going to get the greatest licking a dog ever got, for the griffon and the mastiff are always very chummy, and he will be sure to tell of the treatment he has been receiving from you' (113–14). Chastened by this prospect, the Dachshund concedes that he must be 'American, not German,' in America. While this scene is obviously allegorical, it does not seem overly didactic, perhaps because Boy is so compelling a protagonist that he gives life even to such cardboard characters as the little Dachshund.

Another incident demonstrating Saunders's view of war involves human characters. When Mrs Waverlee, an Englishwoman living in New York, receives a telegram announcing the death of her husband on the battlefield, she attempts suicide. Fortunately, she recovers. But her son Egbert, understanding that his father was killed by the Germans, takes out his anger on his toys:

> … with his little face disturbed with rage, he jumped up and down on the heap, smashing and demolishing animals, birds and games, and toy-carts and engines. (165)

The toys, it turns out, were made in Germany, and Egbert's destructive rampage is obviously a nursery version of the Allied response to German aggression. While his rage is cathartic, the 'disfigured, ugly mass' of ruined toys demonstrates the futility of war. The reaction of Mrs Bonstone (the wife of Boy's master) to what Egbert has done demonstrates Saunders's belief in the intrinsic pacifism of women:

> Her face grew scarlet. 'The whole war isn't worth the flame of rage in this one childish breast,' she said furiously. Then almost in the same breath, she calmed down, 'but oh! my child – forgive, forgive. They are your enemies, but only more war can come from vengeful feelings. Don't let us have the hate-song in this country.'
> ... Your darling mother forgave, for the words she wrote in her anguish ... [in her suicide note] were: "I do not want my boy to be a soldier."' (165)

Although it was published in 1916, *The Wandering Dog*, in its second section, moves ahead to the post-war years. In the aftermath of war, both humans and dogs express their opposition to conflict. Mr Bonstone, for example, addresses his baby son with a powerful pacifist vow: 'I had rather have you die now, than see you live to grow up and shed the blood of a fellow-man' (191). An American bloodhound speaks up for the animal victims of war:

> 'What gets me most of all,' said the dog in his melancholy voice, 'is the unappreciated devotion of dogs. I heard your master telling the other day of a friend of his who was in Belgium during the late war. He said that no human beings were more faithful than dogs; that the red-cross animals were simply magnificent, and even the poor house-dogs who were left in the Belgian villages, when their owners fled for their lives, were so devoted that they sat by their kennels till they dropped dead. Even when food was offered them, they turned their heads away. The poor starving brutes thought it was right for them to stay by their ruined homes, and not to take food from strangers.'
> 'Don't talk about that war,' I cried, 'don't talk about that awful war – I'm trying to forget it.' (219–20)

These references to war in *The Wandering Dog*, none of which is necessary to the plot of Boy's rise through society, suggest that Saunders was a pacifist. In an earlier novel, *The Girl from Vermont* (1912), Saunders had created an activist heroine, Patty Green, who campaigns not only for child welfare but also for settling disputes through 'arguments and reason and willingness to compromise,' not with guns (Waterston 158). This would have been an attitude in keeping with the liberal pacifism that many in Canada espoused before the war but which was, as Thomas Socknat has put it, 'a superficial façade which quickly shattered upon impact with the Great War' ('Canada's' 336). Saunders, who had moved to Toronto in 1914, was certainly part of the reform-minded, religious milieu in the city, but even among such people, pacifism ceased to be an acceptable attitude once stories of German atrocities began circulating. Nonetheless, in *Wandering Dog* Saunders found a way to advocate it: by setting her book in the United States and choosing a dog for her narrator, she was able to argue for pacifism as an essential part of reform-minded concern for animals and for human beings.

# 6 The Adventure of War

... we are going to give the Huns such a corking good lickin' they'll never want another war as long as the world lasts. We'd all be over there, fighting alongside your brothers and mine, if they would only take us, but they won't, durn 'em.

Harold C. Lowrey, Young Canada Boys with the S.O.S. on the Frontier

Long before 1914, Canadian children were reading adventure tales about war. In a study of nineteenth-century Canadian historical fiction for children, Elizabeth Galway notes that 'there was a great amount of literature being produced that dealt with Canada's military history,' the two favourite topics being the defeat of the French in Quebec and the War of 1812 (24). Galway claims that 'tales of earlier victories of the English over their enemies in North America – be they French, Americans, or Indians – were designed in part to bolster a sense of pride in Canada's place within the British Empire' (29). While young Canadians undoubtedly did take pride in the military exploits of their own heroes and heroines, they read war literature not because it was patriotic but because it was thrilling.

As Martin Green has pointed out in his study of the adventure tale, war is 'the supreme adventure' and 'the great test and field of display for manhood' (41). It is not at all surprising that writers and publishers quickly seized on the Great War as a rich new source of adventure plots. Even before the war, there had been in Britain, as in Canada, a highly successful war story industry: Michael Paris notes that 'patriotic novels ... had long been established as a popular sub-genre of the adventure story – a patriotic response to Britain's military adventures across the world and a vibrant justification of British imperialism' (xiii). Paris credits G.A. Henty (1832–1902) with inventing the juvenile war story.[1] From the publication in 1880 of his first story, a tale of the Indian Mutiny, 'Henty quickly gained a reputation for enthralling action novels that reflected the aggressive masculinity of an age of almost incessant imperial warfare' (xiii). Henty's success was soon imitated by many others, and 'the Henty style almost dominated the world of boys' fiction' (xiii).

Paris sees Henty's fiction as an expression of what he calls 'the pleasure culture of war' – 'heroic and romantic representations of war that offered exciting entertainment for many Victorians and were part and parcel of the popular militarism that increasingly infected British society towards the end of the nineteenth century' (xvii).[2] Mark Moss, in *Manliness and Militarism: Educating Young Boys in Ontario for War*, asserts that a similar attitude existed in Canada:

> The dominant ideas and values of manliness and militarism had permeated virtually every facet of society since Confederation. To be sure, there were voices of dissent from working-class, labour, feminist, and Francophone residents of Ontario, but, in general, young boys were exposed to enthusiastic support for war and war culture. (6)

Given that 70 per cent of those who volunteered for the First Contingent of the Canadian Expeditionary Force were 'British-born and -bred' (Morton, *When* 278), this 'support for war and war culture' must reflect at least in part the experience of popular militarism brought here by British immigrants.

While Britain was the source and chief market for boys' adventure fiction, Canadians read it too. Larry Nelson, one of the Toronto residents interviewed in *The Great War and Canadian Society*, remembered that the *Boy's Own Annual* and *Chums* 'were commonly read ... by boys, youths from the ages of ten to fifteen or so ... [and] frequently given, at least in my case, as Christmas presents' (Read 59). One veteran quoted by Desmond Morton in *When Your Number's Up* explained why he tried three times to enlist (succeeding on the third try): 'We felt that we were fighting for what was right ... We were brought up on the *Boy's Own Annual* and *Chums* and on novels like those of Henty and Ballantyne' (52). Moss claims that 'boys living in Ontario probably devoured more British adventure stories than anything else' (75).[3] Members of The Order of the King's Own, the readers' club for the Presbyterian paper *King's Own*, mention adventure books in their letters: Lloyd Farrell, aged thirteen, of Glencoe, Ontario, listed G.A. Henty among his favourite authors; Arthur E. Markert, also thirteen, of South Woodslee, Ontario, wrote that his favourite books were Henty's *Facing Death* and *Under Drake's Flag* (4 May 1918: 72). Moreover, adults approved of this kind of reading and therefore bought it for their children. An article in the *Canadian Magazine* in 1896, 'Our Children and Their Reading,' praises Henty's works – 'What delightful tales these are, and what a taste for history they engender' – and the British annuals – 'Think of all the reading there is for a boy between twelve and eighteen years of age, in the *Boy's Own Annual*, for two dollars' (Merton 283). In the *Sunday School Banner*, the Rev. F.J. Hayden advised Sunday-school teachers about what boys liked to read:

> Boys of to-day want the stories of lives lived in the world with the smoke of battle thick upon them. They want to read of men and women, and boys and girls, upon whose crown is written 'hero,' not 'hermit,' 'Soldier,' not 'Softy.' To this change of mind we must cater, and if we do, we shall see the heroes and the soldiers reproduced in the boys of our classes. (Nov. 1916: vi)

While adventure stories were obviously aimed at boys, 'girls were known to be devoted readers of the adventure story from its inception' (Reynolds 26).[4] Eleven-year-old Jean Gilchrist, writing to the *King's Own*, noted that 'my brother has a War-Book, and I read it sometimes. There are a lot of stories in it about the first part of the war. He also has a book entitled The Boys' Book of Heroes. I like it also' (9 March 1918: 40).

War adventure stories read by Canadian boys and girls also came from the United States. American publishers produced new series about the war: the Boy Allies, the Boy Ensigns, the Young Aeroplane Scouts, the Big Five Motorcycle Boys, the Red Cross Nurses. And in established series like the Boy Scouts, the Campfire Girls, and Ruth Fielding, new war-related titles appeared. Just how many of these American books actually were sold in Canada or acquired by Canadian libraries is now impossible to estimate, but, given that most of these series contained multiple titles (there were twelve volumes in the Boy Allies series, for example), there must have been large numbers of American war books in the hands of Canadian children.[5]

In contrast to the abundant supply of war adventure reading from Britain and the United States, there was very little home-grown Canadian material. While many stories in the Canadian Sunday-school periodicals deal with war, they do not depict combat or even fist fights with German spies. The Sunday-school stories are confined to home-front settings and second-hand accounts of the fighting (as reported in letters from fathers or brothers).

As a consequence, young Canadian readers drew their impressions of the battlefields either from works reflecting a British tradition of imperialist adventure, or from ones steeped in an American ethos of self-help and resourcefulness. In the following discussion of these two types of war adventure tales, I have not attempted to be exhaustive, only representative, in my selection of British and American war adventure tales read by Canadian children. In choosing works, I have been guided by advertisements and reviews in Canadian publications such as the Eaton's catalogue, the *School,* and the *Ontario Library Review and Book Selection Guide*; in some cases, inscriptions serve as additional evidence that works were owned by Canadian children. Only in the case of thoroughly Canadian works – that is, written by Canadians and published in Canada – have I attempted to cover all the available published material.

Whether British, American, or Canadian in origin, the boys' adventure tale of war was written, more or less, to a formula. It was founded on the classic adventure tale and therefore absorbed most of its conventions. First and most obvious, the boys' adventure tale is what Martin Green terms a 'masculinist' genre, depicting males in an essentially all-male society; the reason for this focus is that the adventure tale deals with 'the forbidden world of violence,' a world in which ordinary social relations between men and women cannot exist (4). War as a setting is, of course, a 'world of violence' par excellence. The hero of the adventure tale is usually solitary, although some variants feature the legendary 'band of brothers,' the Three Musketeers being the obvious model. (This is one of the types discussed by Green in his *Seven Types of Adventure Tale*.) The adventure story also requires its hero to leave ordinary human society in order to accomplish something great; often the hero has to escape his past and remake himself in the forge of hardship and violence. This pattern of flight from civilization (a force which in the boys' story is often represented by Mother or School) echoes a central theme in the 'Frontiersman' adventure tale, a type that Green identifies as essentially American.

In the adventure tale of war, the boy is an accidental hero. He doesn't set out to get into a tight spot, but he does, and, despite his youth, he ends up doing a man's job and doing it well. No matter how dangerous the adventure, the boy comes through without a scratch (or with only a scratch). Others may die: sometimes the boy has a comrade who dies, but the hero is miraculously impervious to harm. He is also proof against all temptation, for it is essential that the hero be a 'clean' lad. Though he lives among grown men, he is not corrupted by their tastes or appetites. In the special conditions of war, the boy hero is in the thick of things, but he is rarely part of the regular army. The reason is not just that he is too young to serve; more important is the fact that the narrative needs him to be free and mobile and subject to no one's orders. The boys' adventure tale may feature some kind of romantic initiation, but if so, it is very chaste. Indeed, references to relationships with women tend to be perfunctory. With the emphasis on the splendid physique of the boy-hero and his strong relationships with other men, these stories have, at least to modern ears, a pronounced homoerotic quality.

Another hallmark of the boys' adventure tale is the hero's racial pride. This pride reflects the deep affinities between the adventure tale and modern nationalism. In Green's words, 'The two sprouted from the same cultural tendency, and adventures ... supplied national movements with their icons and liturgies' (77). Thus, while the British, American, and Canadian adventure tales of war have much in common, each reflects a distinct set of national types and values.

## British War Stories

In her 1917 recommendations for a Boys and Girls Collection, Lillian Smith of the Toronto Public Library included twenty-one titles by Captain F.S. Brereton (1872–1957); his listings were second only to G.A. Henty at thirty-two and far ahead of the third-ranked Beatrix Potter at twelve. But despite Brereton's evident popularity and approval rating with librarians, he has had no staying power. His works have disappeared from modern children's reading lists, without even the afterlife of cult popularity enjoyed by Henty (who, as it happens, was Brereton's cousin [Kitzan 53n2]). Brereton produced nearly fifty books, almost all of which were about war. Many deal with imperial wars of the nineteenth century, like *A Hero of Lucknow: A Tale of the Indian Mutiny* (1905) and *With Roberts to Candahar: A Tale of the Third Afghan War* (1907), but Brereton also found the Great War a fertile source of stories.

Brereton's 1917 book, *With French at the Front: A Story of the Great European War down to the Battle of the Aisne,* does not really deal with Field Marshal Sir John French's campaign. There is just one reference to the head of the British Expeditionary Force – 'that dashing leader of cavalry who had returned from the Boer war with laurels of the highest' (123) – and, despite the subtitle, Brereton's main concern is not the opening month of the war, but the exploits of two manly British heroes, Jim Fletcher, intelligence officer and airman, and his friend, Dicky Dance, sailor and captain of a submarine. Many of the lads' exploits have to do with rescuing Miss Gladys Fairchild, first from the cruel, war-hungry mobs in Berlin in August 1914, and then from the clutches of two German spies. The abduction of the heiress Gladys by one spy and then by the other (they are double-crossers as well as enemy agents) has nothing to do with the war; their motives are money and lust, not national interest. But rescuing Gladys gives plenty of scope for Jim and Dicky to demonstrate their skill and daring on land, sea, and air. They escape from a German police station before they can be 'shot in the morning' (49), commandeer a vehicle and are pursued across the countryside, and finally, in order to get Gladys back to Britain, manage the daring theft of a German coast guard boat. Gladys, of course, shows throughout 'spirit, pluck, just what a Britisher likes in one of his own nation' (17). (But not too much: after freeing the two men from prison by obtaining a janitor's uniform and keys, Gladys, who has been 'wonderfully plucky up to the moment when all depended on her alone,' breaks down in tears once 'she was with the two gallant men ..., when, as it seemed, there was no longer need for personal exertion or for nerves to be braced' [48].) Later they have to rescue her again, this time by plane, with a dogfight in the air to put an end to her German kidnappers.

Jim and Dicky do occasionally show up for war service. Jim, for example, drives in his 'quick car' with his man-servant down to the English coast so he can cross the Channel and join the Flying Corps in France (92). Although he is supposed to be in the air on a surveillance flight, he happens to get involved in the Belgian defence of Liège. Dicky, for his part, manages to sink a German destroyer. But the real focus of the two men is the rescue of Gladys, whom, at the end, Jim claims as his own bride: 'I've got to see this business through to a finish. When we've reached Berlin, then there'll be time to talk of marrying' (292).

Throughout the ramshackle plot and highly repetitive prose, three central themes dominate. The first is the British national character. In Jim's first appearance in the novel, Brereton emphasizes his Britishness:

> A more pronounced and essentially British subject, too, it would have been difficult to discover ... For Jim had the head and shoulders of our islanders. A small, fair moustache set off a handsome face which was resolute and firm, and had none of the floppy stodginess so often found among the beer-drinking subjects of the Kaiser. (10–11)[6]

When Gladys and Jim run into Dicky on the streets of Berlin, he is immediately recognized as different from the natives:

> 'Another Englishman,' Gladys told herself, feeling a glow of pride that Englishmen should be so distinctive. Indeed, no one could have mistaken the one to whom Jim called as anything else but essentially British. He was a tall, active young man, somewhere about Jim's age, with clean-shaven face and a decidedly nautical appearance. (32)

These physical qualities are matched by moral ones. Jim and Dicky are keen, dashing, honourable, cool in times of stress. Jim has 'nerves of steel' (44). When a young subaltern with 'the same coolness and nonchalance as those fine fellows under his immediate command' (142) is killed in battle, Jim reflects on death in war:

> Well, he had died the death of a man – his face to the foe, his courage prime and inspiring. Soon there would be widows and fatherless children in all parts of the Empire, and perhaps some weeping and wailing. Not that people would parade their grief. No. Jim knew his countrymen the world over too well for that. (146)

That phrase, 'the world over,' includes young Canadian readers in the British club. If they doubted their membership, they would have been reassured by Brereton's assertion that 'the onset of war' found 'in the Colonies … a younger Britain just as ready for the fray, all shoulder to shoulder' (122).

Moreover, the fine British character is not restricted to public-school products like Jim and Dicky (who, when he first meets Gladys, 'lift[s] his hat to her with an elegance which betray[s] his breeding') (33). Even the working classes have it. There are frequent interludes, evidently intended as comic relief, in which working-class soldiers or sailors, usually Cockney or Irish, but sometimes Scots, discuss matters in highly stylized dialect. These scenes demonstrate what gallant, cool, and loyal fellows the ordinary men are. They look up to the young officers, but Brereton assures readers that his heroes are not snobs. Jim, for example, is fair in his dealings with his man-servant:

> … there was no hard-and-fast line drawn by discipline between Jim and Matthews – nor, indeed, between the British officer and his men generally. With them it was not as it obtains in the German army, where an officer is superlatively above his men – in his own precious opinion … (92)

The contrast with the Germans exemplifies the way in which Brereton highlights the evil of the enemy. For every British virtue there is a corresponding German vice. The British, for example, are fair, but the Germans are sneaky. While Brereton concedes that not all Germans in Britain were spies, he claims, in one of the many passages in which he lapses into an authoritative and historical tone, that 'vast numbers were, without shadow of doubt – aye, and amongst them those duly naturalized – men who had eaten our salt and partaken of our hospitality for years' (169). Germany demonstrated its lack of honour when it tore up the 'scrap of paper' guaranteeing Belgian neutrality, but Britain respected the treaty because 'it carried the honour of millions of us, millions of simple, plain-dealing Britishers, with scrupulous minds and an idea of fairness and of what is proper far transcending ideas in the minds of Prussians' (41). The unappealing appearance of the Germans in the novel, in contrast to the 'clean-built, and active, and alert' demeanour of the British (133), further demonstrates their turpitude.

The theme most likely to impress young readers is the consistent message that war is exciting. Jim, the airman, and Dicky, the submarine captain, have chosen glamorous branches of the military: 'The danger in it, the spice which the unknown risk, the possibility of difficulty, brings, were there to lead them, and with them the subtle call which draws all brave men – the call to surmount those difficulties and dangers, to triumph and live in spite of them all' (53). When Jim happens upon a British cavalry unit about to charge, he acknowledges that 'it's just the very thing I've often longed for' (157). Jim rides into battle with the unit, sharing in their 'delirious excitement' (161). Brereton plays up the bloodthirsty thrill of the charge and then, in a direct address to readers, justifies it:

Jim dodged, and shot the [German officer] with his revolver. Then, as he shot forward against our hero's leg, Jim seized his sabre. What joy it brought him, too! Not that he loved slaying for the sake of slaying. But this was duty, this slaying of the Germans. Think, you tender people who have ever stayed at home and never given a blow in anger; think of the Belgian homes wrecked by the Kaiser's vandals. Think of helpless women and children slain by grown men, armed men, brutes encouraged to be brutal. Then imagine a German host in England! Too long we have withheld our hands. Too long we have listened to those who would have had us grow up a timid nation, who would not encourage us to make preparation for the Armageddon which all guessed must be coming. And now it was on us. Was Jim to hold his hand? Were those gallant troopers to be chary of taking German life? A thousand times no! ... Remember that we entered the war with reluctance. We have now put our hands to the plough. Brothers, let us not look back till the huge work is fully accomplished. (164)

The lofty style of this passage – Brereton uses anaphora, rhetorical questions, parallelism, biblical allusions – does not disguise the nationalist bluster, nor does it conceal the fact that this scene presents killing as joyous and guiltless.

Another Brereton Great War novel, *On the Road to Bagdad: A Story of the British Expeditionary Force in Mesopotamia* (1917),[7] has many similar elements: two brothers-in-arms, German spies, prison escapes, cavalry charges. But this time, instead of overlaying the war scenes on a melodrama, as he does in *With French*, Brereton borrows from Kipling's *Kim* (1901). (As Seth Lerer has observed, '*Kim* was immediately brought into the canon of imperial adventure literature' [167].) Brereton's central character, Geoff, is, like Kipling's hero, an English boy born in India: '... you would not for a moment have imagined that Geoff could speak Hindustani just as well as he could speak English; that he could gabble Turkish in the markets of Bagdad with such ease and such precision that even a native would not have suspected – that is, provided he were dressed as a subject of the Sultan' (29). Geoff has learned about the Middle East in the company of his guardian, Major Joseph Douglas, a 'political' who, with the genius for languages of a Sir Richard Burton, has managed to roam throughout the Middle East, gathering secrets for the British (21).

Geoff's knowledge of Turkish and Arabic allows him to pass for a Turkish officer and an Arab shepherd; he also manages to extract valuable information from captured informants. Lest boys at home feel that their lack of facility with languages would rule them out of the excitement, Brereton supplies another boy hero, Philip, who makes up in 'natural dash and courage' (31) and 'splendid spirits' (188) what he lacks in linguistic preparation. The ease with which Geoff and Philip carry off their masquerades (also very evident in *With French*, where Jim and Dicky disguise themselves as Germans on several occasions) must have added to the novel's pleasure for young readers. Like children

playing dress-up, the protagonists of Brereton's novels transform themselves into enemy officers or inconspicuous enemy
civilians. By making disguise and transformation seem so easy,
these adventure tales indirectly suggest that just by putting on a
uniform, a boy could turn himself into a dashing young soldier.
*On the Road to Bagdad* covers the events leading up to the
siege by the Turks at Kut-el-Amara. This campaign can only be
regarded as an utter failure for the British, at great cost of life
for the Indian units they employed, yet Brereton manages to
present it all as a 'ripping' and 'splendid' adventure for Geoff
and Philip. Those two adjectives appear dozens of times; many
of their encounters with the enemy are described as a 'little affair' (148, 154) or even 'a very pretty little affair' (79). Geoff and
Philip have so much fun that on two occasions their irrepressible
laughter nearly betrays their presence to the enemy. When, at
the end of the novel, Brereton at last refers to the march towards
Baghdad, the withdrawal into Kut, and the subsequent siege, he
brushes aside the losses and focuses on the 'most masterly' way
in which the retreat was managed (382). Geoff and Philip are
not downhearted that the British were nearly annihilated; indeed, 'as we write, our two heroes are in harness once more and
are preparing to fight beside their new comrades right on towards the heart of Mesopotamia' (384). This novel, too, conveys
the unmistakable impression that war is fun.

   *Young Canada: An Illustrated Annual for Boys throughout the
English-speaking World* originated in London at the Pilgrim Press,
with a Canadian edition being simultaneously issued by William
Briggs. Despite its title, this periodical was not especially or exclusively for Canadian boys. It simply capitalized on the inherent
glamour of 'Canada' to promote a publication that was produced and written in Britain with no special focus on Canadian
content (there are as many Australian items as Canadian ones
in the 1915/16 edition of the Annual). In the 1915/16 *Young
Canada*, the editor explains that he has 'striven to make it as useful a war-year Volume as could be produced':

> The valour of our soldiers, the intrepid feats of our flying-men,
> the patient service rendered by the watchers of our coasts – all
> have had due justice done to them ... At the same time we have
> not forgotten that even while this tremendous fight is being waged

school sport must still go on, and cricket and 'footer' claim attention as usual. (436)

Certainly sports articles, with titles like 'A Word to Boy Cap-
tains.' by Jos. W. Bache (Captain of England's Eleven and Aston
Villa F.C.), and 'Hints for the Player Who Is Not a Genius,' by
W.O. Davis (Welsh International and Millwall F.C), appear in
each monthly section, as do a serialized school story, a serial set
in an exotic locale, short natural history fillers, how-to items,
and jokes. But of the 1915/16 edition, approximately half is concerned with war. A series of articles by Patrick Vaux, for example,
deals with various nautical themes: submarines, the work of the
ship's engineer, minesweepers, midshipmen. (Similar articles by
Vaux appeared in the Presbyterian children's paper, the *King's
Own*.) In each monthly section is an illustrated item on new
technologies of war. There are the usual items on the Victoria
Cross and on French child heroes. And several of the monthly
frontispiece illustrations are of scenes of war, ranging from 'How
the Indians Cleared the German Trenches' (42) to an image of
gunners entitled 'A Hot Corner' (282). One of the few explicitly
Canadian items, 'A Canadian Soldier's Story: An Extraordinary
Career,' describes a 'young Britisher' whose 'father gave him
£20 and a ticket to Canada' (290). The story purportedly appeared first in the *Westminster Gazette*, but the man's adventures
sound like the invention of a *Young Canada* staff writer, so neatly
do they sum up the clichéd vision of Canada in the boys' magazines. While in Canada, the man worked as an actor, trick rider,
lion-tamer's assistant, 'Buffalo Bill's' cowboy, chauffeur, valet,
Mountie, big-game hunter, and a member of Stefansson's last
expedition. But, after a 700-mile trek carrying dispatches from
the Arctic explorer, the man arrived at Fort Norman, where he
heard of the war. He 'immediately set out on a two months' trek,
quite alone, to get to the railway station, where he spent £38
on a ticket for England.' The article concludes with a ringing
endorsement of this supposed 'Canadian' type: 'Of such men is
the British Empire composed, and such are the men who have
been attracted to the ranks of the British Army in defence of liberty, honour and humanity, and all that civilisation holds dear.'
    The vast majority of the British war writers for boys focused
on the Western Front or on some other theatre of war. But a few

British boys' stories about the war are set in Canada, a choice that allowed authors both to capitalize on the appeal of a Canadian setting and to write about war at a safe distance from the misery of the battlefields. (As R.G. Moyles has pointed out, the British boys' magazines 'stereotyped the Canadian wilderness as a place of perpetual excitement and romance' ['Young' 11.]) There was, of course, a difficulty: how could they import to Canada a war that never crossed its borders? The answer was the threat of German spies and saboteurs.

Fanciful though such a notion may seem now, German sabotage was considered a very real danger. There were nearly 400,000 German-born residents in Canada; a further 130,000 had come from parts of the Austro-Hungarian Empire (Granatstein 66). Moreover, just south of the border were hundreds of thousands of immigrants from enemy lands. Not only German Americans but Irish Americans too represented a potential threat, particularly for those Canadians to whom the Fenian Raids were still part of 'living memory' (66). Jeffrey Keshen asserts that one of the main thrusts of wartime propaganda was to convince Canadians that there were 'countless fifth columnists' working on behalf of the Germans (24). In 1914 the Royal North-West Mounted Police were given an extra $100,000 to hire additional men for internal security; Canada even hired private detectives 'to frequent, both in Canada and the United States, saloons and social clubs in German neighbourhoods' (6). These precautions must have seemed justified when, in 1915, a German reservist blew up the international railway bridge at Vanceboro, Maine (7). Given this atmosphere of imminent peril, adventure stories about foiling German spies were not so far-fetched.

Brian Kingston's *Sons of the Empire!* (1917?), described on the opening page as 'A Thrilling, long story, telling How Two Young Britishers Foiled the German Attempt at Sedition in Canada' (1), was published in Britain by the Boys' Friend Library. Kingston was the pseudonym of Percy Longhurst, a frequent contributor to boys' magazines. The plot revolves around an uprising by German Canadians, complete with trench warfare and aerial attacks in Saskatchewan. Kingston spells out the reasons why a German insurrection was possible in Canada:

It seemed too absurd to suppose that the Germans could make

themselves masters of Canada, but when one considered the tens of thousands of Huns available, the depletion of Canada of the fine young fighting-men sent to fight for England in Belgium and elsewhere, of the ignorance of the country of Teutonic aims, of the enemy's wonderful organisation and the initial success of the appeal to arms, the absurdity of the supposition was not so apparent. Of course it would all work out right in the end, but – . (32)

Before the end comes, the two young Britishers of the title, Jack Harvey and Terry O'Rorke, are embroiled in a variety of skirmishes with the German rebels and their ringleader, Anton Moritz. The plot affords many opportunities for Jack to display his British manliness. He is a skilled wrestler, so, despite his slim build, he can beat a brawny German-Canadian boy. Jack is also a 'good swimmer and diver,' so he manages to survive when one of the spies attempts to drown him (9). But more important are his moral qualities. When first captured by the Germans, he remains cool: 'His life was in danger, but there was no white feather about Jack. A Britisher isn't of the breed to back down, or take water, as the Canadians say, from anybody, least of all from a German bully' (20). Jack is not only cool but honourable: he escapes from the Germans by taking an officer captive, but he refrains from killing his captive because 'Englishmen don't take advantage of an enemy's helplessness' (26).

Kingston works in the elements that young readers would have expected from a 'Canadian' story. 'Redskins,' for example, are introduced when the German agent tries to instigate an uprising: '... the cunning representative of Germany had been using his art to bring about what not one man in Canada would have believed possible – the rebellion of the Indians against British rule' (57). The notion that Canada's aboriginal people could be easily induced to rebel does not reflect their actual attitudes towards the war; rather, it seems a variant of the 'persistent and reflexive' portrayal of the Native in the adventure tale as 'an essentially savage creature, controlled only by the firm hand and gentle patience of Canadians' (Moyles and Owram 175). When Jack and his Mountie comrades visit an encampment where Moritz is attempting to turn the Indians against the British, Jack manages to tie up Moritz and cover him with feathers and molasses. Then he holds a gun to the head of an old medicine man and orders the Indians – Bloods, Piegans, and Blackfeet – to stop the Sun Dance and disperse. Kingston thoroughly approves of Jack's strategy: '... it was not mere bluff. It was the expression of the Anglo-Saxon power to rule. It told the redmen that they were more than two ordinary policeman; they were representatives of their race – the race that rules, and rules justly' (69).

The rest of Jack's adventures mix conventional 'Canadian' adventure elements with what young readers would have expected of a war story. Jack and the Mounties are pursued across the prairie by Blood Indians; then the British lads lead a cavalry charge against several hundred Germans. German aircraft strafe the British as they ride over the prairie. Then there is a full-scale assault with shellfire and trenches somewhere in Saskatchewan. At last, after much machine-gun fire and another cavalry charge, 'the sons of the Empire had conquered – as they were conquering nearly six thousand miles away' (104). Having saved Canada from the threat of a German-led Indian insurrection, Jack and Terry expect no special thanks for their great deeds: 'They had done their duty. That was sufficient. Sons of the Empire, they could do no less; sons of the Empire, to do more was impossible' (105).

J. Merivale's *The Fallen Flyer, or Camping in Canada* (1919) is also set in Canada, but the geography is somewhat muddled: four young lads are camping in 'a very solitary part of Howe Sound, where the long spurs of the Rocky Mountains ran down to the shore. To the north and east of them it was wilderness, to the west was the sea, and southward there was the civilization of the little town of Langley Corner ...' (13). Tom, Phil, Jim, and Bert ('whose father was away doing his bit on the battlefields of Europe' [13]), are planning to go camping in the wilderness. This would be exciting enough, but soon they come across evidence of spies at work. Tom discovers a downed plane in a gully, and, being 'a boy of resource,' he takes the valuable-looking items from the plane (55). When he opens a box that was in the plane, he finds it contains documents in German. As Tom observes, 'There is something downright fishy in this business, and I say we ought to get this lot of papers into the hands of the police as quick as we can' (59). Meanwhile, two of the boys happen to overhear men speaking German. (Conveniently, the men switch to English so that the boys can eavesdrop.) It turns out that they are German saboteurs who have come to British Columbia to destroy a hidden factory where the Canadians are making 'that deadly gas by secret process from the bark of the Douglas pines' (78). The boys alert the authorities, who apprehend the spies and give the boys a reward for the valuable German documents they have found. The main reward for the boys, however, is 'the satisfaction of having done their bit for the country' (124).

That Canadian boys read and absorbed war adventures of this kind is evident in a student contribution to *Victoria*, the magazine published for children in the Victoria School District. Fred McIntyre, aged twelve, won first prize with 'A Spy Hunt,' in which a group of boys catch a spy who is planning to blow up a bridge. They hand the spy over to the police and are 'highly congratulated, being each presented with a fine gold watch' (April 1918: 43).

## American War Stories

The American war books, like their British counterparts, offered derring-do and invulnerable boy heroes, but they did not serve up the imperial message that permeates the British war adventures. As Paul Litt puts it, 'American cultural products ... deal[ing] with the war treated it as a topic of great contemporary interest rather than an all-encompassing cataclysm' (334). Instead of the clean, gentlemanly Britisher, the American books provided bumptious heroes whose resourcefulness and practical abilities eclipse the rather plodding efforts of the Allies. Although the imperialist ideology of race is not in evidence, the American tales are nonetheless blandly secure in their assumption that American white people are superior beings. Nor, in the American books, is there much high-minded moralizing. The American boy heroes are virtuous, of course – they are devoted to their mothers – but they are not lofty and earnest in quite the same way as their British counterparts. As a consequence, there is very little talk of sacrifice in the American books; instead, the emphasis is on action. And while the British boy heroes are almost invariably public-school boys, American boys are presented as down-to-earth, ordinary lads, even though their knowledge of such things as automobiles and European languages indicates that they are sons of privilege, not farm boys or kids from the

Lower East Side. Indeed, the American war adventures contain just as much snob appeal as the British ones.

For young Canadian readers, the American boys' adventure books provided some elements they could not get from the British publications. There are more car chases, more action, and more weapons. While the situations the heroes find themselves in are preposterous, much of the detail of fights and escapes is realistic. George Orwell, writing in the 1930s, singled out violence, especially fisticuffs, as one of the features of boys' stories in American magazines; to Orwell, the stories sounded as if they had been 'written for devotees of the prize-ring' (194). Even some twenty years earlier, this tendency was evident in the American war stories. It seems to have been part of the American branch of the adventure tale from the beginning: according to Martin Green, 'love of violence' was part of the pattern of escaping from civilization in the American 'Frontiersman' adventure tale (104).

The boy hero in the American books is also a character with whom Canadian boys might readily identify. The American boy hero knows about camping and paddling canoes and riding horses and using rifles. These attainments might not have been possessed by every Canadian city dweller, but they were certainly the kinds of things a true Canadian lad could do. The American heroes are also presented as modern, up-to-the-minute boys who know about motorcars and aeroplanes, and can handle and repair just about any kind of machine.

One American series sold in Canada was The Boy Allies with the Army, written by Clair W. Hayes. Between 1915 and 1918, Hayes wrote thirteen books in this series. Remarkably, during the same period, writing as Ensign Robert L. Drake, he produced ten books in a companion naval series, The Boy Allies with the Battleships, featuring an American boy named Frank Chadwick and an English boy named Jack Templeton.

The two heroes of the Army series, Hal Paine and Chester Crawford, come from Illinois. But in the first book of the series, *The Boy Allies at Liège* (1915), the boys happen to be staying with Hal's mother in a hotel in Berlin when war breaks out. Hayes introduces his characters by striking the requisite note of racial pride and warrior pedigree: Hal's father died 'leading a charge at the battle of El Caney in the Spanish-American war,' and his

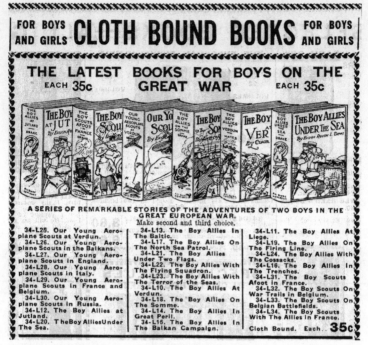

15 This advertisement appeared in the Fall-Winter 1917/18 issue of the Eaton's catalogue (314). From the Collection of the Archives of Ontario; used with the permission of Sears Canada Inc.

grandfather 'died of a bayonet wound in the last days of the Civil War' (6). On the maternal side, Hal is also from 'a family of fighters': his mother's father, a Virginian, was killed at Gettysburg, and three of her brothers also died 'on the field of battle' (6).

All the Boy Allies novels are picaresque tales in which episode follows episode with no discernible character development. Hal and Chester end each book as they began – chipper, clever, and itching for a fight. Although the varied settings include Belgium, Italy, the Eastern Front, Vimy Ridge, and Washington, DC, the novels are remarkably uniform. Not only do several come in at exactly 256 pages, but also Hayes recycles the same intrigues and encounters. Hal and Chester repeatedly disguise themselves as German soldiers, managing to elude detection for at least some time because of their perfect German. (They learned it working in the Pacific Northwest in one of Chester's father's logging camps.) Then, once discovered, they face certain death: because they are not wearing an Allied uniform, they are presumed to be spies and will be shot at dawn. Of course, one way or another, they escape this fate. In *Boy Allies on the Firing Line* (1915), the Kaiser himself intervenes because he wants to find out what the American people think of him. In *Boy Allies at Liège*, they are being held in a medieval castle, but a servant, 'an old darky' transplanted from Virginia (67), offers to help them escape. Hal's 'confidence in these old-time negroes' is rewarded. Ol' Uncle Billy provides them with horses and, as the boys ride off, exclaims, 'Praise de Lawd! ... May dey git home in safety' (81).

Another ingredient is the car chase, usually in a luxury touring car. In *Boy Allies at Liège*, Hal and Chester make a dash for the German border, with the Germans in hot pursuit. In *Boy Allies on the Firing Line*, Hal, Chester, and a band of hand-picked British soldiers, driving five vehicles abreast, smash right through a line of German soldiers (106). The boys are also adept pilots and on several occasions manage to commandeer aircraft and fly to safety. For example, while prisoners in Berlin in *Boy Allies on the Firing Line*, Hal and Chester come into possession of a secret message that must be delivered to Grand Duke Nicholas. (Not for Hal and Chester some mean prisoner-of-war camp. They are held in the comfortable home of a German general and enjoy sightseeing excursions in Berlin; it is on one of these outings that they come into possession of the message.) By a series of clever stratagems, they slip out of Berlin, get a German flying machine, and head for the Eastern Front. In *Boy Allies in Great Peril* (1916), they escape from the Austrian front lines by stealing a plane; when Austrian planes try to intercept them, Hal and Chester turn the plane eastward and head for Montenegro. Fuel, safety, supplies – these are not concerns for Hal and Chester, who manage to fly hundreds of miles without incident.

Most of the action revolves around special missions. Hal and Chester are spared the brute work of digging trenches or being sentries or carrying supplies. Their reputation precedes them, and wherever they go, they are inevitably whisked into the presence of some great personage such as Haig, French, Joffre, Byng, Foch, or Grand Duke Nicholas. Their audience with the

great man is always the same: after the lads have recounted their
most recent exploit, he expresses astonishment and admiration,
and gives them another vital mission. Sometimes these tasks require the boys to be put in charge of a group of men, whom
they of course command with determination and confidence.
A frequent task is to take a message to another commander or
perhaps to extract some vital piece of paper from under the very
nose of an enemy general. The missions are always successful, but
they involve many reverses, near misses, and other opportunities
for the boys to display 'their skill in the fistic art' (*Trenches* 7) or
their swordsmanship and proficiency with firearms. The fights,
which occur in nearly every chapter, are remarkably bloody: Hal
and Chester kill, wound, or knock unconscious their adversar-
ies, while they themselves rarely sustain anything more serious
than a grazed forehead or a dizzy spell. Hal's and Chester's encounters with the enemy are spelled out in breathless detail, but
when, through some clever manoeuvre, the lads manage to kill
dozens of the enemy or lose many of their comrades, these negative facts are dealt with blithely and summarily. In *Boy Allies on
the Firing Line*, Hal, serving as engineer, with Chester as fireman,
drives a locomotive engine into the midst of a group of German
soldiers, causing many fatalities. But Chester observes, 'It's only
a few more gone to the Happy Hunting Ground in a mistaken
cause' (35).

While these books are full of violence, they never represent
the peculiar savagery, degradation, and corrosive tedium of
trench warfare. The conflict is always presented in terms of dramatic, brief engagements. Hayes has an especial fondness for
depicting cavalry charges, which invariably place Hal and Chester in the thick of the fighting, with their swords flashing. He
even manages to send the cavalry into battle on Vimy Ridge, so
that Hal and Chester can get a bit of glory at La Folie Farm (*Stars
and Stripes* 39–40). To vary the action, Hayes also gets the lads
embroiled in duels with hot-blooded Frenchmen. And in Paris,
Rome, and Berlin, they intervene when mobs set upon an apparently defenceless person; as the lads can't bear to see unfair
odds, they end up in a street fight.

Throughout the series, the boys team up with a Frenchman,
Major Derevaux, and an English lieutenant, Harry Anderson.
Often the older men appear at just the right moment to get the

boy allies out of a 'ticklish situation' ('ticklish' is one of Hayes's most dependable adjectives). Another recurring character, Hal's Uncle John, tries to persuade the two boys to come home to their mothers. Uncle John often gets embroiled in their adventures, as in *Boy Allies in Great Peril* when all three end up the captives of an Austrian spy. The plump and irascible American war correspondent Stubbs, who first appears when the boys rescue him from a band of feral cats, provides comic relief. Although Stubbs seems cowardly, he often turns out to be a daring and ingenious sidekick in the boys' escapades.

Although these novels are peopled by stereotypes, not characters, Hayes does not depict the Germans as the 'brutal Hun,' a label that came so invariably to the pens of British and Canadian writers. Some Germans are cruel, but others (always of the officer class) are kindly, courteous, and honourable. Even the Kaiser is portrayed as misguided, not evil. The French are in some instances heroic. Major Derevaux, for example, is a paragon of courage. But the French are also unpredictable and untrustworthy: those duels that Hal and Chester get into with Frenchmen suggest a troubling impulsiveness and vanity. And on a few occasions, Frenchmen turn out to be spies and informers. The British, kinsmen of the Americans, are shown invariably to be heroic. Even the laughable fop known as His Lordship, introduced in *Boy Allies in the Trenches* (1915) – he has red silk stockings under his puttees and manicures his nails while lounging in the front trench (131) – turns out to be a crack shot who can pick off Germans with ease. Canadians are good fighters too, but their skill comes from frontier experience. In *With Haig in Flanders* (1918), McKenzie, a Canadian who speaks German fluently, is assigned to accompany the boys on a mission to Berlin. He manages to get them out of a tight spot when they are stopped just before the Dutch border: he holds off several German troopers while the boys get safely into Holland. But then 'McKenzie, in his early days, had been reckoned in the Canadian northwest as the most deadly shot in the country. He fired from his hips and aimed by instinct and not by sight' (49). In *With Haig*, when Hal and Chester go into action at Cambrai, they are pleased to find 'themselves in the midst of the fighting, alongside the heroic Canadians of Vimy Ridge fame' (74). Hayes describes the Canadians as seasoned, steady fighters:

The Canadian troops advanced calmly and with a sprightliness that seemed strange for men used to the grim work of war. There was something in their carriage that told their officers that they would give a good account of themselves this day. (73)

Indeed, the treatment of Canadians in the series is so laudatory that one wonders if Hayes was given some special directive to appeal to Canadian readers.

Once the Americans enter the war, Hayes describes his own people in similarly mythic terms. The American soldiers are cheerful, rough-and-tumble fellows. While they do not know all the skills required for trench warfare, they can toss grenades because they have played baseball (*Under the Stars and Stripes* 172). The young Americans are 'light-hearted' and 'care-free' (226) and also prone to roughhousing and brawling. They are at war, not for the Empire, but for their own ideals: when, during a German trench raid, one of the young Americans is bayoneted by a German, he is described as 'the first American soldier to give his life in the battle for freedom and world democracy' (215).

Like the Brereton books, the Boy Allies series make war seem like great fun. In the first volume, when Hal and Chester learn that war has been declared, they are dismayed that as under-age Americans 'we cannot take a hand in the fighting. The war will be the greatest of all time, and both sides will need every man they can get capable of bearing arms' (9). At the beginning of *In Great Peril*, when Uncle John has finally corralled Hal and Chester and is about to take them home, the boys regret that their British uniforms have been packed away: 'Every time I look at mine,' says Hal, 'I want to run back to the front instead of going home' (18). But he consoles himself with the thought that 'maybe we'll have a little war of our own some day' (19). When the Americans finally do enter the war, Hal greets this as 'the best piece of news that could possibly come to my ears' (*Under the Stars and Stripes* 4).

Why these books appealed to young readers is not hard to understand. They are packed with action: every chapter gets Hal and Chester into another 'ticklish situation.' The new technologies of the period, such as the automobile, aeroplane, motorcycle, tank, and machine gun, feature frequently. Many of Hal's and Chester's adventures could easily be imitated in a make-believe war game – running through the woods with Germans in pursuit, devising codes for messages, masquerading as Germans. Throughout the series, gratifying role reversals occur in which the boys become cool, quick-thinking heroes while the adults are fumbling and sometimes timid followers. The boys are rarely in unpleasant circumstances: travel, whether by car or train, is almost always via some first-class or luxury conveyance, and they are often put up in fine hotels. Even when Chester and Colonel Anderson have been captured by the Austrians and are yet again waiting to be shot at sunrise, they enjoy special luxury in a 'large tent' with 'comfortable chairs, a table and several books' (*In Great Peril* 239). In short, the boy allies lead a charmed life. Their invulnerability, skill, resourcefulness, relish for fighting, and upright but hot-headed response to any insult make them heroes to emulate. If boys took these books literally, then one would have to judge them pernicious, for they teach that war is thrilling and not really dangerous for active young men. But perhaps the readers of these series books enjoyed them just as a topical fantasy, without taking them seriously as war books. While the appearance in the novels of historical personages such as Haig and French and Pershing and the inclusion of historical events such as the siege of Liège and the assault at Vimy Ridge do have a certain reality effect, it might well be cancelled out by the formulaic plotting and idealized performances of Hal and Chester.

A boys' adventure tale with a stronger claim on the reality effect, though not on realism, is Charles Botsford's *Joining the Colors* (1918). Botsford was born in Toronto and joined the CEF in 1915, but the books in his 'Victory' series are for American boys. *Joining the Colors*, the first in the series, features an American schoolboy named Rodman Van Horne who enlists in the Canadian army (as did some 35,000 Americans [Gaffen 14]). Botsford takes a long time to get to the war: the first third of the novel is set at Dale, a New Jersey prep school, and several chapters are devoted to school-story set pieces such as the football game, the fist-fight between the hero and the school bully, mischief in the dormitory (e.g., frogs escaping from a boy's suitcase), and the misadventures of the plump misfit boy. When, finally, Van Horne goes to Canada and enlists, *Joining the Colors* shifts from the facetiousness of the school story to the more high-minded and suspenseful tone of the war adventure. Van Horne's experiences in Toronto quickly confirm his feeling that he must participate in the war. At a recruiting rally, the revival-meeting atmosphere works its magic, and he finds himself volunteering. He is followed by three Canadian volunteers: a jolly French Canadian, Baptiste Trudeau, dressed in regulation mackinaw; a red-haired Scot from Glengarry named Fraser; and a famed Indian runner, John Longlance (presumably modelled on Tom Longboat). This trio of stock Canadian types go off to training camp with Van Horne, and the four become the familiar band of brothers.

The adventure tale continues in training camp, where Van Horne, aided by the silent and stealthy Longlance and the indefatigable Trudeau, catches a spy among the recruits. Fraser, the Scot from Glengarry, proves to be a poor soldier until a friendly but stern chat with Van Horne convinces him to sober up and tidy up. Thanks to the excellent training in drill Van Horne received at prep school, he becomes an instructor, then a sergeant, and finally a lieutenant. The book is almost over before he gets to the front, but in a few quick pages at the end, Van Horne manages to capture a machine-gun nest, bring back a mortally wounded officer from no man's land, and win a VC.

Like other American war adventures, *Joining the Colors*, despite the fact that Botsford was Canadian, presents Americans as effortlessly superior beings: in class, in strength, in wealth, in courage, they dominate the field. For example, the 'young American giant' Van Horne dwarfs the Canadian recruits. As the Quarter Master remarks, he is 'the tallest and best proportioned soldier yet measured for his uniform in the city of Toronto, and that, I dare say, means in the whole Dominion of Canada' (168).

Mixed in with the school-story and war-adventure elements are long expository passages about the war, presented as unconvincing dialogues between the young hero and various experts; more surprisingly, there are also footnotes, maps, and diagrams. These elements support the impression that the author, identified on the cover as 'Capt. Charles A. Botsford, C.E.F,' is delivering the straight goods about the war. Certainly the reviewer for the *Ontario Library Review* thought so: 'The author, who has been through many of the battles, writes a realistic story that will prove interesting to boys' (Feb. 1919: 76).

But realism and accuracy are hardly this book's strengths.

Take, for example, the stories Van Horne hears about the Germans in Belgium. Captain McCharles, the 'Commandant' of the Dale Academy cadets and 'a veteran of the Great War [who has] been honorably discharged from the Canadian Expeditionary Force ... as medically unfit' (11), tells Van Horne of 'occurrences that I actually observed,' including a tale about a Belgian child with 'the stump of his little forearm ... swathed in field dressings'; the injury had been inflicted by a German soldier who, 'for amusement, had placed a time bomb in the little fellow's hand' (64–5). Certainly many people at this time believed in the myth of the mutilated Belgium child, but Botsford presents McCharles's account as incontrovertible eyewitness evidence from a Canadian veteran. Given that Botsford himself was a veteran, his own authority on matters relating to the war is transferred to the fictional Captain McCharles. Another unrealistic element is Van Horne's 'first real war thrill': on the train journey north to Canada, he witnesses two German saboteurs being apprehended by a secret service officer (111).

Since *Joining the Colors* was not available in Canada until 1919, it could not have influenced enlistment, although encouraging boys to join up certainly seems to have been Botsford's intention. With its explicitly didactic elements, *Joining the Colors* promotes military service as the obvious choice for any healthy, fun-loving lad. The dangers of not enlisting are made evident, too: at the recruiting rally, Van Horne accepts a small item that a pretty girl presses into his hand. He is mortified when he realizes that she has given him a white feather.

Did such books as *Joining the Colors* and the Boy Allies series make young readers long for their chance at war? In writing about Henty's many books of adventure, J.S. Bratton has suggested that boys read them with a certain skepticism: the formulaic quality signalled that these books were 'a game,' very satisfying to engage in, but not to be taken as a guide to the real world (*Impact* 198–9). She quotes A.J.P. Taylor recalling that 'even the most devoted admirers of Henty's books found them comic as well as exciting' (198). The comedy in these formulaic adventure books derived not just from scenes of explicit comic relief but also from the preposterous quality of the action and the unrealistic successes of the heroes. But A.J.P. Taylor, even as a boy, was surely not the average reader. Would less clever

boys have swallowed Henty and other war-adventure books entire? The editors of the Salvation Army *Young Soldier* thought
that such reading was dangerous stuff. An article entitled 'The
Dream of a Dime Novel Reader' warned boys against it:

> You like the thrill and the excitement, perhaps, that such tales
> bring. The deeds of the boy pirate, the boy detective, or the boy
> air scout fascinate you. But you get no real knowledge or informa-
> tion worth a button out of such reading. Therefore it is a sheer
> waste of time.
>
>     And more than that, it is an injurious waste of time, for your
> mind gets so saturated with the unreal that you cannot settle down
> to learn the things that are going to fit you for a useful and hon-
> ourable career. (29 Jan. 1916: 4)

War-adventure tales might well have been a 'waste of time,' as
much pleasurable reading is, in the sense that they taught nothing practical, although the diagrams in *Joining the Colors* were,
arguably, intended to counter this charge. But whether such
reading actually influenced boys is another matter. Bratton
doubts that the values promoted in Henty's novels – courage,
truthfulness, determination, not to mention aggressive imperialism – had much impact:

> How far [readers] were prepared to transfer such notions from
> the deliberately sought and fostered fantasy world into their own
> lives is, I think, questionable; their remoteness from what was actu-
> ally expected of the reader was surely a part of the appeal. (199)

One might similarly question the impact of the American war
series. They were fun to read, but did they convince any lad to
enlist? Did boys go overseas imagining that their war experience
would be like that of Hal and Chester? Or did their knowledge
of the real war from such sources as the newspapers, newsreels,
and letters enable them to keep the boy allies safely in the realm
of fantasy? Such questions are now impossible to answer. Just as
the authors of explicitly didactic works cannot be assured that
readers will learn the appropriate lessons, so the authors of formulaic adventures cannot be sure that young readers will sensi-
bly dismiss them as fantasy. Certainly recruitment propaganda

in Canada appealed directly to young men's desire for adventure, indicating that the picture of war retailed in the boys' adventure tales was in a sense reinforced by other media. As Paul Maroney has observed, the message about enlistment delivered in posters and recruiting speeches was that it would 'mean adventure, comradeship, and healthy fresh air and exercise' – the same 'romantic conception of warfare' that lay behind the boys' adventure tales (88).

In his autobiography, *Homesteader: A Prairie Boyhood Recalled*, James Minifie described how 'war fever' overcame him in 1915: 'I saw myself in heroic roles, sounding amid shot and shell the charge which rallied a hopeless retreat' (161). The diction signals the origin of this vision in the adventure story. While the only adventure reading Minifie specifically alludes to is a British paper called *The Captain* (156–7), the subtitle of the fourth Boy Allies book is *Midst Shot and Shell along the Aisne*. Early the next year, Minifie went into Vanguard, Saskatchewan, and signed up; he was just sixteen years old (162).

**Homegrown Heroism**

There was only one truly Canadian boys' adventure novel about the war – that is, a book written by a Canadian, set in Canada, and published by a Canadian firm: Harold C. Lowrey's *Young Canada Boys with the S.O.S. on the Frontier* (1918). It depicts the adventures of a dozen boy scouts, aged twelve to sixteen, who foil a German plan to blow up the Welland Canal. The boys, members of a Scout patrol from a city school, join the S.O.S. (Soldiers of the Soil) program and go down to Niagara to work as farmhands. Lowrey makes this a distinctively Canadian war adventure in that the spy-catching exploits of the lads are interwoven with history lessons about Canada's previous military actions. If American war adventures incorporate national myths about the frontier and its strong, can-do citizens, Canadian war adventures employ the image of the vulnerable colony, beset by invaders and unreliable Natives.

In Lowrey's novel, the leader of the Scouts is Chester (Chuck) Woodruff, who has selected his patrol members 'with extreme care to represent the different Allied nations at war with German barbarism' (2). Thomas, the Welsh lad, is known as

Cinders. Chuck's little brother, Albert, is called Anzac because he was born in Australia while his Canadian parents were travelling there. Martin is called 'Cod' because he's from Newfoundland, and Harry Douglas is known as 'Jap' because he was born in Japan to missionary parents. Plainly, the boys *are* the Allies, and their ultimate triumph over the German spies will represent the Allied victory in Europe.

Chuck and his patrol members are keen 'to get in the fight' (5). When the principal asks them to volunteer for the S.O.S, they are jubilant: '... after waiting and praying for a chance, they were going to be given the opportunity to serve their country. They were going into the trenches to fight' (5). At first, it seems as if the boys are actually going to France, a confusion that may be deliberate in order to emphasize the importance of the S.O.S volunteers. When the boys (and the reader) realize that the Scouts will be farm workers, not real soldiers, they still describe themselves as part of the war effort. They will 'be the boys behind the boys behind the guns over there in France' (8).

The Allies' Patrol is sent to the Niagara region, home territory for Lowrey, who in his foreword declares that he grew up 'on the very farm where was fought the battle of Queenston Heights' (ii). Elizabeth Galway notes that nineteenth-century Canadian children's literature had contributed to the development of a national mythology with 'its own heroes'; General Isaac Brock, who led the assault at Queenston Heights and died there, was pre-eminent in the pantheon of Canada's military leaders (29). Throughout *Young Canada Boys*, Lowrey connects the Great War to the War of 1812: 'The wonderful deeds of our great-grandfathers during the war of 1812 are just as thrilling and as valorous as those of their descendants' (ii). He even uses names associated with the War of 1812: two characters in his novel, Farmer Lundy and Grandpa Secord, establish a direct link between the present of the novel and the glorious military past.

The chapters alternate between high adventure and history lessons. The history lessons are supplied by Grandpa Secord, whose role in the novel is to tell rambling tales about Canada's military past: 'Yuh call yerselves Soldiers, well jest yuh find out whut your forefathers did tuh make Canada a great country, free an' happy. Take Auntie Laura, thar wuz a great woman, byes, an' a true Canadian, but they wuz common in those days, jest ez they are in this big war' (70). (Dialect was part of the 'fashion of local-colour stories' of the time [Waterston 152], but, in contrast with the subtler suggestions of dialect in the works of writers like L.M. Montgomery and Charles G.D. Roberts, Lowrey's version of rural speech seems overdone; it is hard to believe that any Canadian, no matter how rustic, ever sounded quite like this.) Fortuitously, Grandpa Secord is connected not only to his auntie's war in 1812 but to other conflicts: he remembers 'fac[ing] bullets and cannonballs, first in the scrimmages of 1837, then in the Red River Rebellion, where he lost a leg in hand-to-hand fighting with a massive half-breed' (93). Grandpa Secord, by even the most conservative calculation, must be nearing ninety-five.

The real intrigue of the novel is slow to get started, though there are frequent hints that spies are waiting in the wings. Anzac, the keenest spy-hunter on the patrol, discovers a pretzel in the ruins of 'the famous old stone building' where General Brock was carried when 'mortally shot' (79). The pretzel is 'condemning proof of the existence of a spy' (89). Anzac also discovers 'an everyday commercial letter' that Chuck realizes contains a hidden message: '*Sending you two trusty men. Try it on Aug. 1st*' (90). When they present this evidence to the nearby military camp, the Chief Intelligence Officer recognizes its importance: 'These scouts have done great work. This letter here means that these dirty sneaks are going to try to destroy the Welland Canal or one of the bridges on August 1st' (112). He invites the Allies' Patrol to help him track down the spies; fortunately, the boys have some time off from their agricultural work. When the boys come face-to-face with the spies, they are not afraid: 'They were Canadians and the equal of any Germans, no matter how well armed they were. They were doing just what Grandpa Secord's father and aunt had done a hundred years ago' (162). In the final showdown, the scouts, armed with slingshots and automatic weapons, manage to defeat the spies. Chuck is wounded, but it is only 'the clean flesh wound' so common in the adventure tale (176). Recognition for their good work in foiling the spies is unwelcome to these modest lads, but they cannot avoid it. They are sent to England, where Anzac is awarded the Victoria Cross, and his fellow members of the Allies' Patrol receive the Second Order of Service, 'the new decoration for unselfish devotion to the broader ideals of Empire citizenship' (201).

With its stock characters, implausible coincidences, and daunt-
less boy heroes, *Young Canada Boys* is in most respects an undis-
tinguished specimen of the wartime boys' adventure tale. But
the Canadian context, evoked so specifically through Grandpa
Secord's tales, makes it unusual: here, enunciated in very clear
terms, is the nation-building myth of the war. Through the history that Grandpa Secord relates, the present war becomes the
culmination of a tradition of struggle against the enemies of
Canadian Freedom, whether they be Yankee invaders, English
overlords, rebellious half-breeds, or brutish Germans.

Lowrey's novel was the only Canadian war book specifically
aimed at young readers, but Canadian boys were doubtless also
reading war books intended for adults. As I noted in the introduction, Ralph Connor was named as a favourite author by
young correspondents to the *King's Own*. Francis Pow of Cranbrook, for example, who was just twelve, had read *The Prospector*,
*The Patrol of the Sun Dance Trail*, and *The Sky Pilot* (2 Nov. 1918:
176). It seems likely, therefore, that Canadian boys like Francis
also read Connor's war novels, *The Major* (a best-seller in 1917
and 1918) and *The Sky Pilot in No Man's Land* (1919). In these
novels, they would have encountered a view of the war not so
very different from that in the British adventure tales, but tempered with a strongly Christian outlook and a reverence for the
character-building effects of life in the wilderness. Connor's heroes are the epitome of muscular Christianity; they are frontier-
hardened men who are clean and upright. The war does not
tarnish their faith or sully their morals, nor does it disillusion
them about war. In *The Sky Pilot in No Man's Land*, Connor describes the Western Front as 'that bloodsoaked sacred soil which
[Canada's] dead Battalions hold for Honour, Faith and Freedom' (286).

It was not until just after the war that other wholly Canadian
war adventure tales were published. In 1920, R.G. MacBeth began his *Trail Makers Boys' Annual: An Annual Volume of Stories and
Articles for Canadian Boys by Canadian Boys' Men*; he proudly announced it as 'the first purely Canadian Boys' Annual that has
ever been issued' (1.12). A clergyman and author, well known
in his day for popular histories of the Canadian West, MacBeth
emphasized in *Trail Makers* muscular Christianity, imperial loyalty, and the great potential of Canada – themes that could find

natural expression in stories and articles about the recently concluded war.

The first issue of the annual established the patriotic tone. In 'Our Great Flag,' MacBeth declares that 'overseas there are sixty thousand young Canadians at rest under the wooden crosses because they went forth to defend the flag and the Empire against an attack upon our freedom' (80). In 'The Hero,' W. Smith, who was principal of a Presbyterian theological college, reassures his young readers that 'although the war is over the opportunity of the hero has not passed away': 'If the boys overseas saved the world from tyranny we must look to the boys at home to save Canada from all those evils which threaten our life and destiny as a great nation' (133). Frank Yeigh contributed 'Canada the Best Boys' Country in the World.' (Most often remembered as Pauline Johnson's first manager, Yeigh was also a contributor to children's periodicals such as the *King's Own*.) In enumerating Canada's virtues, Yeigh puts special emphasis on the imperial connection: 'I like Canada because it is part and parcel of the British empire, a partner in the business firm of John Bull and Sons, still doing business at the old stand and doing more of it than ever. I was never so proud of being a Britisher, as well as a Canadian, as during and since the war' (113).

Along with this earnest material were several adventure tales. C.C. Kernahan ('formerly with R.N.W.M.P and C.E.F.') contributed 'Saunders, V.C.,' which recounts the adventures of a dashing Canadian called Bertie, who served in India and then with the R.N.W.M.P. In 1899, Bertie volunteers with Lord Strathcona's Horse in South Africa, where he earns his VC. Kernahan promises that 'Saunders's further adventures in the Great War will be told in the next volume,' but, unfortunately, they were not. In 'A Desperate Ride: An Incident of the British Retreat, France, 1918,' Captain Harwood Steele describes how a young motorcycle messenger manages to dodge shell-holes and a hail of German bullets to deliver vital information. It is, Steele announces, 'a simple story, but ... typical of the bravery revealed by our soldiers' (182). In the second volume, an article by the VC-winning air ace Billy Barker includes several thrilling anecdotes about night bombing, strafing, and aerial surveillance.

The most Canadian of the adventure tales appears in the first volume: 'A Boys' Brigade Hero,' by Herbert Fiddes (identified as 'C.E.F. Captain 5<sup>th</sup> Vancouver Co'y Boy's Brigade'), Tommy, 'a typical Canadian lad' (91), manages to capture 'Fritz Hummer, spy and murderer, the most notorious character that has defiled these beautiful mountains for many years' (95). Tommy is on a camping trip with friends in 'the wonderful mountain scenery of British Columbia' (91) when they encounter Hummer. He is the archetype of Hunnish malevolence: 'dirty and disheveled' and 'drunk to the point of madness,' with 'cunning and evil written all over [his face] and ... an ugly scar on the left cheek,' which is presumably a Teutonic duelling scar (93). When Tommy resists Hummer's attempts to take the boys' food and supplies, Hummer hits the boy 'a blow ... as cowardly as it was unexpected.' Then ensues 'a fight between a drink-crazed fiend and a clean, healthy schoolboy.' Tommy prevails and manages to capture Hummer, who has eluded the R.N.W.M.P. for the entire war. The allegorical message of the story – decadent Germany defeated by youthful Canada – is not hard to detect.

Agnes Laut's 'How the Little Bohunk Made Good' in volume 2 of *Trail Makers* reflects another element in the Canadian myth of the war: the conviction that out of the shared hardship of war had come a new and unifying spirit.[8] Just as men from across the country and from every ethnic group had fought together in the trenches, so Canadians of every kind would work together in peacetime to build a better nation. As Jonathan Vance has pointed out, it was hoped that 'the memory of the war could act as a citizenship primer for children and immigrants, providing a means of Canadianization unlike any other' (*Death* 227).

Laut begins the story by admitting her own and her fellow Canadians' dislike of immigrants – of their strange clothing and strange speech and strange manners. She recounts how, some years before the war, there was a riot in Winnipeg when the Mounties came to take immigrants to their homesteads. There were no interpreters, so the Galicians (Ukrainians) and Russians were afraid and resisted the Mounties' efforts to get them to the train station. In the riot, a small boy threw a stone at one of the Mounties, injuring him on the forehead. Laut drily observes that 'though we were asked not to publish details of the small riot ... – it would hurt the Government's immigration policy – I remember we did publish solemn editorials about not allowing people whose ideas of liberty were different from ours, to come into our country too freely' (157). (Laut had been a journalist with the *Manitoba Free Press* in the late 1890s.) Laut then moves on to the following spring, when the Mountie, along with the narrator and a civil service relief officer, tour a rural district after severe wildfires, looking for survivors. They discover a group of Galician children huddled in a slough. The children have survived because the oldest boy – the very lad who had thrown the stone at the Mountie – had the courage to keep the children in the swamp while the fire raged. The Mountie, who had been expressing anti-immigrant views before the children were discovered, revises his thinking in the face of the courage of the little boy. Twenty years later, the boy enlists, and the Mountie, now a colonel, is the recruiting officer. The boy, who has grown up to be 'a huge river man with a head of tow hair and kinky fierce moustache,' recognizes him: 'You saf' my life in the swamp land twentee year ago, and me, when I wass a leedly poy I heet yo dot lumpel on your highness' brow in immigration hall' (162). The Colonel, remembering the courage of young Petrovsky, immediately assigns him to 'a regiment later to be famous.' In the next section – 'on the firing line in Flanders!' – someone is needed to bomb a 'rat hole' in the enemy trenches:

'Any man in your Company, who can speak both German and Russian?' asks the Colonel, who has a knob above his brow.
'Yes, Sir,' answers the little lieutenant with the toothbrush moustache; 'but he is a foreigner. You can't trust 'em.' (163)

The foreigner, who of course is Petrovsky, volunteers for the mission. The Colonel with the knob on his forehead is none other than the Mountie whom Petrovsky, as a child, had injured. And while the 'little lieutenant,' an Englishman also assigned to the mission, huddles timorously behind the barbed wire, Petrovsky crawls across to the rat hole, bombs it, and sends the remaining Germans 'running with their hands up towards the Canadian line.' Petrovsky does not survive the mission, but the lieutenant does:

'Paid Canada back all right – all right didn't he?' the Colonel was saying over his shoulder to another Canadian officer. 'But Satan's

own luck. That cub [the little lieutenant] will get the credit and
ribbons for it ... and that Bohunk's little finger was worth his whole
carcass! Wish I had a whole regiment of 'em.'

   And back in Canada, Little Bohunk's people didn't find it wise
to vote during elections for fear of being accused of alien sympathies. (163)

By choosing a 'bohunk' for her hero rather than a cool Britisher,
Laut clearly goes beyond the limited ideological range of the adventure tale. Instead of offering the familiar message of racial
pride, her story promotes *avant la lettre* a multicultural vision of
Canada. Moreover, one has to admire her courage in alluding to
the provision of the Wartime Elections Act of 1917 that took away
the vote from persons of enemy-alien birth.[9]

   Other items in the *Trail Makers* also promote a more diverse
picture of Canada. In volume 1, 'Han, The Carpenter,' by O.D.
Austin, describes how a Christian convert from China, a volunteer on the Western Front with the Chinese Labour Corps, heroi-
cally puts out a fire caused by a shell landing on an ammunition
dump. After the war, Han travels back to China via Canada, but
his heroism goes unrecognized: 'And no one of the hundreds
of Canadians who saw this big, brawny kindly-faced Chinaman
passing through Canada on his way home knew that he was
one of the heroes of the great war. Had they but known, would
they not have honoured him as they have their own Canadian
heroes?' (219). The inclusion of a non-British, non-white man
in the ranks of war heroes suggests that MacBeth and his writers
were indeed trying to make of the war experience a 'citizenship
primer' (to use Vance's expression). But Han, it must be noted,
is not Canadian; he is on his way back to China. Perhaps Canadian readers were not yet ready for a Canadian-born Chinese war
hero, returning home to be honoured in his own country.

# 7 But What Can a Girl Do?

'I'm going to enlist just as soon as I can make things right to leave home
... it looks now as if we shall need every man the Empire can send to
bring this war to a successful finish' ...
    Sara lifted shining eyes to Rob's face. 'O, if I could only go too! If I
were only old enough and trained for a nurse. But what can a girl of
fourteen do?'
                                                    Christina Ross Frame,
                                'With Chin Up,' *King's Own*, 10 Feb. 1917

In their lively study of British girls' illustrated papers and annuals, *You're a Brick, Angela!* Mary Cadogan and Patricia Craig
suggest that war adventure tales were only for boys: 'During the
early years of the first world war popular fiction for boys urged
them to become heroes in defence of their country, while girls'
magazines offered their readers mainly the vicarious thrill of
knitting for the boys in the trenches' (87–8). This, however, is
one of the 'platitudes' about war books that, according to Mitzi
Myers, 'need scotching' (328). Myers claims that they cannot be
neatly divided into 'combat books from "over there" for boys'
and 'domestic contribution stories for girls on the home front.'
Indeed, in the range of wartime reading material that Canadian
girls had access to, there is much more than 'domestic contribution.' While the majority of stories for girls in the Sunday-school
papers reinforce the view that girls must do their war service
on the home front, there are nonetheless British, American,
and Canadian war stories in which girls catch spies, foil invasion
plots, and even get to the battlefields.

This high degree of involvement and agency might seem to signal that the modern girl arrived in the literature of the First World War. The typical protagonist of the war story is certainly resourceful, courageous, and even outspoken, able to stand on her own and eager to do her part. This ideal of an independent girl, so frequent in the girls' stories, was surely reinforced by the peculiar conditions of society in wartime, when so many women were forced to assume the jobs and responsibilities of the men who had gone to the front. The absence of fathers and other dominant adult males, a near-universal condition in the war stories, creates both problems and opportunities. Girls and mothers have to do things they have never done before, a frightening prospect but also a liberating and exciting one. Donna Coates has suggested that women war writers could be seen as 'war profiteers, seizing the chaos occasioned by war to vanquish women's subordinate status' ('Best' 68). There are definite glimmers in the stories for girls of just such a move towards independence.

Yet ultimately the authors and their protagonists cannot shed the conventions of their time, narrative or social. The requirements of the female genres of the romantic love story and the didactic domestic tale assert themselves, even in stories that incorporate adventure tale elements. The result is that the resourceful and independent heroine crumples at the end, compliantly withdrawing into a more conventional female role. This kind of mixed message was, according to Anne Scott MacLeod, 'absolutely characteristic' of girls' fiction in the early twentieth century: '... again and again, authors showed young girls fully capable of both the spirit and the physical skills routinely attributed to boys, but they always drew back at the implications of such equality for adult life' (*American* 165). Jacqueline Bratton has pointed out the problem facing writers of fiction for girls in the early twentieth century:

> ... new narratives and character models, which would maintain the old values but offer a more modern standard of activity for girls, were not easy to set up. A century of writing for girls had established the norm of the domestic tale, in which the trials of the heroine were involved with the learning of discipline, the internalization of the feminine values of self-abnegation, obedience and subordination. ('British Imperialism' 197)

In the wartime girls' stories, the heroines make sacrifices for the national cause, but glory rarely accrues to them; girls and women are *expected* to be self-sacrificing in quiet, unobtrusive ways. In girls' war stories, obedience and submission – to parents, to teachers, to nation – are frequently reinforced by recourse to the example of the soldiers. This emphasis on the soldier as a model for obedience also appears in stories for boys, especially in the Sunday-school papers. But whereas boys are encouraged to be obedient so that they will be good soldiers, girls must submit to authority so that they will be good women. Whether the protagonist is a British schoolgirl, a Canadian girl on the home front, or the heroine of an American girl's romance, she is only temporarily free to have war adventures; in the end, she must return to some appropriately feminine role or context.

## Schoolgirls at War

Canadian girls were exposed to British schoolgirl war adventures largely through annuals. The *Canadian Girl's Annual* (which, despite its name, was an English production) was first published in Canada in 1916 by Cassell's branch in Toronto. (Later issues were published by McClelland and Stewart for the Amalgamated Press of London, the publisher 'most closely involved with presenting and refining basic images of adolescent girls' in Britain [Cadogan and Craig, *You're* 9].) In addition to this 'Canadian' annual, girls in Canada were reading other annuals from Britain, which, like their counterparts for boys, were advertised and sold in Canada (Moss 84).[1]

The first *Canadian Girl's Annual* (1916) contained several stories in which schoolgirls take an active part in the war. 'Vic and the Refugee' opens with the hearty tone of a conventional school story:

'German spies,' said Vic the Captain emphatically, as we sat at tea on the first night of term, 'are swarming all over the country, and we're too sleepy and trusting to deal with them, and too jolly sentimental.'
... 'Oh, I wish I could kill one German,' I said with energy. 'I wish one would walk in now!'
'So do I,' said Vic. 'It would be awful sport; but seeing there's

not the slightest chance of it you might use some of your energy –
passing the bread and butter.'

I passed it. 'As to that Kaiser – ' : I went on.

'Oh!' said Vic, 'speak not of him, I beg you; the very name sick-
eneth me. Who's that new kid?' (9)

The 'new kid' is Yvonne, who claims to be a Belgian refugee but
is actually a German spy. Her kind uncle in Manchester, who is
paying her school fees, is in fact her husband, and the couple
are plotting to put a German gun on the school tennis court.
After some detective work involving the tennis court asphalt, Vic
wises up to Yvonne's true intentions. She rifles through the girl's
belongings and finds incriminating letters written in German.
Vic then marches Yvonne to the headmistress.

This sort of schoolgirl spy-catcher was a stock character of the
period. Two wartime novels by British author Angela Brazil, *The
Madcap of the School* (1916) and *A Patriotic Schoolgirl* (1918), feature clever heroines who capture German spies.[2] This plot line
was borrowed more or less wholesale from boys' school stories
of the same period (Foster and Simons 202); one might argue,
therefore, that making the spy-catcher a girl is a somewhat progressive choice. Shirley Foster and Judy Simons argue for the
feminist message of Brazil's *Madcap of the School,* noting that it
'locates its girl characters in a world of changing gender relations
and revised concepts of female identity contextualized by the
impact of the First World War'; nonetheless, they acknowledge
that the school in which Brazil's characters grow and learn is a
closed female community (210). *A Patriotic Schoolgirl* also takes
place in the closed world of the school. All the crucial characters
– the spy, the person falsely accused of spying, the spy-catcher –
belong to this world. In a sense, Brazil's wartime stories do not
really enable the female protagonists to participate in the larger
world. They just rework a conventional school-story plot from
the pre-war period in which the heroine discovers some lesser
kind of criminal such as a girl who is stealing things from her
schoolmates.

Another type of girl's war story involved heroines not in
school but on the Continent. The 'young heroine trapped on
the Continent by the outbreak of war' was, according to Michael
Paris, a favourite wartime plot device, especially in fiction for

girls (24). 'Philippa of England: How an English Girl Played Her Part in the Great War,' another story in the 1916 *Canadian Girl's Annual*, depicts just such a heroine: Philippa, an orphan, has been sent by her uncle to study music in Germany, and when war breaks out, she is living at a school for girls run by the tyrannical Fraulein Eckart, devoted to 'instilling German "Kultur" into her pupils' (50).

'Philippa' was written by Dorothea Moore, a Guide commissioner and prolific writer of girls' fiction; according to Cadogan and Craig, Moore specialized in heroines who 'were usually in danger of drowning in the vacuity of their own pseudo-heroics' (*You're* 149, 156). In this story, Philippa engages in her fair share of 'pseudo-heroics.' For example, she is chased by a mob when she stands up for her country against defamatory newspaper headlines: 'England *isn't* treacherous, and couldn't ever be, and you're telling wicked untruths if you say she is, so there!' (52). On her journey from Germany to Belgium and home to England, Philippa gets embroiled in various adventures. First, she discovers that Belgian nuns on a hospital train bound for Liège are actually German soldiers in disguise. She gets a warning to Liège so that the phony hospital train is stopped. Her next exploit is to warn the Royal Corps of Engineers that the German Uhlans are on the way: to do this, Philippa climbs a bell tower and unwraps the clapper, which a German spy had muffled. Then, after being taken prisoner by the Germans, she helps two British officers escape. One of the officers exclaims, 'Who are you, you wonderful kiddy, who think nothing of carrying prisoners from under the noses of the Germans?' (81). Philippa is certainly in the mould of Moore's unwaveringly patriotic and 'irritatingly resourceful' heroines (Cadogan and Craig, *You're* 148). Philippa ends up 'in a place where no petticoat, even that clothing a person of only thirteen, had ever before been allowed – in the headquarters in the British firing line' (81).

Another story in the 1916 *Canadian Girl's Annual*, Olaf Baker's 'Between Love and Loyalty: A Story of the German Invasion of Poland,' also depicts an English girl trapped by war. Clare Lorraine has been living in Poland as companion to the Countess Dubetzkoi. She displays British sangfroid when a Prussian officer arrives at the castle and demands to be billeted. The officer, Von Kastner, is duly impressed: 'Here was a young girl, utterly defenceless, and in the hands of the bitterest enemies of her country, who yet could afford to carry her head high, and speak as lightly as if she were sitting out a dance in a London ballroom' (153). Clare is in love with Count Nicholas Dubetzkoi, son of her employer, who is now a prisoner of the Germans. Von Kastner makes a sinister proposition: her sweetheart will be freed if Clare will show the Germans the path through the treacherous terrain that lies between the castle and the Russian lines. But even with a gun at her head, Claire refuses to show him the route: 'I may be a woman, but I am also an Englishwoman. Even for the sake of her love, an Englishwoman does not betray' (157). Fortunately, a loyal boatman shoots Von Kastner, thus saving Clare; even more fortunately, 'the next day the Russians gained a tremendous victory' (158). Count Nicholas is freed and sent home to the castle to convalesce under Clare's devoted care. Older and more sophisticated than Philippa, Clare is more clearly a romantic heroine. Perhaps this explains why, despite her courage and resolve, Clare is relegated to the suitably feminine role of caretaker.

What, one wonders, did Canadian girls make of such stories? Certainly these British war adventures offer no practical examples of how a girl in Canada might contribute to the war effort. Canadian girls might have identified with the proud Britishness of these heroines and the pluck that is purportedly their British birthright; after all, Canadian girls lived under the same flag. But the lack of realism in these stories, in which coincidence and miraculous escapes play so great a part, and their pervasive snob appeal make them very distant from the average Canadian girl. Perhaps girls who lived in England and went to boarding schools could trap spies; perhaps girls so fortunate as to be sent abroad to study or to be companion to a countess might find themselves face to face with the Germans. But it would have been hard for a girl in Winnipeg or Orillia to imagine herself into such a story.

**Canadian Girls on the Home Front**

To find war stories reflecting their own situation, Canadian girls had to turn to the Sunday-school papers, especially the Presbyterian paper the *King's Own*, which regularly published war stories specifically aimed at girls. While the Sunday-school authors never lose sight of their didactic purpose, they are not above including some adventure.

A seven-part serial in the *King's Own* by Christina Ross Frame, 'With Chin Up,' features a young heroine whose actions prove that she is as patriotic and resourceful as any boy. Yet it also demonstrates that for girls, adventure must always be subsumed within the pattern of domestic duty. The story begins with the arrival of the family – Mother, Eileen, Sara, and Rob – in the fictional Maritime town of Bayville. Their own father is dead, so they have come to live with Mother's half-brother William. When war breaks out, Uncle William joins up, leaving Sara's family to run the farm. With no adult males in the household, roles in the family must change. At first, Sara feels deeply sorry for herself: '... the remote, far-away evil of war had stalked into this happy Bayville home, as suddenly and relentlessly as into millions of other homes, even to the uttermost parts of the earth' (6 Jan. 1917: 1). But she takes herself in hand, and 'that August noontime' proves to be the beginning of a new era for Sara. She collects for the Belgian Relief Fund. She also displays her courage: sent to do a boy's job – bringing in the cows – Sara encounters a bear, and although it is her brother Rob who shoots the animal, Sara is regarded as 'very brave and resourceful' for having outrun the bear and found a safe perch on a shed roof (13 Jan. 1917: 6).

When the first war Christmas comes, Sara is sick and again feeling sorry for herself, especially because there won't be a Christmas tree. But Sara upbraids herself:

> For shame, Sara McNeill, here you sit before a good fire, with plenty of food, and warm and comfortable, while hundreds of poor Belgian and French girls have been driven from their homes, their families scattered, fathers and brothers dead and our own brave soldiers fighting for the world's liberty in the trenches. Uncle William, too, keeping cheery and hopeful amid the mud and sickness at Salisbury Plain. I'm ashamed of you, Sara McNeill, you're a slacker of the worst kind. Instead of sitting grouching, try to plan some way in which to help, even if you haven't the money to buy Christmas gifts. (27 Jan. 1917: 14)

Sara sells the bearskin (her reward for having survived the encounter) and uses the money to host a Red Cross tea. Although her hat is shabby, she resolves not to buy a new one:

> 'There are dozens of things that I'd like to have, a pretty party dress like Edith's for instance, but I've been reading about those Belgian women and children to-day, and it seems to me that I'll wear any old thing willingly if I can only do something to help them.'
>
> 'Yes, Sara,' put in her mother, 'that is the right spirit. It is a spirit that is making Canada great, the sacrifice of self in the noble cause of liberty.' (14)

Sara's sacrifice results in a highly successful Christmas entertainment with 'patriotic recitations and five-minute addresses by the different ministers.'[3]

A new challenge is presented when the family hires a troublesome lad named Tom to help out on the farm. The fine spirit of the McNeill family and a wartime sense of urgency transform Tom from proto-delinquent into patriot: 'Maps, war conditions, military and political leaders, movements of troops, equipment, Tom studied it all, until he became a walking encyclopedia of the European tragedy' (3 Feb. 1917: 18). Then a strange man shows up at the McNeill homestead asking for work. Although he works hard, the man, who 'gave his name as Angus Maclean,' arouses Sara's suspicions (18). When Tom reports that 'Maclean' kicked the dog and 'jabbered away in some kind of gibberish,' Sara is convinced the man is a spy (19). Sara discovers that 'Maclean' has cleared out of his room, and so while everyone else is in church, she decides to check the railway trestle herself, bravely walking over the stringers 'forty feet above the red raging current of the river.' She discovers no sign of Maclean or of sabotage, but, making her way back to town along the tracks, in the darkness she stumbles: 'The cause of her disastrous fall was plain enough. Rolled straight across the track and tied fast was a huge log placed for a work of death and destruction.' Although bruised and bleeding, Sara races back to town to alert the townspeople just in time to clear the tracks for the troop train. Sara is the heroine of the day.

As 'With Chin Up' progresses, the scope of Sara's adventures begins to narrow. After showing her mettle in escaping the bear, organizing her community, and foiling the spy, Sara ends up taking care of aged relatives and knitting for her uncle at the front. In another serial, entitled 'When the Corner Class Came,' the same pattern manifests itself: a girls' story that starts out with determined modern girls ends up with sweetly conventional heroines. The girls of a Sunday-school class are sad when their teacher, Miss Manson, goes off to work in a munitions factory. This is a most unusual detail: in no other Canadian girls' fiction of the period have I seen a reference to women's work in the munitions industry (or any other form of factory work). One reason may be that, as Joan Sangster has pointed out, the number of Canadian women working in munitions factory was actually not great: the claim of the Imperial Munitions Board that Canadian munitions factories in Ontario and Montreal were employing some 35,000 women is 'highly unlikely' (164). Another reason why the Sunday-school stories for girls are silent about industrial war work may be that it was regarded as socially degrading and even morally compromising for young readers.[4] But Miss Manson makes her choice sound noble: 'It would be a poor soldier who would question the word of his commander when ordered to start off at a moment's notice, and this is my bit of soldiering ...' (23 June 1917: 97). The 'Corner Class' decide that they too can do their bit, so they volunteer to work on a farm. In the next instalment, the girls set off to spend the summer in Fernbank at the McClure farm. Now, at last, they are doing something serious: '"If only I were a boy," Margaret had said more than once at the beginning of the war, and now she was going to be given a chance to show what "even a girl" could do in helping to win the victory' (30 June 1917: 103).

The berry picking is hard work, but the girls soon discover that the real war work on the McClure farm isn't bringing in the harvest; it's raising morale. The McClures' young son Jimmy has a heart problem so he has not been able to join up: '... since the war he has been brooding so over his inability – his utter uselessness as he calls it – that it is telling against him, and he is going down hill again' (7 July 1917: 106). The girls manage to get Jimmy to take over the unruly older boys at the local Sunday school. Through teaching them first aid, Jimmy rediscovers a sense of purpose, and his health improves. He even ends up wearing khaki when he gets a clerical post in a military hospital.

But by the last instalment, the question of war work has been sidelined. The girls donate their earnings to the local Sunday school, and the real victories have been in cheering up Jimmy and in admitting a new girl into the charmed circle of their Sunday-school class. So, instead of carrying through on its apparent message that girls can do practical war work too, the story of the Corner Class girls retreats into a domestic and emotional realm.

In principle, young Canadian women could go to war as Red Cross nurses or VAD workers; indeed, there is much evidence that young girls aspired to this role as fervently as their brothers did to that of aviator.[5] Yet some stories in the Sunday-school papers suggest that for a girl to go to war is unseemly. 'At the Sign of the Maple Leaf' begins with young Edith sitting on a park bench, weeping after the send-off for a troop train (*King's Own*, 1 Sept. 1917: 139). A wounded soldier attempts to comfort Edith, thinking her distress is related to the departed troop train. But Edith admits she is 'crying over myself, because girls can't do anything for their country ... they can't do anything really worth while, like belonging to the army, and suffering hardship, and going into danger, and all that.' The soldier's response disabuses Edith of the idea that women cannot contribute to the war effort:

'Really worth while!' repeated the soldier, and if his tone was not indignant, it certainly was full of surprise. 'Do you suppose I would allow anybody to say that there was a soldier in the army doing more for the country than my wife? Well, maybe I couldn't keep a slip of a girl like you from saying it; but a man had better not try, even if he has got two legs.'

'What is she doing?' asked Edith, very meekly indeed. The man's pale face took on a sort of glow, and a far-away look came into his eyes: 'She is helping to make it a country worth saving,' he said, in a husky voice. 'Whatever is mean and crooked and unkind and dirty, she is working to make clean and straight and good and true. Whatever is weak and helpless and troubled she is trying to lift up – ' The soldier's voice failed him, and ... he drew his sleeve across his eyes.

Because the wounded soldier has suffered for his country, he speaks with moral authority, and his words give Edith a new sense of purpose. She 'dreams no more of going to war to fight for her country' and instead starts a settlement house for the poor children of the city, where she is 'helping to make their beloved country worthy of the sacrifice being offered for her on foreign fields.'

This story ostensibly instructs young women to make a practical contribution to Canadian society, not to 'dream' of action on the battlefield. But the real point is that the value of women lies not in any work they can do but in their inherent virtue and purity. Like the soldier's wife, Edith becomes a model of that 'spiritualised, disembodied femininity' so central to Victorian depictions of womanhood (Bratton, 'British' 197). In the context of war, this idealized femininity takes on special value, for only the pure woman can be worthy of the soldier's sacrifice.

The Sunday-school papers also present war as a force that will teach girls humility and self-denial. 'Doing Your Bit' in the 14 December 1918 issue of the *King's Own* exhorts girls to give up sweets and shopping:

> Many girls are wearing patched shoes and darned stockings and last year's wraps, not because their parents cannot afford new clothes for them, but to save the wool and the leather and the labour of making them. The leather is sorely needed for the army, and any girl who can make her old shoes and clothes last a little longer is serving her country. (199)[6]

A story entitled 'The Noon-"bit," a Nehemiah Weapon,' presents a similar message of self-denial. After a guest speaker encourages girls at a city school to make more war sacrifices, Helen – the 'richest girl in the class, generous and a social leader' – persuades the other girls to change their ways:

> ... Oh, yes, I know that we have given, and have made sacrifices, very great ones, some of us, and we all know the heartache of missing brothers and chums. These are the big things – but the little pinching everyday self denial we have slacked. Just think of our café orders for this term.
> All in favor of the noon-bit – national service – say aye! (7 Sept. 1918: 146)

The story ends with a challenge to the reader: 'How about your

school? Is it doing a plain-lunch bit in food conservation?' Thrift
and self-denial were of course widely promoted virtues in wartime; all citizens were expected to practise them. But here, the
message that self-denial is a form of war service reflects more
than wartime necessity. It reinforces the traditional view that it is
unseemly for girls to be undisciplined or greedy.

One unusual story in the wartime *King's Own* does show a girl
taking an active role in armed conflict (although on the home
front in northern Alberta). In 'Keeping the King's Peace,' Ida
Irwin is appointed as postmaster for the day when the local Royal
Northwest Mounted Police officer goes to town to enlist. Ida also
gets the revolver that goes with the position. Meanwhile, a German agent is stirring up trouble among the local 'colonies of
Austrian Slavs.' When the German gets into a quarrel with a patriotic Englishman, the two men trade national insults, and the
enraged Englishman rounds up a bunch of friends to go after
the agent. It is Ida, wielding the revolver, who stops the vigilantes:

> 'I'm awfully sorry,' said Ida again. 'But it's no use sending our sol-
> diers to fight to keep the king's peace respected if we break it
> here at home ourselves. And you know the king's peace means
> that in Canada not even the wickedest German or anybody could
> be killed or have anything taken from them unless they were tried
> first. Nobody but our police must touch that man.'

Ida holds them at bay until Donald, the Mountie, returns. The
spy is captured, and order is restored. In contrast to other spy
stories of the period, which build shamelessly on fears about 'enemy aliens,' 'Keeping the King's Peace' champions the idea that
all citizens, whatever their origin, are entitled to justice. In its depiction of an active Canadian patriot who happens to be a girl,
'Keeping the King's Peace' goes far beyond more timid pictures
of girls on the home front. In the conclusion, Ida's idealism is
still evident:

> Donald and Ida rode back together in the sunset, and as they
> neared the barracks with the Flag of the Empire waving against a
> golden sky, Ida exclaimed with flashing eyes – 'It's worth fighting,
> and living for. It means so much in justice and law for everybody
> alike.'

## THE RED CROSS GIRLS
### Make second and third choice.

**A New Series of Books for Girls on the European War.**

**34-J90.** The Red Cross Girls in the British Trenches.

**34-J91.** The Red Cross Girls on the French Firing Line.

**34-J92.** The Red Cross Girls In Belgium.

**34-J93.** The Red Cross Girls With The Russian Army

Cloth Bound.
Each.............. **35c**

*The*
**RED CROSS GIRLS**
*in the*
**BRITISH TRENCHES**
MARGARET VANDERCOOK

16 This advertisement appeared in the Fall-Winter 1917/18 issue of the Eaton's catalogue (314). From the Collection of the Archives of Ontario; used with the permission of Sears Canada Inc.

The picture of girl and man riding into the sunset, however, suggests a very conventional restoration of order. Ida, after all, has been just a temporary stand-in as the champion of justice, and when Donald goes off to the front, it is not Ida who will be hired as his replacement.

### American War Books for Girls

American publishers turned out many series books about the war, but most were aimed at boys, not girls. This difference reflects the general pattern in series production of the period: for example, of the nearly one hundred series produced by the Stratemeyer syndicate, only nineteen were for girls (D. Johnson 29). But it also reflects the simple truth that there were not many ways to involve girls in the war.

Of the few active war roles to which girls could aspire, the Red Cross nurse was unquestionably the most glamorous. It is clear,

for example, from many of the stories in the Sunday-school periodicals that girls aspired to being Red Cross nurses. In letters to
the *King's Own*, girls describe dressing up in Red Cross uniforms
for pageants or bazaars. In *Rilla of Ingleside*, Montgomery's heroine envies her sisters who are doing 'Red Cross work in the training camp,' and even though Rilla's father assures her that her
own home-front work is valuable, Rilla complains that 'it lacks
the *romance* theirs must have' (170; italics in original). Even before the war, the Red Cross nurse had been used in girls' stories
as an exemplar of female professionalism and independence:
L.T. Meade's *A Sister of the Red Cross* (1900) shows a heroic young
woman during the siege of Ladysmith. Rilla's mother, Anne
Shirley, cherished the same ambition; as a young girl, she declares to Marilla: 'I think when I grow up I'll be a trained nurse
and go with the Red Crosses to the field of battle as a messenger
of mercy' (*Anne* 192).

The Red Cross Girls series began appearing in 1916; there
were ultimately ten books in the series, but only the first four
appear to have been sold in Canada. Their author, Margaret
Vandercook, was, like so many series writers, highly productive:
she also wrote fourteen books in the Camp Fire Girls series, and
others in the Ranch Girls and the Girl Scouts series.

If the Red Cross nurse is a model 'New Girl' – independent, professional, useful, sturdy – then her appearance in a war
series for girls might suggest something progressive is afoot.
Perhaps these girls have more on their minds than frocks and
marriage. But it is hard to derive any clear message of female
independence from Vandercook's series. On the one hand,
her four girl protagonists do choose to train as nurses and put
themselves on the battlefields. One of them defies her parents
to do so (the others are conveniently orphaned). Yet despite
their choice of a demanding and dangerous profession, the Red
Cross girls never escape the preoccupations of formulaic fiction.
Courtship, friendship, fashion, and status: these are what matter, not gaining independence or making a contribution to a
larger cause. One illustrative example is the incident in which
the girls meet Dr Louisa Garrett Anderson in London and visit
her military hospital staffed entirely by women (*Red Cross Girls
in the British Trenches* 127–8). Garrett Anderson is not fictional:
the daughter of Britain's first female doctor, she too became

a doctor and served as the first female army surgeon. She was also a suffragette who never married and chose to live with a female colleague. In short, Garrett Anderson is unequivocally a model of the independent professional woman. Barbara, one of the Red Cross girls, is impressed by Anderson's accomplishments but offers the opinion that 'I'll bet you the English won't give the women the vote when the war is over, just the same. They can go back home then, although a good many of the poor things won't have any homes to go to' (128). Instead of using this remark to discuss the issue of women's suffrage, Vandercook abruptly changes topics: one of the other girls reproaches Barbara for her use of 'slang.' (I assume it is the expression 'I'll bet' that is considered objectionable.) What matters is not women's suffrage or their war work but that quintessential feminine attribute, refinement.[7]

The very premise of the Red Cross Girls series – that privileged American girls would turn their backs on society to dedicate themselves to war work – is on the surface rather daring and progressive. But the response of the only extant mother in the series, the New York society matron Mrs Thornton, suggests that it is essentially conservative. At first she is utterly opposed to her daughter's plan to join the Red Cross, but Mrs Thornton comes round when she realizes that 'instead of Mildred's engaging in an enterprise both unwomanly and unbecoming, actually she was doing the most fashionable thing of the hour' (*In the British Trenches* 49–50). Mildred's decision earns her much admiration from eligible young men and their mothers, and 'letters of introduction to a number of the best people in England' pour in (50). Vandercook's tone makes it clear that she intends some satire of Mrs Thornton's shallow concern with society, but the point remains that the Red Cross girls are not doing anything that might compromise their essential femininity or their value on the marriage market. Throughout the novels, Vandercook fails to use the girls' war work to show the value of training, self-reliance, and professional work; instead, she succumbs to the gravitational pull of the girls' story conventions.

At the heart of these conventions is female friendship. The four girls who work together throughout the war are really displaced schoolgirls: frequently their lodgings have a boarding-school quality, with plenty of opportunities for cozy chats over cups of tea or coffee. They are not isolated heroines but part of a cheerful, supportive band of friends. The girls are evidently chosen to provide an attractive array of American types – Mildred, the wealthy New York socialite; Nona, the gracious but steely Southern belle; Eugenia, the severe and old-maidish Boston Brahman; and Barbara Meade, the diminutive beauty from Nebraska with the 'the vivacity, the alertness and the "goaheadiveness" of the western girl' (*In the British Trenches* 98). They represent a certain geographical range, but they are all drawn from the same stratum of society. The snob appeal in the Red Cross Girls series is quite remarkable, despite Vandercook's efforts to represent Americans as essentially egalitarian. For example, Barbara (who has promised Mildred's brother that she will look out for her) is alarmed when Mildred seems smitten with a poor journalist: 'Could anything much more disastrous occur than to have Mildred become interested in an unknown and presumably poor newspaper reporter?' (107). Nona, the Southern girl, is attracted to a soldier whom she believes to be of the servant class; she is surprised 'to find the son of a gardener possessed of so much intelligence' (121). But she cannot consider him seriously:

> She was a democrat, of course, and came from a land which taught that all men were equal. But she was a southern girl and the south had been living a good many years on the thought of its old families after their wealth had been taken away. Therefore, there were limits as to what degree of friendliness, even of familiarity, one could endure from a gardener's son. Nevertheless, the young fellow was a soldier and, one felt instinctively, a gallant one. (122–3)

Wherever the girls go, they are surrounded, not by the squalor of war, but by wealth, beauty, and luxury. Just as the boy allies interact with generals and ambassadors rather than ordinary soldiers, so too the Red Cross girls find themselves consorting with the elite: on board ship, they sit at the captain's table and befriend the mysterious Lady Dorian; once in England, they are invited to the estate of the Countess of Sussex; in France they meet a countess; in Russia they visit the Czar and Czarina. Of course, the girls are all attractive, each in her own way. Barbara is diminutive but 'bewitching' (*In the British Trenches* 19); Nona is fine, slender, with hair 'of the purest gold' (56). Mildred, although a failure on the dance floor and considered plain by New York standards, has redeeming features. And severe Eugenia, the Bostonian, appears old-maidish in her drab, worn clothes, but she 'might almost be called handsome: Her features were well cut, her dark hair smooth and abundant, and her expression peaceful' (85). For Eugenia, war has the gratifying effect of a makeover: danger improves her colour and loosens her too-severe hair, thereby revealing her true beauty (114).

Allied with this emphasis on beauty and class is the attention given to clothes. When the girls have to attend a ceremony at the Winter Palace of the Czar, they have only one concern:

> Of course, in the excitement and nervousness due to such an important and unexpected occasion, the three Red Cross girls had the same problem to settle that attacks all women at critical moments: 'What on earth should they wear to the presentation?' (*Red Cross Girls with the Russian Army*)

Ultimately, they settle on their uniforms, and 'they were as handsome and far more dignified on the afternoon of their appearance at the Winter Palace in the costumes of American Red Cross nurses, than if they had been appareled in the court trains and feathers of more gala occasions.' But even arrayed in their uniforms, the girls do not forget fashion:

> ... over her uniform Mildred wore the magnificent sable coat in which she had appeared at her friends' lodgings in Petrograd.
> This afternoon, in spite of her excitement over what lay ahead of them, Barbara did not allow the coat to pass unnoticed a second time. 'For goodness' sake, Mildred, where did you get that magnificent garment?' she demanded, just as they were about to go downstairs to get into their sleigh. '... This is the most wonderful sable I ever saw.'

Midst the privations of wartime Russia, the girls go shopping: Mildred gets a fur hat to match the sable coat, and Nona is 'unable to resist a set of black fox.' After all, 'furs were so much cheaper in Russia than in the United States that it really almost seemed one's duty to buy them.' The girls also manage to go shopping in Paris (even though the Germans, in this volume, are breaking through the French lines); thanks to Mildred's mother, they buy cashmere kimonos 'too pretty for nursing use' but just right for 'the evenings alone at home' (*French Firing Line* 117). Vandercook's grasp of the seriousness of war is perhaps revealed in her description of the girls on the crossing from England to France: 'Except that the four American girls now wore their Red Cross costumes, they might have been taken for four girls on a spring shopping journey to Paris' (*British Trenches* 136).

In the Red Cross Girls series, all action tends towards courtship. Each girl's heart belongs to a particular man. Mildred, ill-advisedly, falls in love with Brooks Curtis, the supposed journalist who is ultimately unmasked as a German spy. Nona is attracted to an Italian aviator and an American captain. Barbara's heart belongs to Dick Thornton, Mildred's brother. (She actually marries him in the course of the series and produces a baby.) In New York, Dick seems like a lazy, self-indulgent rich man's son; but when Barbara meets him again in France – he has volunteered to serve as an ambulance driver – she realizes what he is really made of, and her initial infatuation turns to love. Eugenia falls in love with a French officer, a proud but impoverished aristocrat; her New World wealth turns out to be the perfect complement to his title. In every case, the relationship deepens because the girl nurses the man. Barbara, for example, rescues Dick when a shell falls on his ambulance. Eugenia hides the wounded French officer when Germans overrun the French lines. Nursing serves not so much as a skilled profession but as an opportunity to display tenderness and devotion to a wounded warrior.

Although the Red Cross girls work in field hospitals, and Barbara and Nona even travel to the casualty clearing stations, one would get no idea from these books of the injuries actually sustained in trench warfare. Whatever the girls see, it is sufficiently awful that spunky Barbara faints away in an operating room, but Vandercook is too fastidious to supply details: 'It is not worth while to speak of the scene at the field hospital. If one's own imagination cannot picture it, perhaps it is better never to know the horrors of a battlefield' (*British Trenches* 243).

A particular feature of these books, with respect to their Canadian readers, is the treatment of the American role in the war. These American girls enjoy immunity to the worst of war. They can always go home. For them, this is merely an exciting excursion, attractively bathed in the warm light of noble service. The girls also enjoy the comforting security of American wealth. For example, when they are not happy about serving with a group of snooty British nurses, they decide that 'we have just to remember that we came over here to preach the gospel of peace, not war, and not dislike anyone'; besides, they take comfort in the fact that the hospital to which they are assigned 'is partly supported by American money' (135). They owe no particular allegiance to any of the Allies, and consequently are free to attach themselves to whatever army they wish, finally joining an American hospital in 1917.

If young Canadian girls read these books uncritically, then they were deceived into thinking that for girls, as for men, the war was a great adventure. But perhaps young readers understood the conventions of this kind of series and read Vandercook's books without believing in her version of girls' lives. Helen Bittel has suggested that girls might have been perfectly aware of the foolishness of conventional narratives with their romantic coincidences and tidy resolutions and were 'thus encouraged to question – rather than to accede to – the inevitability of conventional narratives of girls' lives, "real" and fictional' (par. 35). Bittel assumes that it is young readers' knowledge of fiction, not their experience of life, that protects them from the excesses of formulaic romances.

Canadian girls reading the Red Cross series must have known enough about war to recognize the falsities in Vandercook's version. Still, these stories appeal to such strong fantasies – to live a life of beauty and glamour, to have a group of loyal friends, to find a heroic husband, to be his self-sacrificing helpmeet – that the disregard for fact might not have interfered with their imaginative power. Perhaps, in their own way, these books did some good for young girls. In spite of all the snobbery and silliness, the Red Cross Girls series affirm that love and friendship can transcend war. Girls could read about the battlefields, thereby allaying their anxieties and satisfying their curiosity about what was happening there, and at the same time indulge their taste for the reliable pleasures of formula girls' stories.

Another American war series, the 'Somewhere in ...' books by Martha Trent, tell the stories of individual girls in Belgium, France, the United States, England, Italy, and Canada. Promotional materials described the heroines as 'half girl, half boy, and the better half of each.' Although the stories are essentially separate, the books do provide the satisfaction of a continuing series: for example, Marieken from Belgium and Helen from America appear in the story of Valerie from France. These books build on the 'little folks from other lands' tradition of children's stories, originating probably in stories of foreign missionary work. Here, the picturesque qualities of other cultures and countries are interwoven with the adventure of war. As Susan Ingalls Lewis points out, in the 'Somewhere' series, 'rather than representing a fearful threat to world civilization, the Great War simply provides the girls with greater opportunities to shine' (131).

*Phoebe Marshall: Somewhere in Canada* (1919) demonstrates the oddities of the series and its author's uncertain grasp of, or indifference to, geography, culture, and history. Phoebe Marshall has volunteered to care for convalescent soldiers in a converted hunting lodge in Quebec. The location is hard to determine. It is remote enough that there is a nearby Hudson's Bay trading post, complete with a gruff but kind Scots factor, who has to keep a tight rein on the local Native people. It is close enough to the ocean that Phoebe gets involved in intercepting a spy who is being picked up by a German U-boat. And it is close enough to Montreal that a company of soldiers and their tanks drive up for manoeuvres in the countryside. Trent seems to have gleaned her ideas of Canada from magazine stories of fur trappers and restless redskins. The aboriginal characters embody primitivism: they communicate only through grunts and are easily suborned by the German agent with a few bottles of firewater. They also engage in strange rites: Phoebe is quite overcome when she witnesses an old woman go into a trance. The French-Canadian characters are equally objectionable. One is a half-wit: although Jean is a wounded veteran back from the front, he functions at the same mental level as his 'playfellow' Nancy, the impish little granddaughter of the fur trader (24). The other French Canadian, Jacques Laval, is a swarthy, violent man who betrays his country by spying for the Germans. The Mountie who features in this book is an Irishman, bold and friendly and cheery, but not very bright. The officers of the visiting group of soldiers are all English Canadians.

In addition to her role in foiling the U-boat rendezvous in

It was Lucky who discovered her a few minutes later.

17 Frontispiece of *Phoebe Marshall: Somewhere in Canada,* by Martha Trent, illustrated by Charles L. Wren. In the public domain; reproduced from author's collection.

Canada, Phoebe travels to the front in order to search for her brother, reported missing in action. En route to the front, she copes bravely with a train wreck, discovers a secret message concealed in a shoe belonging to the treacherous Quebecker Jacques Laval, and sets out alone to deliver the message into the hands of a British colonel. But after these exploits, she faints at the news that her favourite officer, Lucky Struthers, is missing in action. The story winds up rapidly with Lucky successfully returning from battle, miraculously bearing in his tank Phoebe's missing brother. Again, Phoebe collapses and has to be carried tenderly back to the Colonel's dugout by her sweetheart. The good news that Lucky has also rescued her brother initiates a chaste love scene, set among the trenches:

> 'Oh, Lucky, I never heard anything so wonderful!' Phoebe sat up, her eyes flashing and her cheeks scarlet.
>
> 'I have,' Lucky said very seriously. 'Finding you crying against those sand-bags was far more wonderful to me than anything else that has ever happened. I could hardly believe my eyes. You see, dear,' he added tenderly, 'I had been thinking of you all day long and I wanted you – '
>
> 'The car is ready, sir.' The orderly stood in the doorway. (214–15)

*Phoebe Marshall* concludes back in Quebec at the trading post. It is just 11 November 1918, but miraculously, Lucky and Phoebe's brother arrive on the doorstep. (Other Canadian soldiers did not get home so quickly: transporting the men of the Canadian Expeditionary Force back to Canada took until February of 1920 [Morton, 'Kicking' 360].) Phoebe and Lucky are now engaged, fulfilling the standard requirement of such books to find a partner for the heroine. And the merit of Phoebe's enterprise and courage is neatly undermined when her brother thanks the trader and Lucky for looking after his sister: '… it seems there was no need for either of us to worry for old Lucky decided to take over the responsibility for her quite a while ago, and I must say he does uncommon well' (220–1).

Lewis points out that the plots of the Trent books 'follow a somewhat unusual, and surprising, trajectory' in which 'the climax of most of the girls' greatest heroic adventures comes not at the end of the story, but two-thirds or even halfway through'

(133). In the Phoebe Marshall book, for example, the U-boat
has been sunk by page 134, with nearly a hundred pages to go.
Lewis argues that the purpose of this plot pattern is 'to rescue
these girls from the logical implications of their bold actions.'
Phoebe and her sister heroines can display 'extraordinary courage, resourcefulness, effectiveness,' but only up to a point. Then
they have to be meek and fragile.

Other established American series available in Canada, such
as the Camp Fire Girls and the Ruth Fielding books, included
individual titles which used the war as a backdrop. Ruth Fielding, a creation of the Stratemeyer syndicate, is a girl detective
(the prototype for Nancy Drew), and in two novels by Alice B.
Emerson, Ruth does her sleuthing in the war zone: *Ruth Fielding
in the Red Cross; or, Doing Her Best for Uncle Sam* (1918) and *Ruth
Fielding at the War Front; or, The Hunt for the Lost Soldier* (1918).
In the first, Ruth manages to 'clear up the mystery of a trio of
criminals who had come from America to prey upon the Red
Cross,' to quote the plot summary that appears at the beginning of the second Ruth war book (*War Front* 10–11). Then, in
*Ruth Fielding at the War Front,* she has to find out who is giving
secrets to the Germans, lay to rest the mystery of a werewolf that
is terrifying the locals, and rescue an American boy who is spying
behind the German front lines. On this rescue mission, as she
treks across no man's land, Ruth shows herself an unusual heroine. Although at first frightened, she thrills to the adventure:
'Now a feeling of exultation gripped her. She was fairly into this
adventure. It was too late to go back' (168). Even when forced
to don rubber overalls and boots in order to cross the mud of
no man's land, Ruth does not flinch, for 'she had camped out
in the wilderness, ridden half-broken cow ponies on a Wyoming
ranch, and gone fishing in an open boat' (172).

Once behind the German lines, Ruth and her escort, the
French spy Major Marchand, must disguise themselves. Ruth
puts on a German uniform, pulls on 'the long, polished boots'
(183), and picks up the swagger cane. Then the Major adds the
finishing touch: 'With a camel's hair brush dipped in grease
paint he darkened her lip and her cheekbones just before her
ears – as though the down of immature manhood were sprout-
ing' (184). Seeing herself in the mirror, Ruth cries, 'I *am* a boy
now!' (184; italics in original). Does Ruth have to become a boy

in order to do what no mere girl could do – undertake the most dangerous part of the rescue mission, which is to pass through the German lines?

Throughout the successful rescue, Ruth shows courage and zest, but on the return to the American trenches, she nonetheless crumples and has to be carried back by the men. When they arrive back, the Major congratulates Ruth for her 'sublime' courage, but also for her 'modesty and goodness' and 'graces of person' (201). Evidently Ruth's brief career as a boy has not diminished her femininity.

Back at the Red Cross hospital, Ruth's two American friends, unaware of her secret mission, believe that she has eloped:

> 'Two whole nights and a day! It is disgraceful! Oh, Ruthie! Are you really wedded?'
>
> 'I am wedded to my work,' replied the girl of the Red Mill [Ruth] quietly. (202)

This ironic ending brings *Ruth Fielding at the War Front* to a close, not with the convention of romantic union, but with Ruth's commitment to more adventure.

Ruth Fielding's unusual tomboy spirit reflects the assumption, often on display in these American books, that American girls enjoy more physical freedom and fewer behavioural constraints than British or continental girls (Foster and Simons 16). This assumption is strikingly evident in Trent's 'Somewhere' series, when an American soldier explains to Valerie Duval that 'our girls are a little more independent than most French girls – I mean they do pretty much as they please' (*Valerie Duval* 36). Valerie gushes, 'They are very brave, yes?' and the officer replies, 'Oh, I don't know, it isn't exactly bravery, but they *do* things' (36–7). He then describes how Helen Carey (the heroine of Trent's *Somewhere in America*) 'has a good deal of spunk' and has saved his life on two occasions. Valerie herself is no shrinking violet. She cut her hair and tried to enlist in the French Army, and she has rescued two soldiers, an act for which she earned the Croix de guerre. But her spunk is not really French: it is attributed to her American grandmother.

As Lewis points out, each girl in the 'Somewhere' series reflects a national stereotype. Lucia of Italy is mischievous and lively; Valerie of France is obsessed with glory; Alice of England is a sports-loving squire's daughter; Helen or 'Missy' of America is a healthy outdoorsgirl; Marieken of Belgium, though prodigiously energetic, is also the youngest and physically weakest of the heroines (perhaps, Lewis speculates, to represent 'poor little Belgium' [137]). But the heroine of *Phoebe Marshall Somewhere in Canada* is 'the most introspective, self-sacrificing, emotional and timid' of them all (134). Lewis explains Phoebe's comparative weakness as reflecting the moral exhaustion at the end of the war – the book was published in 1919 – but a more likely explanation is that Phoebe is merely exhibiting a stereotypical version of Canadianness.

Given this kind of fictional representation, did Canadian girls envy the freedom of American heroines? Those who lived in rural areas had the same physical freedoms as American girls: they too could play outdoors, skate, ride horses, and roam about in the forest. Foster and Simons count the Canadian heroine Anne Shirley among their examples of typical American protagonists, such as Jo March and Katy Carr, who 'find opportunities for self-expansion through the expression of physical energy in a way denied their English counterparts' (17). But Canadian girls were more constrained socially than American ones. One has only to think of the way the Meredith children in L.M. Montgomery's *Rainbow Valley* (1919) shock the community with very minor transgressions, such as Faith wearing no stockings with her boots, to realize that Canadian children, at least those of the church-going middle classes, were held to rather strict standards of conduct. So the confident, out-going manner of American girl protagonists, when added to the glamour of American wealth and the apparent immunity of Americans to the privations of war, must have made series from the United States attractive reading for young Canadian girls (despite the occasional unflattering portrayal of their own kind). At least there was nothing in these books about thrift or knitting or self-denial.

These American girls' books surely would have been regarded by Toronto librarian Lillian Smith as examples of the 'vapid serial reading matter' that she deplored (11). While some Canadian adults did not judge the books quite so severely (inscriptions in extant copies indicate that they were given as school reward books), others disapproved strenuously. A dialogue in the *Young*

*Soldier* of 26 February 1916 entitled 'What's in a Bag?' takes aim
at formulaic romances as a form of feminine self-indulgence.
(The dialogue was designed for two girls to present in a 'demonstration' or church entertainment.) In her bag, Maud has a
novelette entitled 'Gipsy Nell, the Long Lost Heiress.' She de-
fends her choice of reading matter: 'It's not so bad but they're
all the same, these tales, all about dukes and plots and elope-
ments and all that' (4). Connie, the other girl in the dialogue,
is carrying a Salvationist booklet in her bag: 'The Warrior and
Life Saving Scout and Guard.' Maud has peppermints in her
bag, while Connie has given up sweets in order to buy wool: 'All
the Guards are making mittens, you see, for the soldiers and
sailors. I'm getting quite an expert, Maud, and it's ever so nice
to feel you are helping your country, nicer than a hundred bags
of peppermint!' And while Maud is carrying 'complexion-beau-
tifier powder,' Connie claims that a pair of dumbbells are her
beautifier: 'Breathing deeply and taking in fresh air and doing
plenty of exercise keep one's health good and one's cheeks rosy,
too.' The romance novelette, like the candies and cosmetics, is
regarded as harmful and selfish, especially in time of war. The
Salvation Army, of course, had a certain interest in promoting
wholesome reading, for their own publications were positioned
as an alternative to the racier commercial books and papers.
An editorial in the 16 October 1916 issue of the *Young Soldier*
described the 'real uneasiness' felt by 'a careful father [who]
observed that his little girl of about ten years was beginning to
get very engrossed in the serial stories running through some of
the magazines taken in at their home'; his solution is to take the
*Young Soldier* even though the family is not Salvationist, because
'they knew a good thing when they saw it' (8).

### A Canadian Romance of War

In certain respects, L.M. Montgomery's *Rilla of Ingleside* (1920)
is not so very different from the American girls' series books.
Montgomery herself referred to it as a '"story for girls,"' and
she advised her correspondent Ephraim Weber to 'read it from
the standpoint of a young girl (if you can!) and not from any sophisticated angle' (Tiessen and Tiessen 88). Like the formulaic
American girls' series books, *Rilla* deals with fashion, friendship,

and courtship. But Montgomery's novel handles these themes with such humour and balance that, 'story for girls' though it may be, *Rilla* rises far above other books of its kind. Take, for example, the matter of fashion. Rilla, whom even her mother describes as 'abominally vain,' cares about clothes (7). So did Montgomery: the suite of photos she had taken of herself in her trousseau demonstrates her love of fashion (Walford 74–7). But every incident in *Rilla* that deals with fashion is at once detailed, comic, and gently didactic. After Rilla's first dance, the eve-of-war set piece at the beginning of the novel, the party is broken up by the sombre news of the outbreak of war, and in the confusion Rilla discovers that she has been left behind and must walk home with Mary Vance. Rilla takes off 'the frail, silver-hued slippers with high French heels' and her 'dear silk stockings' and walks barefoot down the 'deep-rutted pebbly lane' with her blistered feet (37). She is angry and humiliated, especially when Mary Vance recommends goose grease to soothe her sore feet. It is a comic scene but also a subtly ironic one that creates an effective starting point for Rilla's maturation. At this point, Rilla is consumed with her own adolescent disappointment; readers can see how petty her reaction is in light of what has befallen the world on this August evening.

The incident of the velvet hat similarly shows that fashion is a trivial concern in the great scheme of things. In her diary, Rilla exults over the first hat she has chosen on her own:

> I found the dearest hat – it was simply bewitching. It was a velvet hat, of the very shade of rich green that was *made* for me ... Well, as soon as I saw this hat I felt that I simply must have it – and have it I did. The price was dreadful. (84)

Back home, Rilla realizes that the hat is 'too elaborate and fussy for church going and our quiet little doings in the Glen,' and she is guilt-stricken over its cost when she thinks of 'the starving Belgians' (84). Montgomery supplies girls with the satisfaction of reading about the velvet hat, but she also gives Rilla the intelligence and conscience to regret her extravagance, especially 'in war-time, too, when everybody is – or should be – trying to be economical' (84). Stuck with her costly purchase, Rilla vows to wear it 'three years or for the duration of the war' as a form of penance for her foolishness (85). Another fashion-related scene similarly leavens its didacticism with comedy. When Rilla sets off to visit the snobbish Irene Howard, in an effort to cajole her into helping with the Belgian Relief concert, she is so preoccupied with 'the coming distasteful interview' that she neglects to check her appearance (109):

> On one of Rilla's feet was a smart little steel-buckled shoe and filmy blue silk stocking. The other was clad in a stout and rather shabby boot and black lisle! (110)

The adjectives 'smart' and 'filmy' suggest Montgomery knows her audience – girls who might themselves own or covet just such a shoe and stocking. But her aim here is not to satisfy girls' interest in fashion; it is to show that girls like Rilla do understand that there are more important things in life. Rilla has so wanted to impress 'pretty and stylish' Irene (28) that she is deeply humiliated. But she persists. Her exchange with Irene shows just how much Rilla has grown since the night of the party when war began:

> 'But I haven't anything to wear. My new evening-dress isn't home from Charlottetown yet, and I simply cannot wear my old one at such a big affair. It is too shabby and old-fashioned.'
> 'Our concert,' said Rilla slowly, 'is in aid of Belgian children who are starving to death. Don't you think you could wear a shabby dress once for their sake, Irene?'
> 'Oh, don't you think those accounts we get of the conditions of the Belgians are very much exaggerated?' said Irene. 'I'm sure they can't be actually *starving* you know, in the twentieth century. The newspapers always colour things so highly.'
> Rilla concluded that she had humiliated herself enough. There was such a thing as self-respect. No more coaxing, concert or no concert. She got up, boot and all.
> 'I am sorry you can't help us, Irene, but since you cannot we must do the best we can.' (112)

Irene's focus on clothing, although partly just a stalling manoeuvre to reduce Rilla to begging for her participation, marks her as someone who cannot rise above personal vanity. When Rilla takes the moral high ground, her stand is thoroughly inspiring and not at all self-righteous. An instructive contrast is with the many scenes in the Red Cross Girls series devoted to clothes and appearance; never does Vandercook suggest that wearing fine clothes and going shopping might be inappropriate in time of war, or that girls supposedly dedicated to alleviating the suffering of war might have better things to do than buy furs or dressing gowns. Montgomery wrote that she intended *Rilla* as a 'tribute to the girlhood of Canada' (Tiessen and Tiessen 88), and by showing that her heroine is not just an empty-headed, vain creature, but a morally complex one, she does indeed pay tribute to girls' capacity to understand their world.

Montgomery's treatment of the theme of courtship is similarly subtle. It is true that at the end of the novel, Rilla is reunited with Kenneth, who reappears on the very last page, scarred but handsome and manly, to claim 'Rilla-*my*-Rilla' (277). From all the trials of the war years, Rilla has emerged 'a woman altogether beautiful and desirable' (277). Montgomery is bound, in Laura Robinson's words, by 'a generic and social imperative to marry the female characters off' (13), and when Kenneth and Rilla pair up at the end of the novel, it does read 'like a formula romance' (Epperly 124). Yet, even if the reunion of Kenneth and Rilla does seem to tie up neatly Rilla's fate, it does not negate all the hard work she has done for the war effort or the tremendous strides she has made in acquiring self-discipline, humility, and charity. The emotional high point of the book is not her reunion with Kenneth but the loss of her idealistic brother Walter on the battlefields (Epperly 117). This is what makes Rilla change from girl into woman. And because of the peculiar incident that has made Rilla into an adoptive war mother – she has taken on the care of an infant whose mother has died and whose father is overseas – she doesn't need love and marriage to display her capacity for nurturing motherhood. Moreover, in contrast to the time spent on courtship in other girls' war books, Montgomery is very restrained: only three scenes feature Kenneth. When Rilla receives her first love letter from Kenneth, she cherishes it, feeling sorry for 'other girls whose sweethearts could never have written them anything half so wonderful and exquisite' (140).

But Montgomery devotes only one longish paragraph to Rilla's private joy and then turns to the greater news of 'a big Allied victory in the West' (140–1).

Courtship as a theme is also ironically undermined by Montgomery's elevation of a stock secondary character to a central role. Susan, the eccentric servant, is, as Elizabeth Epperly puts it, 'the most colourful heroine' of the novel (124), and she too has a suitor: Mr Pryor, the pacifist and bullying eccentric of Glen St Mary, known as Whiskers-on-the-moon. Whiskers thinks that Susan ought to be grateful for his attentions. When she refuses his proposal, he 'blurt[s] out the truth: "Why, I thought you'd be only too glad to get a chance to be married"' (220). This courting scene does not end well: Susan goes after him with an iron pot full of boiling dye (she had been dying her rug rags when he arrived). By alternating between Rilla as the romantic heroine and Susan as the comic one, Montgomery adds some astringency and humour to the formulaic girls' story.

While Rilla's transformation from girl into woman suggests Canada's own growth into nationhood during the war years, Susan is more clearly the embodiment of Canada. She is, as Rilla puts in her diary, 'a perfect dynamo of patriotism and loyalty and contempt for slackers of all kinds' (223). When, in the summer of 1918, the tide begins to turn, Susan raises the flag:

> As it caught the breeze and swelled gallantly out above her, Susan lifted her hand and saluted it ... The wind whipped her grey hair about her face and the gingham apron that shrouded her from head to foot was cut on lines of economy, not of grace; yet somehow, just then Susan made an imposing figure. She was one of the women – courageous, unquailing, patient, heroic – who had made victory possible. (247)

Susan here transcends her comic function and takes on her symbolic one as the spirit of home-front Canada.

Whereas other girls' stories deal in pseudo-heroics – with heroines catching spies and eluding the Germans and pulling wounded officers from danger in the most unrealistic way – *Rilla* never loses its steady focus on the courage of ordinary Canadian girls and women. What Rilla does for the war is, in its own way, undramatic: she cares for a war baby, she knits, she organizes a patriotic entertainment, she collects funds, she helps out in a store. But Montgomery makes clear what it costs this vain, empty-headed girl to transform herself into a useful person. Rilla's hardest work in the war, however, is to wait:

> If she were only a boy, speeding in khaki ... to the western front! She had wished that in a burst of romance when Jem had gone, without, perhaps, really meaning it. She meant it now. There were moments when waiting at home, in safety and comfort, seemed an unendurable thing. (144)

Montgomery's heroine – or heroines, since Susan's role is so important to the novel's celebration of the women of the Canadian home front – reveal their courage not through battlefield derring-do but by carrying on despite their fear and their grief.

Another way in which Montgomery's novel demonstrates the shallowness of other girls' stories is her attention to events as they unfold. Other novels are maddeningly vague about where and when events are taking place. Montgomery, using her own journals from the war, follows events precisely, introducing names like Vimy, Courcelette, and Passchendaele into the dialogue. This sort of realism – Canadians were devoted followers of the news during the war – makes *Rilla* less a girls' story than a documentary novel about Canada during the war years. In November of 1921, Montgomery copied into her journal parts of a letter she had received from a Vancouver librarian who presciently praised *Rilla* as 'a book that will live, I think, when most of the ephemeral literature of the time will be forgotten' (Rubio and Waterston 3: 27). He wrote to Montgomery that 'you have visualized the soul of the Canadian people in the war; you have given a true picture of what we went through during five long years of agony.' Montgomery reported herself to be 'especially pleased with this because that is exactly what I tried to do in my book.' On 4 August 1922, Montgomery noted in her journal that she had received a letter 'from a fifteen-year-old reader (who would of course be only seven when the war broke out) [and] she told me how *Rilla* had made the years of the great war (which she only remembered dimly) "seem so real to her"' (Rubio and Waterston 3: 65). More recent readers have also praised the documentary qualities of *Rilla*. Sandra Gwyn in her *Tapestry of War* describes it as 'virtually the only Canadian work of fiction to describe everyday life on the home front from direct experience' (165).

Perhaps the most profound way in which *Rilla* transcends the confines of the girls' story is in Montgomery's treatment of war itself, not with respect to the depiction of trench warfare (though Jem's letters are frank and authentic-sounding), but in her exploration of the moral problem the war presented. Though *Rilla* unmistakably endorses the war and Canada's part in it, it also introduces elements that seem to question how Christian nations could kill each other's young men. One of these elements is the speech given by Mr Pryor, Whiskers-on-the-moon, at a 'khaki prayer-meeting':

> He prayed that the unholy war might cease – that the deluded armies being driven to slaughter on the western front might have their eyes opened to their iniquity and repent while yet there was time – that the poor young men present in khaki who had been hounded into a path of murder and militarism, should yet be rescued – (174)

A public uproar over this 'sedition and treason' ensues (175). Rilla's father, Gilbert, approves of the harsh treatment Whiskers gets, though not of the unseemly way in which it is meted out; thus, it would seem that Montgomery, too, approves of it. Moreover, on the eve of the signing of the Armistice, Mr Pryor has a 'paralytic stroke,' apparently a divine punishment for his disloyalty (270). Yet the fact remains that Mr Pryor has made his lucid and eminently Christian comments at a morally problematic event, the khaki prayer meeting. Perhaps Montgomery was troubled by the thought that churches were being used for recruitment and other war-related activities. J.S. Woodsworth, a minister and a pacifist, condemned as 'absolute sacrilege' a Methodist Sunday service in which the pastor appealed for recruits (5).

The strongest counterweight to the patriotism of *Rilla* comes from young Bruce Meredith, when he drowns his beloved cat Stripey. He explains that 'I thought if I sacrificed Stripey God would send Jem [Blythe] back. So I drownded him' (261). Stripey is to be the ram for Jem as Isaac. Bruce's own father, gentle Mr Meredith, the Presbyterian minister, has preached on

Hebrews 9:22: 'Almost all things are by the law purged with blood; and without shedding of blood there is no remission of sins.' Paraphrasing scripture, Mr Meredith asserts that 'our race has marked every step of its painful ascent with blood' and that war 'is the price humanity must pay for some blessing' (50). In the abstract, this position may seem to make sense of war, but when taken literally, it leads only to the sort of primitive slaughter symbolized by Bruce's drowning of his pet. Is blood sacrifice necessary for human progress? This seems to be Mr Meredith's belief, and it is a very literal reading of the Abrahamic covenant – the notion that in order for Abraham's people to become a great nation as God has promised, they must be willing to sacrifice their sons. Montgomery's questioning of this rationale for war is not overt; she does not explicitly challenge the war or the Christian churches' endorsement of it. As a Presbyterian minister's wife, Montgomery was presumably aware of 'The War and the Christian Church,' the Presbyterian statement on the war, published in 1917. While the report deplored the war, it nonetheless made the familiar comparison between the soldiers and Christ: 'The Cross of Christian sacrifice spreads its arms over the field of war' (Kilpatrick 15). The reference to Christ's sacrifice implicitly reinforces the Abrahamic covenant as a fundamental guarantor of the nation's future, for Abraham's readiness to sacrifice Isaac is a biblical type prefiguring the sacrifice God will make of His son. In other words, God requires Canadians to sacrifice their sons, just as He and Abraham were ready to sacrifice theirs. Certainly the death of Rilla's beloved brother Walter is regarded as a sacrifice that will earn some future benefit. As Walter puts it in his final letter, 'I've helped to make Canada safe for the poets of the future – ... The future not of Canada only but of the world – when the "red rain" of Langemarck and Verdun shall have brought forth a golden harvest' (192).

Whether Montgomery intended the drowning of Bruce's kitten to be a critique of the Christian rationale for war is impossible to determine. It may be, as Owen Dudley Edwards has suggested, that Montgomery put this 'subversive' passage into her novel 'in spite of herself' (134). He suggests that *Rilla* 'is far less comfortable in its support of the war ... than its critics have imagined.' Montgomery may not have set out to write a pacifist critique of Canada's war, yet at the same time she did not intend *Rilla* to be pro-war. In a journal entry written in 1928, she expressed her impatience with a reader in New Zealand who had written Montgomery to decry *Rilla* 'because it "glorifies war"' (3: 387):

> I wrote *Rilla* not to 'glorify war' but to glorify the courage and patriotism and self-sacrifice it evoked. War is a hellish thing and some day it may be done away with – though human nature being what it is that day is far distant. But universal peace may come and may be a good thing. But there will no longer be any great literature or great art. Either these things are given by the high gods as a compensation – or else they are growths that have to be fertilized with blood. (Rubio and Waterston 3: 387–8)

Montgomery's thinking takes an odd turn here, for, after calling war 'a hellish thing,' she ends up arguing that blood sacrifice is culturally necessary. This position is firmly in the tradition of the Abrahamic covenant, and it just does not square with the powerful impact of Bruce's drowning of his kitten (which, as Edwards puts it, 'seems deliberately designed to make [readers] ill' [134]). Perhaps Montgomery could not reconcile her essential pacifism with her patriotic acceptance of the necessity of the war. She imploded, to use Edwards's term, building into her novel scenes and allusions that undermined the very justification for the war. Montgomery's problem, of course, was not unique. A whole generation of Canadians were similarly tormented by the contradiction between their detestation of war and their reluctant conviction that this one must be fought. That such conflicts and questions are even adumbrated in a girls' story is in itself a remarkable accomplishment.

# 8 A War for Modern Readers

In the first edition of *The Republic of Childhood*, published in 1975, Sheila Egoff lamented that writers for children had neglected many 'incidents or themes that have influenced our history,' such as 'our flood of immigration in the nineteenth century, the Fenian Raids, the collapse of the Quebec Bridge, the sinking of the *Empress of Ireland*, the *Bluenose*, John Booth's lumber camps' (110). She did not mention the First World War as one of the neglected stories of Canadian history. There is only one reference to the war in *Republic*: a bibliographic listing in the chapter on history and biography of John N. Harris's 1958 *Knights of the Air: Canadian Aces of World War I* (232). By the time of the second edition in 1990, many of the neglected historical themes had been tackled, and Egoff and her collaborator, Judith Saltman, observed that there had been an 'interesting development in historical fiction' of 'a concentration on our recent rather than our distant past' (18). Still, virtually no one was writing about the First World War for Canadian children, an omission that Saltman and Egoff did not remark on.

But since 1990, more than thirty children's books have been published in Canada that deal in some way with the First World War.[1] These books are, in their various ways, profoundly different from what was written in the war years. Gone are the adulation of soldier-heroes, the emphasis on duty, and the enthusiasm for war. In their place are disillusioned soldiers, pacifism, and battlefield realism. The first part of this chapter examines how the new historical novels about the war treat these themes. The second part examines how modern information books and picture books represent the war.

**Heroes of Today**

The soldier-hero, that figure whom Graham Dawson has described as 'one of the most durable and powerful forms of idealized masculinity within Western cultural traditions since the
time of the Ancient Greeks' (1), was a central ingredient in the
writing of the war years. Both solemn didactic works such as Parrott's *Children's Story* and the racier boys' adventure tales and
series celebrated the hero and his virtues. A common understanding of the hero's qualities ran through all the war literature: pluck, gallantry, courage, endurance, and selflessness. But
this kind of hero is rarely to be found in the modern war books.

Jim Hay, the central character in John Wilson's *And in the
Morning* (2003), is the antithesis of the traditional soldier-hero.[2]
At the Battle of the Somme, confused by the shelling and slaughter all around him, he walks away from the battlefield. He is
arrested, court-martialled, and shot as a deserter. Yet, up to the
point of his breakdown, Jim has shown courage and endurance:
he is not yet eighteen, he has lost both his parents, and he has
lasted in the trenches for several months. As the lieutenant
writes in a letter to Jim's young widow, *'Please do not think Jim
a coward. No one who has not suffered in this war can understand
the extraordinary pressures it puts on a young man'* (192; italics in
original). During the war years, a book that treated a deserter
so sympathetically would hardly have been publishable, given
the watchfulness of the censors towards anything that smacked
of pacifism; moreover, it is hard to imagine any publisher of the
time thinking that it would appeal to boys.

A similar situation occurs in Jean Little's *Brothers Far from
Home: The World War I Diary of Eliza Bates* (2003). The narrator's
brother Hugo dies in disgrace after a great battle (in this case,
Vimy Ridge):

> ... he had gone to help get a wounded man out of the line of fire.
> The soldiers had been ordered not to turn back no matter what.
> But the wounded man was a father with a new baby. When Hugo
> went to help him, a Canadian officer shot Hugo and killed him.
> (97)

It is instructive to compare Hugo's fate with that of Walter in *Rilla of Ingleside*, a book which in many respects serves as Little's model for *Brothers Far from Home*.[3] Rilla's brother Walter performs a similar act of generosity on the battlefield, but when he 'dashe[s] back from the safety of the trench to drag in a wounded comrade,' he is awarded a DC (166). He later dies, not as a disgraced victim, but as a hero in action at Courcelette (188). In Little's novel, the beloved brother is executed rather than apotheosized as a soldier-hero, a shift that suggests how profoundly our ideas about heroism have changed. Death in war (at least in the First World War) can no longer be presented as a beautiful sacrifice that would earn a better world. The only kind of heroism that seems to make sense is the kind that Hugo displays – an individual gesture of kindness and bravery. This is a modern view of what a hero should do, more palatable to us now than Walter's romantic notions of dying for his country and its future. By giving Hugo a fate so very different from that of Walter Blythe, Little rejects Montgomery's rhetoric of sacrifice. She also makes explicit the contradiction between Christian charity and the logic of the battlefield: what Hugo does is good and selfless, yet it is a military crime.

Allan Hayward, the protagonist of Kevin Major's *No Man's Land* (1995), is a quiet sort of hero. In this sombre account of the Newfoundlanders at Beaumont-Hamel, Hayward does nothing daring or ostentatiously gallant. Just before he is to take his men over the top, Hayward learns that the German guns and barbed wire have not been disabled by the bombardment. But the colonel will not be persuaded to hold the men back. In the minutes before the battle, Hayward acts with confidence and resolve:

> He had a word for each of them, the encouragement that was his duty. There was not the fire that had sometimes been in his voice, though he would not have them think anything but that there was a job to be done and they were the men who could do it. (228)

When the whistle blows, the men of the Newfoundland Regiment go stoically to their deaths: 'They trudged on, shoulders pressed forward, heads pulled into them, as if they were making their way home across a frozen harbour in the driving snow' (239).[4] Major's novel presents the engagement as a horrible

mistake, redeemed only by the courage and steadfastness of ordinary men. What the Newfoundlanders did was heroic by anyone's standards, yet Major avoids words like 'sacrifice,' 'noble,'
and 'gallant,' epithets that writers of an earlier time would have
found indispensable.

In Colleen Heffernan's *A Kind of Courage* (2005), the central
male figure is a pacifist. David Ross, son of a prominent Toronto
Methodist family, refuses to go to war because 'he just couldn't
kill anyone'; his piano teacher is German and has taught him
German music, so David cannot find it in himself to hate the
enemy (76). (Perhaps his surname is Ross because of Robert
Ross, the protagonist in Timothy Findley's *The Wars*, also the
sensitive scion of a prominent Toronto family.) As an alternative to imprisonment, David accepts farm work and is sent to
the prairie homestead of the Tamblyn family.[5] At first, young
Hattie Tamblyn despises David because her brother Will and his
friends are fighting in France. But David shows that he is not a
coward when he rescues Hattie from the unwelcome attentions
of a neighbouring farmer and then fights off a crowd of bullies.
David's earnest principles, his quiet confidence, and his devotion to music make him an admirable character, though most
definitely not a soldier-hero. The only candidate for this role
is David's cousin Julian, a dashing young officer who earns a
medal. But Julian is a sadist: David recalls in detail a childhood
incident in which Julian cheerfully drowned unwanted kittens.
Thus, Julian's heroism on the battlefield – he wins a medal for
'killing all those Huns on his last raid' (87) – is rendered sus-
pect. It is evidence of bloodlust, not courage. As if to underline
the virtue of the pacifist and the depravity of the warrior, Heffernan gives Julian a pathetic fate. He comes home from the
war shell-shocked and disabled, and when David visits him in a
convalescent hospital, Julian sits blankly in his wheelchair, taking wings off flies.

Edward Bathe, the narrator of Arthur Slade's *Megiddo's
Shadow* (2006), perhaps comes closest to the old-fashioned type
of hero. He goes to war at age seventeen (the recruiting officer
ignores his obvious deception) in order to avenge the death of
his brother Hector. Through the somewhat implausible inter-
vention of Colonel Hilts, an old South African War comrade of
his father's, Edward gets transferred from the Canadian army

to the British and ends up with the Lincolnshire Yeomanry, a mounted unit, in Palestine. Edward rides into battle against the Turks, and he does not flinch when the time comes: 'I thrust my sword into his shoulder, jarring my arm and knocking him to his knees' (233). Afterwards, he feels proud and excited that he has done his job and survived. But Edward also feels deep ambivalence about battle: as he surveys the scene of a preliminary bombardment – 'The Turkish side was a mess of body parts – an arm here, a leg there, a head here, smaller parts everywhere' – he reflects that 'the world was upside down when mothers and girls made shells that killed' (224). Slade's intention to write against the grain of the old ideas of heroism is evident in his references to the *Boy's Own Paper*. To the impressionable Edward, still in training camp, a cavalry squadron, with its 'horses snorting, steam rising from their flanks' and the men with 'lances steady, their faces stern, helmets shiny,' is 'a *Boy's Own Paper* illustration come to life' (46). And when the jingoistic Colonel Hilts praises the courage of his Gurkha man-servant, Edward is awed: 'This was the kind of derring-do I'd read about in *Boy's Own Paper*' (83). But Edward's belief in the *Boy's Own* version of warfare is clearly ironic, setting him up for later disillusionment when some very un–*Boy's Own* events occur, such as the deaths of his sweetheart Emily, his comrades, and his beloved mount Buke, not to mention the murder of a prisoner by a British soldier. Another undercurrent that from the outset works against any conventional notion of heroism is the condition of Edward's father. He is a decorated veteran of the South African War, but he is 'broken' (8) and 'won't get out of bed' (16). The only time he shows any animation is when Edward announces that he is going to join up. Then Mr Bathe sits up and tells him, 'Duty is what kills young men' (9). Even the minister in Edward's town in Saskatchewan, also a veteran of the South African War, warns Edward that war lasts a lifetime: 'Killing doesn't ever leave you' (16).

While some modern characters like Edward Bathe briefly express excitement about the war, it is soon extinguished by the horrors of the fighting. In contrast, the boys of the wartime books were keen to get into the fray, and their first experience of battle sharpened their appetite for more. But that zest for war has gone. The heroes of the new war books, once exposed to the realities of the battlefields, know only revulsion and bitter disillusion.

This shift in the motivations and emotions of the soldier-hero is, in a sense, the fictional counterpart of the shift in recent studies of the Great War (post-1990) from armies to individual soldiers, described by Antoine Prost and Jay Winter in their historiographical study:

> The representation of the army has broken apart: it is no longer units that manoeuvre or fused collectives, but rather a place where men suffer, toil, or, in the excitement of combat, become infuriated and kill; the army has, in a sense, faded behind the figure, both individual and multiple, of the soldier, of individuals crushed by a instrument of suffering and death which they cannot resist ... in a society characterized by the rise of individualism, historians have become seemingly fascinated by the singularity of individual fates. (280)

In the new historical fiction about the war, a similar fascination with the individual – with his choices and decisions and suffering – has taken over from an earlier vision of the soldier (and child) as part of a collective cause.

**Patriotism and Pacifism**

Canadians during the war years knew only too well the human cost of the war, yet most continued to believe in it as an honourable and necessary conflict. An editorial in the *Christian Guardian* of 14 April 1915 expressed the strained optimism of the times: 'We do not offer any apology for war; we do not condone its frightfulness and cruelty and crime; but we think it wise to look also at the brighter side, and to cheer ourselves as best we may with the vision of the good that may follow this awful period of unprecedented carnage' (6).

The war years in Canada were marked by what Suzanne Evans has described as 'a kind of fervour – some might call it madness or fanaticism – that parallels the structure and intensity of the stories of martyrs who have died for causes in other lands' (6). Nowhere was this fervour more evident than in what was written for Canadian children. They were taught that the war was bringing out the best in all citizens, and that the training in service and sacrifice it imposed would be invaluable moral preparation for adulthood. But most of the recent children's novels about the First World War start from the assumption that patriotic talk was entirely propaganda, lies that would lead soldiers to a pointless death. In these books, pieties about duty, a righteous war, and the nation's common cause with the Empire come only from unlikeable authority figures or gullible youth. Female characters, especially young girls, are presented as seeing through the bellicose and patriotic statements of their elders. Margaret Brown, for example, the protagonist of Barbara Haworth-Attard's *Flying Geese* (2001), recognizes that the war enthusiasm of her brother Edward is something that he has uncritically imbibed from a recruiting rally:

> 'A man all the way from Ottawa was talking. A doctor and a reverend both,' Edward marvelled. 'I didn't catch his name. He said every Canadian, every man, woman, and child, must have a part in the struggle for freedom from oppression.' Edward's voice took on the man's sombre tones ...
> 'More war talk,' Mrs Brown said, voice taut. 'It's over there, in Europe, it doesn't affect us.'
> 'But it does, Mama,' Edward protested. 'We're part of the British Empire and all Canada's young manhood must answer the call to fight.'
> Repeating the man again, Margaret guessed. Edward didn't know words like that. (11)

When she sees Edward in uniform, Margaret is dismayed: 'Why did he have to go to a war so far away? Just because they were part of the British Empire didn't seem reason enough to go over the ocean to Europe' (15). Later in the novel, Margaret and her friend Jean are engaged as companions to a severe older woman, Mrs Ferguson, who has lost a son on the Western Front. When Mrs Ferguson declares that 'God is on our side in this war, the right side [and] He will help our men to cleanse the world of evil,' Jean responds, 'Perhaps the Germans think God is on their side, too' (142). But it seems unlikely that a young pauper girl like Jean would express such a disloyal sentiment, especially to a person like Mrs Ferguson, who has money, class, and age to give her authority. While Jean's outspokenness and her skepticism make her attractive to readers of today, they also make her a girl of today, not of 1916.

Another female protagonist resistant to the *idées reçues* of her time is Claire, the hero's sweetheart in Sharon McKay's *Charlie Wilcox's Great War* (2003). When Claire tells Charlie about life in Brigus during the war, she decries the human cost of war:

> What about their parents? What about the people they were to marry? What about the children they were supposed to have? What will Newfoundland do without more children? They were fighting for the King – the King! Do you think the King knows that Phil's mother is all alone now? Does he care? ... Why did it go on, and on, and on? (30)

Claire's questions are forceful, but they imply that the deaths of the Brigus boys were pointless, a suggestion that would have been profoundly shocking, even blasphemous, to people of the time.

Deploying female characters as the voices of skeptical pacifism is not unique to Canadian books. According to Esther Mac-Callum-Stewart, modern British children's books about the war 'heavily suggest[] ... that women naturally oppose war' (184). She claims that the pacifist heroines are 'placed as a moral guide for the reader.' There is some historical basis for this strategy: maternal feminists of the war years did argue that women, especially mothers, naturally oppose war. Because they have given birth, they know how precious life is, and 'if women would react on the basis of their "mother-hearts,"' then surely they would unite to stop the war (Roberts 24). But they did not. Although before the war many feminists had advocated mediation and arbitration as alternatives to war, they did not remain pacifist once the war began. Nellie McClung, for example, who initially wrote and spoke against the war, gradually came to a different position after her own son enlisted (Coates, 'War' 1190).

It is instructive to compare the unfettered expression of antiwar sentiment in the modern war books with the fate suffered by the pacifist heroine of Francis Marion Beynon's 1919 novel *Aleta Dey*, who dies when she is injured at an anti-war rally. This incident was not pure fantasy on Beynon's part: it was based on the experience of the labour activist F.J. Dixon, who was seriously injured when returned soldiers broke up an anti-conscription rally in Winnipeg (R. Cook 200–1). Beynon, herself a pacifist, left her job at the *Grain Growers' Guide* in 1917, probably because the editor feared that the 'Press Censor was unhappy about her anti-war views' (200). In *Witness against War*, Thomas Socknat offers other examples of radical pacifists who were persecuted for their opposition to the war. Francis Beynon's sister Lillian and her husband, A. Vernon Thomas, found life in Winnipeg so uncomfortable that they went to New York for the duration of the war (*Witness* 66). When Alice Chown, who called herself a 'strenuous pacifist,' spoke against the war, there was a public outcry, demanding that she 'be confined in an asylum or jail' (57). It was not just a matter of hostile reaction in the press or on the streets: public statements that undermined the war effort were specifically prohibited by the War Measures Act passed in 1914. In other words, being a pacifist in wartime Canada took courage; anyone who spoke against the war was liable to encounter a great deal of unpleasantness, if not outright persecution. [6]

Using young women or girls as the representatives of pacifism is undoubtedly convenient. It permits anti-war notions to be added explicitly, in more or less natural dialogue; authors do not have to lecture readers in a voice detached from the action, nor do they have to rely on readers to infer the anti-war message from scenes of battle. But giving the pacifist lines to young females understates the patriotic mood of the country, and it obscures the moral problem that the war posed. There was terrific pressure on children and young people – in school, in church, and in virtually everything they read about the war – to support the nation's cause. Even getting to the point of being able to form an independent anti-war position would have been difficult, let alone expressing it publicly.

It is true that the occasional young person did adopt a pacifist viewpoint. In 1917, a thirteen-year-old Saskatchewan girl wrote to Gertrude Richardson, a pacifist and feminist, requesting pacifist literature. 'I do so want to do something to end this terrible war,' she wrote (quoted in Roberts 25). And in July of 1918, in a letter to the socialist paper the *Canadian Forward*, twelve-year-old Harold Parkkonen declared that 'I want to work so that the war will stop, and the nations will learn to love one another' (24

July: 8).[7] But these two children were hardly typical. Both had access to dissenting points of view: Harold described himself as the child of socialists, and the Saskatchewan girl probably was too, if she had read Richardson's columns in the *Forward*.

By including characters who oppose the war, modern authors undoubtedly intend to promote pacifism, but this strategy has the unfortunate side effect of diminishing the courage that being a pacifist in war actually required. It also obscures the fact that many who supported the war did so, not because they were brainwashed patriots, but because they saw no other ethical course of action.

John Wilson's *Red Goodwin* (2006) focuses on one of Canada's real-life war resisters, the socialist and union organizer Albert 'Ginger' Goodwin. When conscription was declared, Goodwin went into hiding on Vancouver Island. He was tracked down and shot by a police officer, who claimed that he had killed Goodwin in self-defence. In Wilson's novel, an English boy named Will Ryan is sent out to British Columbia when his father is killed in the war. Will arrives on Vancouver Island in 1918, just as the search for Goodwin is underway. He is drawn into the clandestine effort to support Goodwin and other deserters by Morag, the beautiful daughter of a Scottish miner and workers' leader. Predictably, Morag is an outspoken young person with pacifist and socialist ideals. Despite this reliance on anachronism (Morag being a modern character in period dress), Wilson presents Will's inner conflict convincingly. Will loved his father and cannot accept that he was a dupe or that he died in an evil war, yet he is moved by Morag's convictions and by Goodwin's speeches. *Red Goodwin* has the great merit of showing, on the one hand, a positive character who supported the war (and died in it) and, on the other, an equally positive character who opposes it. No YA novel can resolve which attitude was 'right,' but Wilson's *Red Goodwin* does not disguise just how hard it was for individuals to decide for themselves. For his decision to resist the war, Goodwin paid with his life.

Eliza Bates, the twelve-year-old narrator of Little's *Brothers Far from Home*, combines in a plausible fashion both an enthusiasm for war and disquieting doubt about its real costs:

War is confusing. One minute you are excited. The flags are flying and the march music makes you stride out ... Then you hear about the wounded men and you see the lists of missing and dead. I cannot understand how it can all be part of the same thing. (52)

When her father, a Presbyterian minister, is not sufficiently war-like, Eliza is disappointed:

> When Father prayed for the families of all those fighting in the War or suffering because of it, and did *not* pray that the Kaiser get struck down with lightning or something worse, I could feel the congregation tightening their mouths and giving him cold looks. I wish he would pray for God to be on our side and for us to *win*. The Germans are such vile beasts, killing those Belgian babies and sinking the *Lusitania* and using mustard gas. (51)

Little's strategy here and in her second war novel for the Dear Canada series, *If I Die before I Wake: The Flu Epidemic Diary of Fiona Macgregor* (2007), is to give the young female narrator contradictory perceptions of war, but not to make her the spokesperson for pacifism. That role is taken by the fathers. Both Rev. Bates of *Brothers* and Mr Macgregor of *If I Die* are shown as precisely the kind of liberal reformers who found themselves torn between their essential pacifism and their reluctant acceptance of the war. For both men, the church's support of war represents this dilemma in its most painful form. When Fiona of *If I Die* records in her diary how her father reacts to a patriotic sermon, his deep ambivalence about war is evident:

> The minister prayed for our army again. He asked God to strike down our enemies and lead our gallant troops to victory. I think it is fine but Father always gets restless as though something about it bothers him. I was going to ask him about this but he seems a bit like a stranger when we come home from church and he shuts himself up in his study.
>
> I thought about going after him but I asked Aunt instead. She says he reads the names of those who have fallen and he thinks of all the other fathers in England and even in Germany reading the same sort of lists.
>
> 'We humans made this War, not God,' she told me. 'David thinks it is up to us to work it out and we should not be expecting God to

strike down our enemies when most of them are young men just
like ours.'
  'Is Father a pacifist?' I asked her.
  'He would have enlisted if he had been physically fit,' she said.
'They would not take a man his age with a limp and five children.
But he certainly believes there are better ways to settle problems
than going to war and killing people.' (68)

Aunt's explanation of the war as a human error exonerates the
Christian God, and it resolves, at least for Fiona, the problem of
how He could permit the war to go on. These two novels are unquestionably pacifist; no one could mistake their protagonists'
excitement over military bands for an endorsement of the war.
Yet Little manages to provide an anti-war perspective – to provide a 'moral guide' – without violating what is known about
how Canadians viewed the war. Little was born in 1932 and grew
up among people who had experienced the war. Perhaps this is
why her characters Eliza and Fiona display an ambivalence not
shared by the girls in other modern war books. Another reason may be her reliance on Montgomery's wartime journals and
*Rilla of Ingleside* as sources (*Brothers* 217). Although she departs
in many ways from Montgomery's patriotic tone, Little does not
lose sight of the fact that many thoughtful people felt, as Montgomery did, that war was terrible yet in this instance necessary.
In other words, Little does not operate on the premise that only
'bad' or naïve characters can support the war or that all good
characters oppose it.

**Battlefield Realism**

Modern children's writers do not disguise the awfulness of
trench warfare. To 'embrace explicit realism about the costs of
historic wars' is, as Winfred Kaminski has noted of German war
books for children, a way 'to reject sentimentality' (61). Explicit
descriptions of shrapnel injuries and rat-gnawed corpses in the
mud are deployed as antidotes to clichés about dying for one's
country. Reading about such things will, it is assumed, impress
upon young readers just how awful trench warfare was and thus
inoculate them against war fever. But perhaps war books with
'honest representation of the human capacity for evil' simply

'overwhelm the young mind with despair' (Higonnet and Rosen vi). There is also the opposite danger that they may inure young readers, who will perceive explicit descriptions of warfare as an aesthetic formula familiar from cartoons and video games, and not as descriptions of real acts done by human beings to each other. As I noted in the introduction, many stories, games, and toys produced for children during the war years were part of what George Mosse has described as a 'process of trivialization, cutting war down to size so that it would become commonplace instead of awesome and frightening' (126). Modern war books for children aim for the opposite effect: to depict war honestly, in all its horror. But inserting a few gruesome facts about trench warfare and then moving on to more 'child-friendly' matters such as sibling rivalry can amount to just another form of trivialization. The oft-repeated details about lice and mud and shell shock become quickly familiar and thus stripped of their power to shock and disturb, which surely they should never lose. How to combine a realistic treatment of the battlefields with an appropriate degree of gravity and sorrow, how to represent war without trivializing it, remains a very great challenge for children's authors.

One way to achieve realism while avoiding excessive violence is to set a book on the home front. In her discussion of British books about the war, Kate Agnew notes that 'few late twentieth-century children's novels concentrate primarily on the lives of young men in the trenches, preferring to juxtapose scenes of the battlefield with those set in hospital wards or on the home front' (57). But even on the home front, in Uxbridge, Ontario, Jean Little's protagonist Eliza of *Brothers Far from Home* encounters realistic evidence of the war's cost. On a train journey, she and her siblings sit near a soldier who has 'one pant leg folded up' (111). Eliza's brother asks him 'what the men thought was the hardest thing to bear in the War.' After some teasing answers – 'No dry socks' and 'having no mother to tuck me in' – he says that it was not his wound that was worst.

> 'No, no,' the soldier said. 'Losing that leg got me sent home.' He told us he was being eaten alive by bugs of every kind imaginable, and drowned in the mud of the trenches. (111–12)

Eliza also encounters a shell-shock victim. Richard Webb, the boy who lives next door, is brought home so shattered that he screams in the night. Eliza records in her diary that 'he dreams he's back in the trenches and is buried alive and keeps begging someone to get him out' (65). One day, Eliza discovers Richard about to cut himself with a kitchen knife, and she has to disarm him. But Eliza's most disturbing encounter with the damage inflicted by war occurs when brother Jack comes home. A pilot who was shot down and burned, Jack is so disfigured that Eliza does not recognize him:

> ... he looked like a man in a monster mask. It was made of pink rubber and, in those first few seconds, it did not look human. An ugly scar ran from his hairline down the whole left side of his face. One corner of his mouth was twisted down and the end of one eyebrow was caught in the puckered up skin. (168)

Children's books and stories of the war years certainly mentioned wounded soldiers, but they rarely provided any detail about what had actually happened; the one adjective 'wounded' was supposed to be sufficient. Nor did children's books from the war years ever depict shell-shock victims or (for obvious reasons) the enduring psychological damage of war. Here, Little provides enough explicit detail that readers will be, like Eliza, frightened and appalled; they will realize that neither Richard nor Jack will ever be whole again. But *Brothers Far from Home* also shows human resilience in, for example, the good humour of the wounded soldier on the train, and in Eliza's own actions – her kindness to shell-shocked Richard, and her helpfulness to her disfigured brother. From these positive elements, Little manages to provide hope midst the horror.

Letters from the front also bring some degree of battlefield realism into the home-front novels. Most of Julie Lawson's *No Safe Harbour: The Halifax Explosion Diary of Charlotte Blackburn* (2006) deals with the explosion and its aftermath, but the backdrop is the nation at war. Charlotte's brother Luke has enlisted, and she faithfully copies into her diary his description of the battlefields:

> ... it's grim, this letter, the way he describes the open stretch of ground called No Man's Land – the mud and shell holes, the smell

of dead bodies – where a line of Huns on one side faces a line of Allies on the other. All of them stuck in their trenches until the order goes out – 'Over the top!' and the killing begins.

... every minute feels like a year with the 'earth-shaking bombardments' and 'fireworks night after night,' and 'no picnic' when it's raining, which is most of the time. And the place is overrun with giant rats.

He has to do chores, too. Horrible chores like digging latrines or draining a trench with the mud to his knees. (16–17)

It seems to me unlikely that a protective brother would have mentioned such things to a twelve-year-old sister. In their letters, soldiers seem to have focused on personal discomforts – hunger, cold, and mud – rather than on the horrors of battlefields, perhaps both to spare those at home and to avoid problems with the censor.[8] This information about the trenches, while accurate, is unconvincing in a twelve-year-old's diary; still, it does introduce realistic details without excessive gruesomeness.

Another book focused primarily on the Halifax Explosion, Cathy Beveridge's *Chaos in Halifax* (2004), similarly introduces the war as a backdrop to the circumstances of the explosion. In this case, it is not letters but the device of the time slip (or 'time crease' as Beveridge's characters call it) that allows three modern-day characters, the twins Jolene and Michael and their grandfather, to travel back to 1917 and meet men who have been at war. On their first foray into the past, Jolene and her grandfather fall into conversation with a major and a blind soldier, sitting on a park bench. The soldier was blinded at Ypres; the major explains the gas attack and the Canadian response. Later in the novel, Jolene and Michael meet Rory, a veteran of Vimy Ridge. He describes the digging of the tunnels, the careful practice before the assault, and then the wintry April conditions in which the Canadians fought. Rory's account (which, despite the rustic Scottish dialect attributed to him as a Cape Bretoner, reads like a barely digested excerpt from a history book) culminates with how he got the wound that allowed him to come home:

I stumbled into a dugout with two German soldiers and struck the first one down with my bayonet. His comrade lunged for my heart, but I jerked away and the blade severed my shoulder. I plunged my own bayonet into him and left him slumped in the mud. (151)

This is not excessively gruesome either, although it does refer plainly to killing, and while as a story of Vimy Ridge it is much more muted than the exultant version given in wartime adventure tales or information books, Rory does say that 'the Canadians saved the day and the other troops respected our audacity and courage' (152). The time crease device in this novel is creaky, but it has the merit of separating the past from the present, of placing the sorrows of war in a different realm. Thus, when Jolene and Michael return to modern-day Halifax, the contrast between the stories of war and the banal happiness of a modern-day family vacation does not trivialize the war material.

Modern books that take readers to the battlefields, like Sharon McKay's *Charlie Wilcox* (2000) and *Charlie Wilcox's Great War* (2003), provide a remarkable amount of information about trench warfare. McKay describes the trenches in a fashion that will simultaneously revolt and fascinate children:

They could smell the trenches before they could see them. The stench rose up in great waves. The entire area reeked of shell fire, gasoline, urine, feces, unwashed bodies, and all things rotting and wrong. (*Charlie Wilcox* 175–6)

Nor does McKay spare young readers when she describes Charlie's work as a stretcher-bearer and unofficial medical assistant: Charlie and his partner bring back a soldier from whom 'blood poured out ... like paint running out of a pot' (*Charlie Wilcox's Great War* 60) and another 'who was cradling the better part of his leg in his arms' (61). Arthur Slade similarly describes the injuries inflicted when a German submarine shells a troop ship. His hero, Edward, receives only superficial shrapnel wounds, but many around him are horribly mutilated: 'I took a wobbly step and stumbled over a leg, reached down and picked it up. It was light, the puttees fluttered like banners. Whose leg was it?' (151). Slade's treatment of the severed limb verges on cartoon violence: it is sudden and shocking, but does not seem to be happening to real people.

McKay and Slade have evidently decided that such details are necessary in order to impress upon readers the awfulness of war. Perhaps they also believe that, in the absence of the old adventure-tale excitement (though both Slade and McKay provide some of this), explicit and graphic violence will hold young readers' attention. In 'Why Writers Write of War,' American children's author Patricia Lee Gauch wonders whether her own focus on war is just 'a cheap trick – to excite the readers, give them a goodly amount of dramatic and violent action to entice them to read my story' (14). She concludes that it is not; for Gauch, though 'war is a terrible thing,' writing and reading about it help us to see 'that man, woman, child, not only survive, they prevail, and that is the basic assurance that supports our life and our behavior' (16). Perhaps this is an overly optimistic assessment of what books about war, especially those with realistic depictions of battle, can achieve. No one knows what impact grim war books actually have on their readers. Perhaps, as Maria Tatar cautions, we ought to consider 'the possibility that the representation of death and dying in children's books might give rise to dread, alarm, or anxiety' (239). Tatar concludes that 'we err when we give [children] too strong a dose of reality, but we also make a mistake when we pretend that nothing is or ever will be out of order in the world' (240). She suggests that in the treatment of war some combination of danger and fantasy, in which fears are dealt with allegorically, is more effective than hard-hitting realism.

Most recent discussion of war in children's literature focuses on books about the Holocaust, clearly an ultimate test of what can and cannot be told to children. Despite the complexity and magnitude of the Holocaust, it has given rise to what Kenneth Kidd calls a 'contemporary children's literature of atrocity' (169): 'Since the early 1990s, children's books about trauma, and especially the trauma(s) of the Holocaust, have proliferated, as well as scholarly treatments of those books' (161). Kidd argues that this phenomenon is intertwined with a psychoanalytical and critical-theoretical concern with trauma, that is, with the enduring effects of terrible experiences, whether some kind of personal disaster or a political-historical one. He also suggests that another contributing element has been the influence of Bruno Bettelheim's persuasive defence of the fairy tale, with all its horrors, as a form of 'self-help or bibliotherapy' (170). Kidd speculates that psychoanalytical faith in the benefits of uncovering trauma has influenced the way writers for children treat the past. The result has been a 'shift away from the idea that young readers should be protected from evil and toward the conviction that they should be exposed to it' (161–2). Behind this shift lies the implicit belief that knowing the truth about the past and experiencing the suffering of others will somehow be good for children.

Recent books about the First World War comprise a subset of this modern 'children's literature of atrocity.' As topics for children, the war and the Holocaust present very different challenges, but both require writers to find some way to make the terrors of the past useful.[9] In war fiction for adults, this is not always an overt or central issue, but didacticism makes it one in children's literature. In discussing books for children on the Holocaust, Hazel Rochman suggests one measure of usefulness: good books on terrible events should 'bring readers up close and make them confront the moral choices and the connections, then and now' (550).

Some of the modern Canadian children's books about the war do indeed provide both 'moral choices and ... connection,' though not always in directly war-related contexts. For example, the young protagonist Cass of Michael Bedard's 1990 novel *Redwork* makes a connection between the cruelty of war and the violent neighbourhood control exercised by the gang in the park. He also makes a spiritual connection. Cass's landlord, Mr Magnus, is a veteran of the First World War; living in Mr Magnus's house, Cass has absorbed the old man's past, as if his memories of the war are so powerful that they seep into Cass's consciousness. The old man survived the war because the spirit of a dead man dragged him off the battlefield. This otherworldly experience made Mr Magnus, in a somewhat demented way, a spiritual seeker and alchemist; it taught him that there is something more than the flesh.[10] By transmitting this understanding to Cass, Mr Magnus, a shabby, frail, despised old war veteran, gives the boy a vision that will sustain him. But this novel may also be read, as Heather Kirk has suggested, as privileging the private world without offering 'anything new about Canadian history' (18). While Kirk praises it as a 'thoughtful treatment of the permanent physical and psychological damage that can be caused by war,' she questions its emphasis on the individual experience of war and the consequent neglect of any public or national themes: '... the soldiers seem to have accomplished nothing, and thus the public sphere is ... depicted negatively' (18).

Major's *No Man's Land*, with its tight focus on the battle at Beaumont-Hamel, poses all its questions in the immediate setting of war. Allan Hayward has the courage to comfort and lead his men, even though he knows that what lies ahead is probable slaughter. We admire Hayward, but is this the right thing to do? Here is a moral choice that goes directly to the heart of what bravery on the battlefield is all about. Should we celebrate a quality that leads to the deaths of others?

In Iain Lawrence's *Lord of the Nutcracker Men* (2001), the moral choice of whether to participate in war is posed allegorically.[11] The 'lord' of the title is ten-year-old Johnny Briggs, and the nutcracker men are soldiers made by his toymaker father. When Johnny's father joins up in October of 1914, the boy is sent away from London to live with an aunt in a country village, and there he begins to act out his war anxieties with the toy soldiers. Gradually he comes to believe that the mock battles he conducts mirror what happens on the battlefield. The first sign of this correspondence comes when he and his friend Sarah conduct a trench raid, with an officer (a lieutenant just like Sarah's dad) leading a toy soldier (a self-portrait carved by Johnny's father) out into no man's land. A few days later, when a letter from Johnny's father describes a trench raid, Johnny realizes that 'his raid was so close to the one that I had imagined that the letter might have been sent by my wooden soldier' (68). Then Johnny and Sarah conduct a pitched battle with a German assault and a British counteroffensive, hurling clumps of mud and stones at the soldiers on both sides. A few days later, a report comes that Sarah's father has been killed in battle.

The meaning of these uncanny parallels is illuminated by Mr Tuttle, the schoolmaster who has been teaching the *Iliad* to Johnny. Mr Tuttle compares the rulers of Europe who have led the nations into the present war with the heartless Olympians who provoked the Greeks and Trojans into fighting: '... all the rulers of Europe are just like Homer's gods, all related, always fighting' (61). Johnny sees his own part in all this:

> ... I was a sort of god to my little soldiers, the savior of the metal
> Tommies, the lord of the nutcracker men. I could stir them up
> however I wanted, and kill them all if I cared. And maybe it *was*
> true that whatever happened in the garden happened in faraway
> France. (132–3)

But Johnny is not really a god; Lawrence's point is not to con-
struct a fantasy in which a ten-year-old boy determines the course
of the war. Johnny's power over his soldiers only makes sense allegorically – as a picture, in miniature, of the thoughtless way in
which the real powers (Lawrence is not explicit about whether
these are politicians, generals, or gods) play with the lives of
men. As Margaret Higonnet has put it in discussing French war
narratives that employ toy characters, '... adults often treat live
people like dolls [and] this inversion may help explain how the
toy fits into our narratives about war' ('War Toys' 116). But if
there is a less pessimistic message in Lawrence's allegory, it might
be connected to the one real soldier who plays a substantial role:
Murdoch, the deserter. He has made his way back to his home in
the village, but is afraid to show himself to his parents. They believe he is dead because Murdoch switched his own ID tags with
those of a dead soldier. Murdoch pops up like an apparition
from time to time, talking with Johnny and watching him play
with the toy soldiers. Although he nearly dies from exposure,
Murdoch recovers and lives in the village, and after the war no
one ever reports him to the authorities. Murdoch is a pathetic
character, confused and fearful, but the fact remains that he did
take action to get out of the war. He refused to be a toy soldier.
Even those who do not desert, Lawrence suggests, can make
choices. At the end of the novel, a German bomber, pursued by
British planes, comes near to the village, and Johnny, instead of
seeking shelter, works frantically with Mr Tuttle to protect his
rose bushes. The German pilot seems to be headed straight for
Mr Tuttle's garden, but then he turns and drops his bombs some
distance away, near the station. In the pilot's surprising action,
Johnny sees a humane decision, an act of resistance to the logic
of war: '... the thought that came to me was that he just couldn't
drop a bomb on a child, that he couldn't kill a boy on Christmas
Day' (198). While Johnny's play with the toy soldiers seems to
emphasize the helplessness of men, this gesture by the German

pilot and Murdoch's desertion affirm the opposite – the power of individuals to choose not to kill.

### Good Stories, Bad History?

In discussing recent American historical novels for children, critic Anne Scott MacLeod claims that 'children's literature, historical as well as contemporary, has been politicized over the past thirty years; new social sensibilities have changed the way Americans view the past' ('Writing'). While these new perspectives have brought positive changes to children's historical literature – more emphasis on girls and women, the inclusion of the stories of marginalized people, a reduction in chauvinism – they have also resulted in books that misrepresent the past. In MacLeod's assessment, 'too much historical fiction for children is stepping around large slabs of known reality to tell pleasant but historically doubtful stories.' Is this the case with modern Canadian historical novels about the First World War?

Certainly the preponderance of pacifist girls and women is one 'historically doubtful' element in the recent war books. Another is the consistent emphasis on private life. The notes on the back cover of Sharon McKay's *Penelope: An Irish Penny* (Book 3 of McKay's four-volume Penelope series for Our Canadian Girl) indicate the relative importance of war and of Penny's private life in the story:

> In Book Three of Penny's story, the Great War in Europe continues to cast its shadow over the world, and Penny worries about her Uncle Robert, who is serving in France. But Penny faces more immediate problems. She misses her family terribly – Emily, Maggie and most especially her beloved Papa. And she's begun school at an exclusive private academy, where the upper-class girls look down on her for her Irish roots. It will be up to Penny not only to discover the meaning of her Irish heritage, but to take pride in it.

The two 'private' themes alluded to, separation and discrimination, are powerful ways to engage young readers, and one can hardly fault McKay for making them central to the book. But they could be treated as problems arising out of the context of war instead of exclusively private ones, as they are in the Penelope books. Moreover, Penny's pride in rediscovering her Irish heritage reflects modern multiculturalism, not the attitudes of the time.

On the back cover of the Penelope books is a note about the Our Canadian Girl series, welcoming readers to 'the continuing adventures of Penelope and many other smart, spirited and courageous girls.' Penelope is indeed 'smart, spirited and courageous.' So is Rilla Blythe. But Rilla demonstrates her intelligence, spirit, and courage, not through her 'immediate problems,' but through her involvement in the greatest concern of her community and her nation – the war. At the Our Canadian Girl series website, editor Barbara Berson explains what she wanted to achieve: 'As someone asked me – are these going to be great stories or history lessons? Obviously, I wanted them to be fantastic stories' ('Letter').

There is no doubt that compelling stories with attractive characters draw children into the study of the past. According to researcher Linda Levstik, there is even evidence that 'the connected discourse of literature' actually helps students to learn and remember the facts of history ('Relationship' 2). But Levstik is also aware that 'the power of narrative is not an unmitigated good' (Levstik and Barton 133). In a classroom-based study of response to historical narratives, Levstik concluded that 'even though [students] could explain the difference between fiction and nonfiction and did spontaneously critique books as literary creations, they tended to accept the history content as unimpeachable' ('Relationship' 17). As Anita Clair Fellman has pointed out in her study of the Little House series by Laura Ingalls Wilder, books that are emotionally and aesthetically appealing to children can be very powerful learning materials, even if what they are teaching is not wholly accurate: '... children apparently tend to accept the veracity of those texts in which they are emotionally involved. If they believe a story, find it credible as a narrative, then they also read it as telling what really happened in a larger sense' (149). This response is surely amplified by the way in which many modern historical novels for children employ documentary or pseudo-documentary elements. John Wilson's *And in the Morning* reproduces newspaper headlines and stories, recruiting slogans, and Jim's father's mobilization notice. Heffernan's *A Kind of Courage* includes a facsimile of the famous 'whiz-bang' or field service postcard (7). Jean Little's novels in the Dear Canada series include photographs and maps, historical notes, and an epilogue explaining what happened to the major characters, as if they had lived beyond the book. Even the design of the Dear Canada volumes – the name of the child 'diarist,' not of the author, appears on the cover, and copyright and publishing information is tucked away at the back – reinforces the sense that these are real diaries by real girls.

Dale Simmons of Library and Archives Canada has observed that 'the growing amount of historical fiction being used to augment history textbooks has made accuracy of information and authenticity of details more important than ever' (16). If indeed, as Levstik and Fellman argue, young readers respond to credible narratives as if they were history, then it matters whether authors present Canadian attitudes towards the First World War as they were, or as we would like them to have been. An instructive contrast can be seen between Montgomery's protagonist Rilla, created during the war years, and the modern character Claire in Sharon McKay's Charlie Wilcox novels. When Charlie Wilcox asks Claire what she did during the war, she responds with impatient disgust:

> 'Me? I've been knitting a million ugly green socks, that's what. I've been having a swell time. And guess what?' Claire skirted around him and blocked his way. 'Once in a while we'd run out of that ugly khaki color, and you know what happened then?'
> Charlie was afraid to ask.
> 'They gave us ugly gray wool to knit with!' (*Charlie Wilcox's Great War* 29)

This is brisk and perhaps even amusing, but would any girl of the war years have complained about knitting? Rilla is not an enthusiastic knitter: in her diary, she flatly declares, 'I hate it' (89). But she does not complain out loud: 'I just think of Jem joking about the mud on Salisbury Plain and I go at them.'

**Information Books and Picture Books**

Information books from the war years tended to be propaganda narratives, full of tales of heroism and British virtue. But the modern information books, with their emphasis on primary materials such as photographs, postcards, and letters, present a very different picture of the war. Instead of championing national interests, they remind young people of the ordinary humanity of individual soldiers. One very powerful example appears in Elizabeth MacLeod's *Kids Book of Canada at War* (2007). A reproduced newspaper clipping, the obituary of Lt Blayney E. Scott of Victoria, recounts the amazing story of how Scott, a gunner on a plane, managed to plug a shrapnel hole in the petrol tank by crawling out on the wing – twice. He survived that episode, flew again, crashed, survived and flew again, and then crashed once more and was 'severely wounded'; he died of his injuries in February of 1919 (43). Then on the following page is reproduced a letter that Scott wrote home in October of 1918, in which he describes the final crash in a jaunty and self-deprecatory tone:

> They shot our old bus to pieces but luckily didn't hit my pilot and only managed to get me with the last burst as we crossed the lines ... the kid [the pilot] sure had them buffaloed to a fare-thee-well ... The kid kept his head all the time and the next think [sic] I knew I was in a dressing station and they were cutting my clothes off. He sure is a wonder that kid and landed me 300 yds from a Field Hospital. The fact that he did, making a perfect landing in a machine that was a 'write off' was the one thing that saved my bacon ... (45)

Knowing that Scott never recovered lends tremendous pathos to this letter; it will certainly bring young readers closer to understanding the courage and dignity of the soldiers.

The best-known of the recent children's information books about the war is Linda Granfield's *In Flanders Fields: The Story of the Poem by John McCrae*. At first Granfield had difficulty finding a publisher for her manuscript: 'I had approached different children's book publishers during the five previous years; none would have any part of the idea' ('In Flanders Fields' 84). Finally, an editor did take up Granfield's idea, and *In Flanders Fields* proved to be a great success; there has even been a special tenth-anniversary edition. *In Flanders Fields* consists of the text of the poem, presented twice – once in a facsimile of McCrae's famous handwritten version and then as printed captions for the illustrations by Janet Wilson. In addition, Granfield supplies background information about McCrae and about the war. Usefully, she outlines McCrae's many accomplishments, for he was much more than the author of a single poem; she even includes one of his sketches.[12] In explaining the war, Granfield describes conditions in the trenches and in the field hospitals. With reproductions of advertisements for the War Charity Fund and the Victory Bond campaign that employed lines from the poem, she documents the impact of 'In Flanders Fields,' the best-known poem of the war and probably the most famous of all Canadian poems. Granfield acknowledges its ambiguity: 'Some people argue that the poem's invitation to battle is unsettling, while others recognize it as an expression of John McCrae's personal beliefs and an example of social attitudes of the time' (n.pag.).

Almost all of the illustrations by Janet Wilson that accompany the poem are dominated by a single colour: the greenish-brown of khaki. In a two-page image of soldiers relaxing (to accompany 'short days ago / We lived, felt dawn, saw sunset glow'), everything – ground, grass, tent, shadows – is suffused with this colour, as if the men were already dissolving into the earth. Wilson's image for the final lines, 'and now we lie / in Flanders fields,' shows a dresser on which are arrayed a teddy bear, toy soldiers, military medals, and a photo of a child in a uniform; in the dresser mirror is reflected the rest of the bedroom, and we see a woman lying across the bed weeping, with a letter under her hand. This illustration, in which once again khaki is the dominant colour, contains an entire life story and an implicit argument about war: did playing with those toy soldiers motivate a young man to enlist? Two final illustrations deal with remembrance, and they depart dramatically from the sombre tones of the other images in the books: green predominates in these illustrations, one showing the laying of the wreath at a modern Remembrance Day and the other showing a military cemetery in France. This is the highly conventional use of nature images – both scenes are full of green and growing things – to suggest that time heals the wounds of war. While Granfield's informed and thoughtful text assumes a fairly sophisticated readership (presumably the teachers who use this book for Remembrance Day), the illustrations work on a different level. Young children will sense the gloom and even horror in the images of war, but they will be restored to a safe world with the green-hued images of the present.

Granfield, who has made something of a specialty of books about war, has also written *Where Poppies Grow: A World War I Companion* (2001).[13] The synopsis on the copyright page identifies the book as 'an anecdotal overview of World War I illustrating how ordinary lives were changed by global-scale conflict, and humanizing the sacrifice made by so many' (n.pag.). Granfield looks at women on the home front, children, animals, training, entertainment for soldiers, living conditions in the trenches, food, spies, propaganda, all illustrated with an impressive array of images from postcards, books, and newspapers. While the major focus is on Canada, Granfield includes American and British materials too. *Where Poppies Grow* is not really a picture book; rather, it packages the experience of visiting a war museum, in which images, documents, and the words of real people are framed by brief commentary. Another Granfield book, *The Unknown Soldier* (2008), focuses on how fourteen nations, including Canada, have commemorated the unidentified fallen soldier; many of the photos are of the First World War, and many of the monuments Granfield discusses were built in response to it.

*Desperate Glory: The Story of WWI* (2008), an information book by John Wilson (the author of *And in the Morning* and *Red Goodwin*), is aimed at upper-elementary-school readers. Wilson manages to cover the entire war, from Sarajevo to war memorials, in just over eighty pages, including maps, sidebar commentaries, and a timeline. Like the other hybrid picture/information books about the war, such as Dylan Kirk's *Canada at War* (2004), Robert Livesey and A.G. Smith's *The Great War* (2006), MacLeod's *Kids Book of Canada at War,* and Norman Leach's *Passchendaele* (2008), *Desperate Glory* is intended, not for gift giving or the individual child, but for the school Remembrance Day market. (Kirk's book, which covers both world wars, even includes a quiz.) All the illustrations in Wilson's *Desperate Glory* are in black and white. This choice might have been made for reasons of economy, but the black-and-white illustrations achieve a kind of documentary sobriety. Even recruiting posters, which were usually in very bright colours, are reproduced here in black and white. Perhaps Wilson and his editor came to the conclusion that too much colour and too many tasteful illustrations would prettify the war.

In the new picture books about the war, the scenes of battle are stylized, reducing the complexity and chaos of the fighting to simple emblematic imagery.[14] In Nicolas Debon's *A Brave Soldier* (2002), this stylization is largely a matter of colour, and of intense focus on one individual's experience – a young man named Frank who joins up 'because he didn't want anyone to think he was a coward' (n.pag.). The illustrations, done with acrylic paints on textured paper, depict some of the grimmer aspects of war. While there are no bloodied bodies on display, reddish-brown and blue-grey tones impart a fearful mood to every page; an orange glow in the scenes of battle suggests flames and bursting shells. *A Brave Soldier*, with its realistic narrative and focus on an individual soldier, is an unusual picture-book treatment of war. According to Christina Desai, picture books on war tend to depict war indirectly, through allegory, folktale, or a toy-soldier story, rather than presenting soldiers as 'true characters' who are 'engaged in the business of war' (89). But then Debon's book, despite its format, is not intended for the usual picture-book audience. The text is simple, but the images, in which the perspective changes sharply from close-ups to aerial views to low shots, seem to owe more to the sophisticated narrative techniques of the graphic novel than to the conventional picture book.

*A Bear in War* (2008), by Stephanie Innes and Harry Endrulat, is based on the story of a Canadian soldier who died at Passchendaele. When the body of Lieutenant Lawrence Browning Rogers was found, in his jacket pocket was a small teddy bear that his ten-year-old daughter Aileen had sent him. *Bear in War*, which is narrated by the teddy bear, is illustrated with paintings by Brian Deines, supplemented with photographs and documents. Some of the photographs show the Rogers family on their farm in Quebec; co-author Innes, the great-granddaughter of Lawrence Rogers, supplied these family photos. Other images, like the photo of the Canadian War Museum, where the teddy is now on display, provide a connection to the present.[15] Documents reproduced in the text include a recruiting poster, school report cards for the Rogers children, and the 'Circumstances of Death Report' for Lieutenant Rogers. While *Bear in War* does show scenes of war, the teddy narrator and the emphasis on daily life for the Rogers children deflect attention away from the battlefields. The description of Rogers's death is simple:

> I continued to watch the war from Daddy's front pocket. I saw him help lots of soldiers.
>
> That's what he was doing in the fall of 1917 at a battle called Passchendaele, when many soldiers died.
>
> Daddy died that day, too, and I stayed in his pocket for a long, long time. (N.pag.)

In the illustration that accompanies this text, a shattered helmet dominates the foreground, while in the upper right two small silhouetted figures carry a stretcher. Another illustration shows a ghost-like soldier walking in a field of poppies; the soldier is an ethereal, unfeatured representative of all the dead.[16] Here again, battle and death are stylized. Through visual metonymy (the helmet), the symbolism of the poppy, and the metaphor of the ghost soldier, the father's translation from life into the ranks of the fallen is conveyed in a highly sophisticated, indirect fashion.

The illustrations by Ron Lightburn in Heather Patterson's *A Poppy Is to Remember* (2004) also stylize battlefields. One shows men advancing towards no man's land, but the figures are indistinct, rendered in light brown and bluish tones, while the foreground is filled with bright poppies against a lattice of barbed wire (4–5). Another painting, to accompany the text of 'In Flanders Fields,' shows John McCrae sitting by the casualty clearing station, writing in a notebook (6–7). In the background are stretcher-bearers carrying a wounded man, but again the figures are indistinct, while poppies, three crosses, and a shining helmet dominate the foreground. As the focus of this book is remembrance (it also deals with the Second World War), a choice has been made not to depict battle directly but to show it as a mediated event – that is, as something we remember through McCrae's poem and through the symbolism of the poppy that the poem invested with such resonance.

Hugh Brewster's *At Vimy Ridge: Canada's Greatest World War I Victory* (2006) abounds in images, predominantly photographs but also diagrams, maps, and paintings. Highlighted quotations quickly convey the significance of many of the images. The visual density of this book reflects the complexity of the war and the variety of evidence we now have about it. Given that it is richly illustrated, Brewster's book is classified as a picture book, but the reading level is too high for the usual picture-book audience. Brewster makes subtle points that are more suitable for a junior-high-school audience or even older. Here, for example, is his closing discussion:

> Today, some people question 'the Vimy myth.' Should Canadians take pride, they ask, in a battle that cost 10,602 casualties and 3,598 deaths? A battle that made little difference to the outcome of the war? The Great War itself (as it was once called) is now seen as having led to World War II, an even more murderous conflict that engulfed the world only twenty years later.
>
> Yet, in remembering the stories of those young men who faced death on that long-ago Easter Monday, what Canadian is not moved by their bravery and sacrifice? (43)

In this conclusion, Brewster tactfully manages to question the value of this mythic victory without diminishing the courage of the men who won it.

# Conclusion

What has the Great War taught? The list of its precepts is long, but a few of them may be mentioned: The pre-eminence of right over wrong, – the blessings of democracy and the perils of autocracy, – the pleasures of peace and the pains of war, – the weakness of strength and the strength of weakness, – the power of unselfishness, of kindliness, of benevolent brotherliness, the triumphs of personal courage, initiative, and resourcefulness.

*Annals of Valour*, Empire Day pamphlet, 1919

Canadian educators, like so many of their fellow citizens, believed that the war would lead to a better, stronger Canada. But this transformation could occur only if Canadian children internalized the lessons of sacrifice and service taught by the soldiers. In many post-war textbooks, these two sacred themes, which had been so central in wartime education, were preserved. Through historical accounts, patriotic verse, and stories of heroes, children were encouraged to live up to the moral example of the Canadian soldier.

The earliest and most patriotic of the post-war texts was J.E. Wetherell's 1919 anthology, *The Great War in Verse and Prose*, published by the Ontario Department of Education. In his introduction, the Rev. H.J. Cody, then the minister of education, called upon teachers to use the selections 'as vehicles of patriotic and moral instruction' (x). In Cody's view, the war would lead to 'a better Canada ... if there is kindled in the souls of our citizens the same flame of sacrifice and service which burned so brightly in the hearts of Canada's citizen-soldiers of the Great War' (xiv). The way to kindle that flame was to ensure that Canadian children studied the war.

Cody evidently had plans to rethink all school materials in light of the war: '... the changes wrought by the war call for fresh treatment of many subjects ... The importance of direct and indirect inculcation of sound moral and patriotic ideals cannot be overestimated' (*Report of the Minister for 1918*, quoted in Parvin 97). But, given the other pressing demands on the Department's resources, there were not the funds at the end of the war to undertake a wholesale revision of the curriculum.[1] Within a few years, however, the textbook revisions that had been delayed by the war were undertaken, and all the major educational publishers embarked on ambitious programs to bring Canadian history and literature to the classroom. At Ryerson Press, for example, which had published just eleven books in 1919, production expanded dramatically throughout the 1920s. In 1930, under the energetic leadership of Lorne Pierce, Ryerson published eighty-three titles, of which more than half were works in the Canada History Readers series (Wallace).

In the new history texts of the 1920s and early 1930s, Canada's wartime experiences crystallized into a single story.[2] Certain events – the Second Battle of Ypres, Vimy Ridge, Passchendaele, and the Hundred Days – became enshrined as the key moments in Canada's war. Sir Arthur Currie was anointed as the great Canadian soldier and leader. The same photo of Currie appears in virtually every text. (In 2006 the Dominion Institute tested Canadians' knowledge of the First World War. Asked to identify the Canadian war heroes from a list of four names – Currie, Billy Bishop, Douglas MacArthur, and Ulysses Grant – only 30 per cent of respondents chose Currie and Bishop [Dominion Institute].) What we now call the Conscription Crisis was treated as a minor political skirmish, satisfactorily resolved with the emergence of the Unionist coalition. And without fail, the history texts concluded their discussion of the war with a balance sheet in which the losses of war were weighed against intangible gains such as national pride and an elevated national spirit. Here, for example, is how Duncan McArthur summed up the war:

Canada had tasted the glories of war, but she had also learned much of its horrors and gruesome reality. Fifty thousand of her men lay buried in Europe; thousands of others were maimed or disabled. Her treasure had been scattered and a heavy burden of debt laid on future generations. The war represented the greatest effort that the Canadian people had yet put forth; it marked their 'coming-of-age' as a nation, with new powers and fresh responsibilities ... Her sacrifices in the war gave her the right to be heard in the councils of the world, where her voice will be raised on behalf of peace and international good will. The heroic achievements of the war have been woven into the traditions of the Canadian people and have helped to form the basis for a strong Canadian national sentiment. (473–4)

In the immediate aftermath, those who had lived through the war believed it would always be central to the nation and thus to its curriculum. Yet the First World War inevitably began to recede. As early as January 1920, a notice in the *School*, responding to 'numerous enquiries regarding the teaching of the Great War,' announced that 'teachers will be delighted to find that this course has been wonderfully reduced in amount – the assignment is pages 7 to 12, inclusive, in *Canada's Part in the Present War*, and pages 15 to 27, inclusive, in *Annals of Valour*' (271).

The war also faded from children's fiction. Some of the girls' and boys' series books from the United States continued to use the war through the early 1920s. British boys' and girls' papers and annuals also continued to exploit the adventure possibilities of the Great War. But in a sense, the Western Front was simply added to the repertoire of heroic imperial settings; it became another possible field for adventure, like the veldt or Lucknow, no longer the great story of the day.[3]

Of course, the war did not fade completely. In the entryway of many Canadian secondary schools hung a memorial plaque listing students or teachers who had given their lives in the war. Many schools across the country bore the name of a person or place associated with the war: Courcelette, Lord Byng, General Currie, Earl Haig, Lord Roberts, Edith Cavell. And through the 1930s, attendance at Armistice Day events actually increased (Vance, *Death* 216). The decision in 1931 to create a special public holiday, to be named Remembrance Day, stimulated the patriotic sentiments of Canadians, who 'made 11 November as important in the 1930s as it had been in 1919' (215).[4] But re-membering the fallen on one day of the year was quite differ-ent from making the nation's war record the moral foundation of education, which was what some educators had attempted in 1919. By the 1930s, teaching the war was no longer seen as a central and sacred duty for Canadian educators.

Once the First World War had ceased to dominate the nation's self-image, there seemed no reason for it ever to return. Another, even costlier war intervened, and then Canada's military role shifted from loyal ally to international peacekeeper. Past military glories as a combatant nation were, it seemed, permanently ban-ished to the sidelines. But in the last two decades, the First World War has made an astonishing comeback in Canadian life.

The recent children's books about the war constitute only one aspect of this phenomenon. Numerous works of adult fiction have also taken the war as their subject: for example, Jack Hod-gins's *Broken Ground* (1998), Jane Urquhart's *The Stone Carvers* (2001), Alan Cumyn's *The Sojourn* (2003), and Joseph Boyden's *Three Day Road* (2005). Plays such as Guy Vanderhaeghe's *Dan-cock's Dance* (1996), Stephen Massicotte's *Mary's Wedding* (2002), and Vern Thiessen's *Vimy* (2008) have explored the war's impact on Canadians. This return to the war has also manifested itself in a rediscovery of older Canadian war writing. Barry Callaghan and Bruce Meyer's *We Wasn't Pals* (2001) and Muriel Whitaker's *Great Canadian War Stories* (2001) have made First World War material by forgotten writers such as Will Bird and Peregrine Acland available once more to Canadian readers. So, too, has Norm Christie's ambitious publishing program at CEF Books, which has produced more than twenty titles, both new works (such as Christie's ten-volume For King and Empire series, based on his successful television programs) and welcome reprints of post-war classics such as Will Bird's *Ghosts Have Warm Hands*. Works by academic historians like Jonathan Vance's *Death So Noble* and Tim Cook's *Shock Troops: Canadians Fighting the Great War, 1917–1918* (the second volume of which was awarded the 2008 Charles Taylor Prize) have found praise and readers out-side the academy; popular histories of the war by writers like Ted Barris and Mark Zuehlke have also been well received.

In other media as well, the First World War has reappeared. The Dominion Institute's Memory Project, the opening of the new Canadian War Museum in May 2005, and the rededication in 2007 of the restored Vimy Memorial brought the war back to the nation's newspapers. On 7 April 2007, the front page of the *National Post* carried a picture of a soldier returning from battle in April 1917; the headline read, 'Vimy Ridge: How Canada marched into nationhood on a French battlefield 90 years ago.' The CBC television series *The Great War*, released in April 2007, occasioned publicity, particularly with respect to the selection of Justin Trudeau for the role of Talbot Papineau (Peritz). In 2008, the ninetieth anniversary of the Armistice prompted a number of works and events. There was the release of Paul Gross's long-awaited *Passchendaele*, the most expensive film ever made in Canada; the novelization of Gross's screenplay spent several weeks on the best-seller list, and the companion book for children was in bookstores in time for Remembrance Day school projects. On November 10 of 2008, the National Film Board released *Front Lines*, by Claude Guilmain, based on 'the war diary and private letters of five Canadian soldiers and a nurse' ('Front Lines'). From November 4 to 11, the Vigil Project 1914–1918, organized by Canada's History Society, arranged a unique memorial: the names of the 68,000 war dead were projected onto the National War Memorial and other buildings across Canada, as well as Canada House in London ('Vigile').

All of these works and projects demonstrate the powerful resurgence of the First World War in the Canadian imagination. It is not surprising that scholars continue to write about the war: its consequences even in domestic terms, such as the imposition of the first income tax, the introduction of female suffrage, and the Conscription Crisis, explain why the First World War remains a topic of interest to them. What is less clear is the source of its interest for other Canadians.

One explanation may be demographic. The novelist and short-story writer Frances Itani, whose best-selling novel *Deafening* (2003) deals with the First World War, interprets the current interest in the war in these terms: 'This was our grandfathers' war. And we are now of an age to write about it' ('Hear' 53). To Canadians of Itani's generation – that is, people now in their fifties and sixties – the men and women who lived through the war were individual human beings, not just figures from history.

As the last witnesses of the war die, and then those who knew them die, the collective memory will disappear. In February 2010, the last known Canadian veteran, John Babcock, died at the age of 109. (In Britain, the last two veterans of the Western Front died in 2009.) We are at the horizon of the collective memory of the First World War, and this fact surely lies behind much of the current interest in the war and its soldiers. Of course, what modern Canadian writers have recorded about the war is not some simple transcription of what their grandfathers or other veterans told them. In virtually every case, these writers acknowledge their reliance on archives and histories. Collective memory may in some sense have sparked their interest in the war, but in order to write about it, these authors must turn to the very sources and institutions that demonstrate the end of spontaneous remembering. The archives, the newly published diaries and letters, histories, films, and exhibitions – these sources, which belong to or derive from what Pierre Nora has called 'devotional institutions,' have emerged 'at the same time that an immense and intimate fund of memory disappears, surviving only as a reconstituted object beneath the gaze of critical history' (12). Now that there is no one left to remember the war, we are reconstituting it, to use Nora's word, through literature, film and other media, and various forms of scholarship.

It is hard not to wonder whether the rediscovery of the First World War might be related to another demographic phenomenon in Canada: our transition from a predominantly British society, with French and aboriginal minorities, to a more obviously and self-consciously multicultural one. 'Old' Canadians – those whose roots in this country go back three generations or more – are the only ones who have some direct link to the Canadian experience of the First World War; they are the people whose grandfathers or great-grandfathers participated in it as Canadian soldiers. Thus, interest in the war may serve as a way for 'unhyphenated' Canadians – those who no longer have close linguistic or cultural ties to any other nation – to see themselves as having had some distinct common experience in the collective past, an experience that marked and shaped their ancestors and thus, indirectly, themselves. Most of the authors who have returned to the war specifically acknowledge the family connection. For example, some books are dedicated to a relative who died in the war; in others, the preface or afterword describes a family member's war service. If, as Antoine Prost and Jay Winter assert, 'to every nation its own Great War' (264), then one of the features of the Canadian Great War is its place in national mythology as Canada's coming of age, the struggle that gave Canada its place as an independent nation. To claim descent from the men and women who were part of that struggle is to announce a particular sort of Canadian identity.

Another reason why Canadians have turned back to the First World War is our recent military history. Through the 1990s and into the 2000s, Canadian troops have served in the Gulf War, in Somalia, Bosnia, Macedonia, and, more recently, Afghanistan. In public discourse, it has become conventional to describe Canadian deaths in these conflicts as part of a tradition of military sacrifice. For example, in July 2006, when the prime minister was planning a 'work-in-progress visit' to the Vimy Memorial (then still undergoing restoration), columnist John Ibbotson noted that 'by visiting Vimy, Mr. Harper is reminding Canadians that our young have laid down their lives before in foreign lands in a just cause.' Speaking in December 2008, Prime Minister Stephen Harper specifically linked the present war in Afghanistan to the First World War. He began by going over the events celebrated in Canada in 2008, including 'the 90th anniversary of the end of World War I, the Great War, the tragic conflict that nevertheless marked Canada's coming of age as a strong and independent country.' In the prime minister's words, it was a 'historic milestone' that 'remind[s] us of the great sacrifices made by those who have gone before us to defend and protect Canada. We are the heirs of the sacrifices and the gains of our ancestors, which we are duty-bound to protect.' This was his cue to turn to the war in Afghanistan, where 'today, at the front lines of protecting Canada are our brave men and women of the Canadian Forces serving abroad'; he went on to say that 'their courage and sacrifice is a credit to all of us.' The prime minister's repetition of 'sacrifice' and 'protect' emphasizes the parallels being implied between the First World War and the war in Afghanistan. According to journalist Michael Valpy, Canadian involvement in global conflicts has led to 'a profound cultural shift': Canadians no longer see themselves as peacemakers but 'have reimagined themselves as a military nation, lauding their army, navy and air force as never before in the country's history' (F1).

There is another reason, specific to children's literature, why books on war seem to have proliferated in Canada: the increasing toll that war is taking on the world's children. It is estimated that in various recent conflicts in the Middle East, as many as 97 per cent of the casualties have been civilians, many of whom, inevitably, are children (Goldberg 5). Deborah Ellis's *Three Wishes: Palestinian and Israeli Children Speak* (2004) presents the following information on its frontispiece: 'In World War I, 15 percent of all casualties were civilians. In World War II, 50 percent of all casualties were civilians. In 2004, 90 percent of casualties in war are civilians.' Ellis then lists the names of the 429 children killed in the Middle East between 29 September 2000 (when the second Intifada began) and 7 March 2003 (11–17). In these modern conflicts that do not distinguish between citizens and soldiers, even children who survive are victims of war: according to Mona Macksoud, a psychologist with the Project on Children and War at Columbia University, 'in some countries as many as 25 per cent of the children have lost a parent as a result of ongoing conflict ... [and] there are places where the proportion of children deprived of a close family member as a result of wartime violence climbs above 50 per cent' (13). Moreover, in some countries, children are not just civilians affected by war; they have been conscripted. While there are no exact figures, a recent report from Human Rights Watch estimated that in 2008 there were still 'many tens of thousands of child soldiers' in the world ('Child Soldiers' 10).[5]

Canadian children are fortunate to live far from such troubles: there has not been a foreign army fighting on Canadian soil since 1812–14. Nonetheless, any Canadian child who watches television can see that children elsewhere are being made the victims, accidental or deliberate, of wars waged by adults. There appears to be widespread agreement among psychologists that children need to talk about war in order to manage their fears about it (National Association). The authors of *Children's Fears of War and Terrorism: A Resource for Teachers and Parents* suggest that 'reading books and stories aloud to children and then talking about these books can be a starting point in helping children cope with their fears in an uncertain time. Books offer many examples of real and imaginary people who experienced hope, determination, and love as well as suffering, injustice and death'

(Moses et al. 47). As Judy Brown puts it in a recent article, '...
there is a need for fictional treatments of war in which child
characters are allowed to emerge from the margins and to demonstrate the varieties of children's experiences of and responses
to war' (40–1). Carol Fox, a member of a multinational project
in the European Union surveying children's literature on war,
asserts the importance of books that 'communicat[e] to children what war is, what it is like, what it means and what its consequences are' (126).

But what are modern books about the First World War teaching Canadian children? To compare the war as it was represented in children's literature of the war years with the way it is
represented now is to see vividly the truth of Prost and Winter's
dictum that 'the meaning that different nations give to the war,
the contents of this apparently simple term, differs in effect according to nations ... but also according to era' (273). Not only
each nation but also each generation has its own Great War.

For Canadians during the war, the meaning of the conflict
rested on certain abstractions – freedom, Empire, sacrifice, service – and was communicated through particular images and
metaphors – the soldier in the arms of Christ, the maimed Belgian child, the testing fires of the crucible. In presenting the war
to children, educators and writers translated these ideas and images into terms that it was felt young minds could absorb. Freedom and Empire were communicated through the symbolic
power of drills, tableaux, slogans, pledges, flags, and patriotic
music. Service and sacrifice were represented in narratives of
everyday life, and the special importance of these virtues was
emphasized by recourse to the example of the soldiers.

As for the central images of war – the Christ-like sacrifice, the
maimed child, the crucible – these too were presented to children. Sometimes they were taught explicitly, as in the 'picture
study' of *The Great Sacrifice* recommended in the *School*; in other
cases, the analogy between Christ and the soldiers was made indirectly, by the incorporation of the war into a broader Christian
schema of suffering and redemption.

The image of the maimed child was not presented to children,
but its meaning was transmitted through a kind of transposition:
this is what the incident of the decapitated Belgian cat in *Me'ow
Jones* does. Another way of communicating it, also indirect, was

to focus on providing aid to child victims of war, especially the Belgian refugees. By aiding the Belgian children, children at home in Canada could do their bit to fight the evil represented by the atrocities.

The metaphor of the crucible does not appear, as far as I have discovered, in wartime literature for Canadian children, despite its widespread use in other writings. Nonetheless, the essential moral dynamic underlying this metaphor – that the war was a form of suffering sent to test Canadians and make them stronger – is present in children's literature, most obviously in the Sunday-school papers. In the Sunday-school stories, children who make some sacrifice for the war gain in strength and maturity; moreover, they often receive some material compensation. Such rewards can be seen as a promise that the larger sacrifices of the war would also be rewarded in some fashion. Another example of this thinking appears in L.M. Montgomery's *Rilla of Ingleside.* Montgomery's protagonist, who suffers deeply when her brother Walter dies, emerges from the trial of the war years 'a capable, womanly girl,' purified of vanity and shallowness (258). Rilla's transformation implicitly affirms that the war has wrought a similar change in the Canadian people.

These ideas belong to the Canadian version of the Great War, but Canadian children were also exposed to war literature from Britain and from the United States. For young Canadian readers, the national version of the war, with its stern elements of service and sacrifice, was supplemented by a British mythology of imperial adventure, gallantry, and racial pride, and tempered by American optimism that the new world would not be scarred by the battles of the old. As Paul Litt has observed, Canadians probably derived some comfort during the war from the many American books and magazines they read: 'However traumatic the experience of being at war, most Canadians lived the experience from the other side of the Atlantic Ocean, immersed in a North American cultural context in which it was business as usual' (333).

In Canadian wartime literature, we see the facts and interpretations that Canadians wanted to transmit to their children: the causes of the war, the great battles, the heroic deeds of the Canadian soldiers. We also see their hope that the terrible costs of the war could be offset by the values it had taught. If Canadian children could learn from the soldiers and from their own war-work the true meaning of service and sacrifice, those two great watchwords invariably invoked in discussions of children and the war, then the struggle would not have been in vain. Perhaps the constant emphasis on heroism, service, and thrift equipped children with a clearer vision of active citizenship, a vision that would sustain them through the troubles of the decades ahead – the Great Depression and then another war. It would be comforting to think that this was the case, but perhaps such speculations are just another example of the consolatory fallacy, the notion that something good must have come of so much suffering.

In recent children's books about the war, we see very different values: a profound antipathy to patriotism, deep cynicism about officers and other authority figures, and a pervasive conviction that the war was a pointless, bloody slaughter. This, of course, is the modern view, and one for which there is much distressing evidence, most powerfully the knowledge we have, which Canadians of the war years did not, that the suffering of the First World War would lead directly to the even greater suffering of the Second. However, this modern view is not the whole story. Some of the modern children's books on war display an unexamined confidence that we know better, that we would not allow something like this to happen, that sensible and good people would resist the war. I am not at all sure that this is an honest or helpful message, for it dangerously underestimates the illogical appeal of war as a decisive, regenerating act, a form of renewal for the individual and for the nation. It also underestimates the power of propaganda and the hazards of resisting war enthusiasm.

Heather Kirk has observed that in pre-1940 Canadian historical fiction for children 'the main characters *take part in* history,' but the protagonists of contemporary fiction 'ultimately *flee from* history, often after rebelling unsuccessfully against societal as well as parental authority' (14, italics in original). The result is fiction that is 'not only anti-historical but antisocial' (14) and which offers its protagonists (and thus its readers) no 'incentive to participate in public life' (16). Kirk's concern about contemporary historical fiction is worth quoting in full because it applies so well to many recent works about the First World War:

> Canadian writers of historical fiction for children must be careful
> that mastering a literary convention that focuses on temporary,
> private concerns does not mean that the broad, public perspective
> of history is distorted or lost altogether. Canada needs novels that
> show the good side of entire, collective events and whole lives, as
> well as of brief, personal experiences. (17)

While I do not for a moment think that we ought to go back
to the old modes of patriotic education and warrior adventure
tales, there was something good in the earnestness of *some* earlier children's war literature and in its commitment to collective
causes. At its worst, the children's literature of the war years was
jingoistic and deceitful: it glorified war, demonized the enemy,
and disguised the true face of battle. But the values it purported
to teach – service and sacrifice – were not bad in themselves. If
everything associated with the war is contaminated by the terrible suffering of the Western Front, then we perforce discard
the idealism and collective spirit that animated the home front;
we also unintentionally but inevitably diminish the value of the
sacrifices men and their families made. How can we decry the
war and see it in all its horror, and yet still honour the men and
women, the boys and girls, who fought in it, worked for it, sacrificed for it? This book has been an attempt, from the perspective
of children's literature, to examine how Canadian ideas about
the First World War have altered, and to salvage, tainted though
it might be, the good side of the collective spirit that animated
the war years.

# Appendix: Recent Canadian Children's Books about the First World War

## 1990–2000

Bedard, Michael. *Redwork.* Toronto: Lester, 1990.

Granfield, Linda. *In Flanders Fields: The Story of the Poem by John McCrae.* Ill. Janet Wilson. Toronto: Lester, 1995.

Major, Kevin. *No Man's Land.* Toronto: Doubleday, 1995.

McKay, Sharon E. *Charlie Wilcox.* Toronto: Stoddart, 2000.

## 2001

Granfield, Linda. *Where Poppies Grow: A World War I Companion.* Toronto: Stoddart, 2001.

Haworth-Attard, Barbara. *Flying Geese.* Toronto: Harper-Collins, 2001.

Lawrence, Iain. *Lord of the Nutcracker Men.* New York: Delacorte-Random, 2001.

McKay, Sharon E. *Penelope: Terror in the Harbour.* Toronto: Penguin, 2001. Our Canadian Girl.

## 2002

Debon, Nicolas. *A Brave Soldier.* Vancouver: Groundwood-Douglas & McIntyre, 2002.

Haworth-Attard, Barbara. *Irish Chain.* Toronto: HarperTrophy-Harper-Collins, 2002.

McKay, Sharon E. *Penelope: The Glass Castle.* Toronto: Penguin, 2002. Our Canadian Girl.

## 2003

Foran, Jill. *Remembrance Day*. Calgary: Weigl Educational, 2003. Canadian Holidays.

Little, Jean. *Brothers Far from Home: The World War I Diary of Eliza Bates*. Markham, ON: Scholastic, 2003. Dear Canada.

McKay, Sharon E. *Charlie Wilcox's Great War*. Toronto: Penguin, 2003.

— *Penelope: An Irish Penny*. Toronto: Penguin, 2003. Our Canadian Girl.

Wilson, John. *And in the Morning*. Toronto: Kids Can, 2003.

## 2004

Beveridge, Cathy. *Chaos in Halifax*. Vancouver: Ronsdale, 2004.

Kirk, Dylan. *Canada at War*. Calgary: Weigl, 2004.

McKay, Sharon E. *Penelope: Christmas Reunion*. Toronto: Penguin, 2004. Our Canadian Girl.

Patterson, Heather. *A Poppy Is to Remember*. Ill. Ron Lightburn. Markham, ON: North Winds-Scholastic, 2004.

Skrypuch, Marsha Forchuk. *Silver Threads*. Ill. Michael Martchenko. 1996. Toronto: Fitzhenry and Whiteside, 2004.

## 2005

Heffernan, Colleen. *A Kind of Courage*. Victoria: Orca, 2005.

Watts, Irene. *Flower*. Toronto: Tundra, 2005.

## 2006

Brewster, Hugh. *At Vimy Ridge: Canada's Greatest World War I Victory*. Toronto: Scholastic, 2006.

Lawson, Julie. *No Safe Harbour: The Halifax Explosion Diary of Charlotte Blackburn*. Toronto: Scholastic, 2006. Dear Canada.

Livesey, Robert, and A.G. Smith. *The Great War*. Ill. A.G. Smith. Toronto: Fitzhenry and Whiteside, 2006. Discovering Canada.

Slade, Arthur. *Megiddo's Shadow*. Toronto: HarperTrophyCanada-HarperCollins, 2006.

Wilson, John. *Red Goodwin*. Vancouver: Ronsdale, 2006.

## 2007

Little, Jean. *If I Die before I Wake: The Flu Epidemic Diary of Fiona Macgregor.* Markham, ON: Scholastic, 2007. Dear Canada.

MacLeod, Elizabeth. Ill. John Mantha. *Kids Book of Canada at War.* Toronto: Kids Can, 2007.

## 2008

Granfield, Linda. *The Unknown Soldier.* Toronto: North Winds-Scholastic, 2008.

Innes, Stephanie, and Harry Endrulat. *A Bear in War.* Ill. Brian Deines. Toronto: Key Porter Kids, 2008.

Leach, Norman. *Passchendaele: Canada's Triumph and Tragedy on the Fields of Flanders. An Illustrated History.* Foreword Paul Gross. Regina: Coteau, 2008.

Wilson, John. *Desperate Glory: The Story of World War One.* Toronto: Napoleon, 2008.

## 2009

Granfield, Linda. *Remembering John McCrae: Soldier, Doctor, Poet.* Toronto: Scholastic, 2009.

# Notes

## Introduction

1 In *When Your Number's Up*, Desmond Morton claims that the youngest recorded member of the Canadian Expeditionary Force was ten years old (279), but neither the Canadian War Museum nor Library and Archives Canada could provide any information about this soldier.

2 All translations, unless otherwise indicated, are my own.

3 Another lurid story associated with the invasion was that the Germans had raped women and then cut off their limbs or their breasts. According to Horne and Kramer, such stories were 'commonplace' but were likely 'symbolic tales' rather than factual accounts (200).

4 In 1915, the British government established a commission to investigate reports of German attacks on Belgian civilians. The commission, chaired by Viscount Bryce, issued a report documenting acts of violence against citizens and the destruction of sites of cultural significance. The report included 'several eyewitness reports on the severing of hands which were "alleged" to have occurred' (Horne and Kramer 234).

5 The tenacity of this myth is evident in British Columbia author Bertrand Sinclair's 1919 novel *Burned Bridges*, in which one returned soldier tells another about the atrocities he witnessed: 'These little children, shorn of their hands – so that they could never lift a sword against Germany – cried aloud to him. They held up their bloody stumps for him to see' (251). Sinclair was not a veteran, but several of his post-war novels set in British Columbia feature returned soldiers as protagonists.

6  This story is identified in the *King's Own* as having first appeared in the *Congregationalist*, an American publication.

7  See, for example, chapter 8 of MacKenzie's *Propaganda and Empire*, chapter 4 of Bratton's *Impact of Victorian Children's Fiction*, Reynolds's *Girls Only*, Castle's *Britannia's Children*, and Dunae, 'Boys' Literature.'

8  Richard Altick points out that some of the children's periodicals 'have a solid claim to the literary historian's remembrance,' for not all the material they published was formulaic trash: '*Young Folks*, for example, published Stevenson's *Treasure Island*, *Kidnapped*, and *The Black Arrow*' (362n29).

9  The circulation figure appeared in the advertisements section at the back of each issue; it was announced in order to solicit advertisements. See, for example, 26.1 (Nov. 1914).

10 Annick markets two editions of Harrison's novel. The new edition, which differs only in the introduction, is described as for readers aged 17+ ('Generals').

11 See, for example, Mosse, chapter 8.

## 1  Doing Their Bit

1  Barbara Wilson notes that teachers 'encouraged their pupils to prepare "News from Home" scrapbooks. Each budget consisted of six or more pages of newspaper clippings of interest to local soldiers far from home, and the children were instructed to fill in spaces between the clippings with "jokes, funny stories, etc."' (xcv).

2  According to Adam Crerar, 'in 1918 18,000 to 19,000 high school students in Ontario – roughly 70 percent of those enrolled province-wide – signed up as "Soldiers of the Soil"' (234).

## 2  Studying War

1  The following chapter deals in more detail with the program of the Strathcona Trust.

2  See Djebabla and Mesli for a discussion of the situation in Quebec.

3  Some material in this chapter also comes from the *Western School Journal*, an independent journal published ten times a year in Winnipeg; I have also drawn on annual reports and other publications of the British Columbia Ministry of Education.

4  This article is signed SWP – probably S.W. Perry, a member of the

Faculty of Education at the University of Toronto, and a contributor of other material to the *School*.

5 The teacher, Harry Erland Lee, later enlisted and was killed at Courcelette in 1916, 'the first Toronto teacher to die in action' (B. Wilson xcviii). There was a controversy over whether a plaque could be erected in his memory; finally, the Board agreed, and a plaque and a portrait of Lee 'procured by the pupils of the school' were unveiled at the school in 1917 (xcviii–xcix).

6 An inspector thought Held had taught a poem by the Irish poet Tom Moore 'too effectively,' indicating her sympathy with Sinn Fein. Another supposed sign of her disloyalty was that Held objected to singing the second verse of 'God Save the King' on the grounds that it was 'inconsistent with the golden rule' (in the words of Professor C.B. Sissons, who defended Held in a letter to the *Globe*) (B. Wilson 156).

7 All examination questions are taken from the Annual Reports of the British Columbia Department of Education, held by the British Columbia Archives.

8 An aggressively international firm based in Edinburgh, Thomas Nelson and Sons had a representative in Toronto as early as 1854; it was the first foreign publisher to enter directly into the Canadian school-book trade (Clark 337).

9 Quotations from *The Children's Story of the War* are cited by issue number followed by page number.

10 The story of Colonel Elkington was regarded as especially appropriate for children. It was related in the December 1916 issue of the *Western School Journal* (published in Winnipeg) with special mention of its educational value: 'In years to come the story of this soldier in the Great War will be read by little children all the world over, and boys and girls will be taught how good a thing it is to try again' (391).

11 Cavell, a British nurse working in German-occupied Belgium, was detained by the Germans in August 1915. Found guilty of helping Allied soldiers to escape, she was executed on 12 October 1915. Cavell quickly became a martyr to the Allied cause: 'Recruitment doubled during the eight weeks after her death' (Granfield, *Where* 37).

## 3 Children of the Empire

1 Ross's memorandum, which was addressed to the president of

the Dominion Teachers' Association, is quoted in full in J. Castell
Hopkins's 'The Origin and History of Empire Day' (14–17).

2  This view of the significance of the First World War was in evidence
at the Rededication of the Vimy Memorial in April of 2007. In his
speech, Prime Minister Stephen Harper said that 'every nation
has a creation story to tell; the First World War and the Battle of
Vimy Ridge are central to the story of our country' (quoted in D.
Saunders A5).

3  The question-and-answer section was designed to assist those who
could not 'comprehend fully' the contents of the Blue Book of
diplomatic correspondence that had already been issued to the
schools (*Empire Day Annual* 1915: 7). The Blue Book 'contain[ed]
159 telegraphic dispatches and notes exchanged between 20th July
and 4th August 1914, and several speeches by leading statesmen in
the British House of Commons.'

4  A 1909 photo of the women's drill team of the St John's Ambulance Corps appears in J.M.S. Careless's *Toronto to 1918: An Illustrated History* (167).

5  Four booklets by Groves – *Fancy Flag Drill, How the Fairies Chose
Their Queen, Canada Our Homeland,* and *Patriotic Scarf Drill* – were
published by William Briggs in the Canadian Drills and Exercises
series during 1900–1. Up until 1916, Groves's drills were still being
published by Briggs, but then McClelland, Goodchild and Stewart
took them over. Spadoni and Donnelly in their *Bibliography of Mc-
Clelland and Stewart Imprints* list only sixteen titles by Groves in the
series between 1916 and 1918; three more are listed in the Appen-
dix as 'not located.' A McClelland advertisement for the All Canadian Entertainment series in the *School* lists a total of twenty-four
titles: twenty by Groves, two by Elspeth Moray (*Dream of the Months*
and *Festival of the Wheat*), one by James MacDougall (*Miss Canada's
Reception*), and one by Allegra Cronk (*The School Fair*) (7.3 [Nov.
1918]: 195). An advertisement on the back cover of *The Soldiers of
the Soil and the Farmerettes* lists an additional title, *The Girl Guides,* by
Marjorie Mountain Jarvis. I have not been able to locate the Jarvis
drill, but of the other four non-Groves works in the series, only
MacDougall's is overtly patriotic.

6  Some of Groves's All Canadian Entertainments are not specifically concerned with war. *A Canadian Fairy Tale: A Patriotic Play*
(1916), for example, does not allude to the war, though it is highly
nationalistic. So, too, is *The Key to Jack Canuck's Treasure House*

(1916), which celebrates Canada's natural resources. In *A Spring Fantasy* (1918), two children travel to a house in the forest where the months live. Despite the benign subject matter, Groves uses military analogies: the tyrant King Winter calls on 'all my allies and friends' to 'come quick to the help of your Monarch and King,' and when Jack Frost arrives to help, he makes a 'military salute' (7).

7  This song, written by Alfred E. MacNutt and M.F. Kelly, appears to be Canadian in origin. On the cover of a copy held by the National Library of Australia is written: 'The Song that has swept Canada like a wave from end to end' (M.F. Kelly). The second verse suggests the tone of the song and its appropriateness for an Anglo-Canadian audience:

Britain's sons have always called her Mother,
Britain's sons have always loved her best,
Britain's sons would die to show they love her,
The dear old Flag laid on each manly breast.
Britain's ships have always ruled the ocean,
Britain's sons will serve her one and all,
Britain's sons will show their true devotion,
And we'll never let the old flag fall.

'We'll Never Let the Old Flag Fall' was one of the music-hall songs (along with Harry Lauder's 'While the British Bull-Dog's Watching at the Door' and 'The Laddies Who Fought and Won') included in *For Freedom and the Right: The Star War Album*, published in 1918 by the *Montreal Daily Star* and the *Family Herald and Weekly Star*. It was advertised in the Eaton's catalogue of Fall/Winter 1916–17 as 'Canada's Great Marching Song' (328).

8  See K. Bird for a detailed discussion of this work.

9  Margaret Higonnet notes that in a French story from this period, a child burns a toy soldier that was made in Germany ('War Toys,' 123). George Mosse's *Fallen Soldiers* includes an advertisement from a Paris department store in which two smiling French children trample a stuffed German soldier; the toy is labelled 'Made in Germany' (138).

10  There were at this time in the Toronto schools Little Mothers' classes, designed to teach girls how to care for their children. See 'Little Mothers' Class, Board of Education,' subseries 11, Board of Education fonds, item 60, in City of Toronto Archives.

11  In the version published later in *Canadian Poems of the Great War*,

edited by Hale's husband, John Garvin, this stanza was revised, making the allusion to Penelope even stronger:
> Whispers of women, tireless and patient,
> 'This is our heart's love,' it would seem to say,
> 'Wrought with the ancient tools of our vocation,
> Weave we the web of love from day to day.' (73)

12 This recitation seems to echo the 1908 song 'In a Child's Small Hand,' with lyrics by Philip Trevor and music by Cecil Engelhardt. The first stanza begins: 'What will you do for England / Dear little English maid? You may be poor, weak and obscure, / Still, you can lend your aid.' The lyrics of this song appeared in the *Girl Guides Handbook*; they were also reprinted in the 7 January 1917 issue of the Anglican children's periodical, the *New Young Soldier*.

## 4 Brave Little Soldiers

1 Presumably, the Agrippa referred to is Henry Cornelius Agrippa von Nettesheim, a German occult philosopher and magician (1486–1535) ('Agrippa'). Zipes identifies him as the famously cruel Roman, but this seems less pertinent, especially given the figure's appearance in Hoffmann's illustrations.

2 *Soldier of the King* was published by Oxford University Press in Toronto in 1915 (Watters 398). I have failed to turn up any information about Stirling. The book was published first in Britain by Oxford, but, according to Martin Maw, the present archivist of the Press, records related to publications for children were destroyed some time ago. The archive of Toronto's Hospital for Sick Children has no material on Stirling or on this book.

3 Stirling's description seems based on the funeral procession of Captain Robert Clifton Darling of the 48th Highlanders, killed on 23 March 1915. His wife brought his body home (a practice that was soon forbidden), and his funeral in Toronto on 6 May 1915 was a public event with large crowds, including children, lining the streets. The procession taking his body from church to cemetery contained the elements Stirling mentions – the riderless horse, the soldiers with their rifles reversed (I. Miller 41–3).

4 Findlater won the Victoria Cross for his actions at Dargai on the North West Frontier of India. Despite being wounded in both legs, Findlater continued to play the bagpipes, thereby encouraging his fellow Gordon Highlanders to take the ridge. See 'Piper Findlater, VC.'

5  The doctor's statement is strikingly similar to what a doctor says to
a sick child in 'A Brave Little Soldier,' a story by Francis McKinnon Morton that appeared in the 6 November 1915 issue of the
Salvation Army's *Young Soldier*. The protagonist of this story is also
a sick boy in a city hospital, and his doctor also likens his little
patient's courage to that of the soldiers:

> 'Well, you know there are two kinds of soldiers,' said the doctor.
> 'One kind wear bright uniforms with gold lace and shining
> swords and go marching off to war; and the other kind wear no
> uniforms at all, but just stay at home and face their duty every
> day as it comes along. Our Little Soldier is one of this kind.' (2)

6  'Bobs' has military associations, for it was the nickname of Lord
Roberts of Kandahar. It seems to have been a popular name for
pets. In a letter to the TOKO club, Wallace Graham of Markham
wrote: 'I have a little dog, an English fox terrier ... He came about
the time of Lord Robert's [sic] death, so we called him "Bobs."
If he grows up to be like his namesake he ought to be a mighty
warrior, even already he barks and growls when he hears a strange
step on the verandah' (*King's Own*, 24 April 1915: 68).

7  See Mark 14.

8  Perhaps this story about the locket was a war myth like the Angel
of Mons, widely circulated, replicated, and embroidered. In the 12
June 1915 issue of the *Young Soldier* appeared 'For the Children's
Sake: A Touching Story of Two Orphaned Belgian Children,' a
story which also turns on the discovery of the sister's picture in a
child's locket:

> She turned the locket over, and saw that it held a photograph,
> and as she looked she could scarcely believe her eyes, for the
> face behind the locket was that of her own sister!
>
> Long ago her sister had gone to Belgium and had married,
> and the two had lost sight of each other.
>
> But now through caring for the little friendless strangers, God
> was giving her the unspeakable joy of being a mother to her
> dead sister's children. (8)

## 5  Dogs of War and Other Animals

1  This poem by the English poet Henry Chappell (1874–1937) is
reproduced at the website of the Animals in War Memorial. See
'Stories' at www.animalsinwar.org.uk.

2  There was a book published in Britain either during or just after

the war entitled *The Animals Do Their Bit*, by Frank Hart. I have not been able to obtain a copy of it or to find any evidence that it was sold in Canada. Some images and text from this book are reproduced at www.greatwardifferent.com/Great_War/Childrens_Books/Childrens_Books_01.htm.

3 Originally called Our Dumb Friends' League, it had been founded in Britain in 1897 as a charity devoted to ameliorating the conditions of working animals. Its early activities involved such matters as the welfare of draught horses in London and the conditions for rail transport of livestock. In 1912 the League created the Blue Cross Fund to assist animals affected by the First Balkan War, but with the outbreak of the Great War, the Fund soon found a much wider scope for activity ('About Us').

4 *Pierrot, Dog of Belgium* was published in 1915 in the United States by Doubleday and Page and was issued in Canada in the same year from the Doubleday sheets by McClelland, Goodchild and Stewart (Spadoni and Donnelly 120). Although *Me'ow Jones*, published by George H. Doran in New York, did not appear in a Canadian edition, it was available here: an advertisement from the Murray-Kay stores in the *Globe* of 8 November 1918 lists *Me'ow Jones* (which it calls *Me and Jones, Belgian Refugee Cat*) among 'better books for children for all ages' (12).

5 One wonders whether he was inspired by the extremely popular, extremely maudlin *A Dog of Flanders* (sometimes subtitled *A Christmas Story*) by Ouida [Marie Louise de la Ramée], published in 1872. Pastrache, the dog of the title, is a working dog like Pierrot.

6 I was not able to find any reference to a fundraising cat in newspapers of the period, so, while Edward Branch Lyman certainly existed, perhaps Me'ow Jones did not. See 'Directing' for information on Lyman.

7 It was published in Canada and by George Doran in the United States under this title; Grosset of New York published it as *'Boy,' the Wandering Dog* (Waterston 160).

## 6 The Adventure of War

1 Henty wrote more than a hundred 'phenomenally popular' boys' adventure books (Dunae 110); collectively, about 25 million copies of Henty's books were sold (Bristow 146–7).

2 Graham Dawson also uses this term in *Soldier Heroes* (1994). As a

member of the Popular Memory Group at the Birmingham Centre for Contemporary Cultural Studies, Dawson became interested in 'the intense fascination and excitement generated for men and boys by the military side of the [Second World] war' (4). In examining various forms of popular culture, Dawson concluded that 'images and stories about military war ... clearly provided pleasure and excitement for very large numbers of men and boys, to the extent that it seemed feasible to speak of a popular masculine pleasure-culture of war' (5).

3 In 'The Boys' Own Annual, 1911,' Margaret Atwood connects this kind of reading to the war. The narrator remembers that, as a child, she had discovered old copies of the annuals in the attic. She thinks of her 'half uncle, gassed in the first war and never right since. The books had been his once' (11).

4 George Orwell, in his famous essay 'Boys' Weeklies,' asserted that two highly successful papers, *Gem* and *Magnet* – 'perhaps the most consistently and cheerfully patriotic papers in England' during the First World War (189) – 'are much read by girls' (183). Orwell was writing in the late 1930s, but there is no reason to suppose that girls' interest in such material was a new phenomenon.

5 American periodicals for children, notably *St. Nicholas* and *Youth's Companion*, were also read by Canadian children. For a discussion of war-related materials in *St. Nicholas*, see Andrea McKenzie.

6 Not all editions of *With French* contain the unflattering reference to the Germans. It appears in the first Blackie edition (1915 or 1916), but it does not appear in a later edition (1916). See both editions at www.archive.org.

7 This book also appeared under the title *On the Road to Bagdad: A Story of Townshend's Gallant Advance on the Tigris*.

8 Laut, a journalist and novelist, was well known for her historical novels about the wilderness: *Lords of the North* (1900), for example, is an adventure tale about the fur trade. Educated in Manitoba, Laut moved to the United States and, during the war years, contributed regular articles on war-related topics to *Maclean's*.

9 The Wartime Elections Act, passed in September 1917, denied the vote to citizens naturalized after 31 March 1902 who had been born in 'enemy-alien' countries (which included not just Germany but all the Austro-Hungarian Empire). Only those with a son, grandson, or brother on active duty retained their right to vote. The same act gave the vote to wives, mothers, and sisters of serving soldiers, as well as to women serving in the armed forces.

## 7  But What Can a Girl Do?

1  See also, for example, Eaton's catalogue, Fall/Winter 1914–15: 269.

2  *A Patriotic Schoolgirl* was recommended in the *Ontario Library Review and Book Selection Guide* (February 1919: 76–7); I have found no similar evidence confirming that *The Madcap of the School* was available in Canada during or just after the war.

3  This serial appeared before *Rilla of Ingleside* was published. Given that Montgomery's husband was a Presbyterian minister, it seems likely that she would have seen the *King's Own*. Moreover, she was a contributor to the paper: her story 'The Cake That Prissy Made' (originally published in the *Congregationalist*) appeared in the 3 August 1918 issue of the *King's Own*. Earlier in her career, in 1906, she had contributed several stories to *King's Own* (Russell et al. 79–80). Perhaps some elements from Frame's 'With Chin Up,' such as Sara's decision not to buy a new hat and her organizing of the patriotic entertainment, influenced the development of Montgomery's war novel.

4  In J.G. Sime's short story 'Munitions!' (1919), a young domestic servant leaves her post to work in a Montreal munitions factory. After the constraints of domestic service, she is at first shocked and then liberated by the casual, open speech and behaviour of the other young women workers. This story (which was not for children) suggests that the factory might have been regarded as a morally questionable environment for young women. Sangster also suggests this (165).

5  The VADs were members of the Voluntary Aid Detachments established by the British Red Cross to assist the military in time of war. The VADs worked primarily in hospitals and convalescent homes.

6  The editors obviously prepared the *King's Own* well in advance of publication. In the December 1918 issues, there is no acknowledgment of the end of the war. This article, 'Doing Your Bit,' was borrowed from the *Queen's Gardens*.

7  See Bratton for a discussion of refinement in Victorian girls' fiction (*Impact* 180–1).

## 8  A War for Modern Readers

1  This trend is not exclusively Canadian. For example, British

authors Michael Morpurgo (*War Horse* [1982] and *Private Peaceful* [2003]), Marjorie Darke (*A Rose from Blighty* [1990]), and Theresa Breslin (*Remembrance* [2002]) have written children's books about the war, as have the New Zealand author Ken Catran (*Letters from the Coffin-Trenches* [2002]) and the Australian Kerry Greenwood (*A Different Sort of Real* [2002]). American author Zibby Oneal's *A Long Way to Go* (1990) is set during the First World War; Kate Cary's *Bloodline* includes characters who serve on the Western Front (2005). See MacCallum-Stewart for a discussion of recent British children's books about the First World War.

2 *And in the Morning* is not about a Canadian soldier, although Wilson is a Canadian author. But in telling this story about a Scot in the Highland Light Infantry, Wilson works in many references to Canada. The protagonist, Jim, dreams of emigrating to Canada and living on a prairie farm. Several of the inserted newspaper stories deal with Canada: 'Dominion Troops Eager for the Fight' (61), 'Canada Promises Britain 20 Million Bushels of Wheat' (84), 'Six Die in Canadian Parliament Fire' (111). While training on Salisbury Plain, Jim meets a young Canadian soldier, whose openness and friendliness make Jim even keener on the idea of emigrating to Canada. Jim's sweetheart, Anne, and her father are Canadians, who have come to Scotland to escape labour unrest in Canada.

3 Eliza's experience of war has many parallels with Rilla's. Like Rilla, she loses a beloved brother. Hugo, like Walter Blythe, joins up after the sinking of the *Lusitania* (18). Eliza, like Rilla, has a second brother who goes to the front but ultimately comes home. Eliza also becomes involved in caring for a war baby. Little acknowledges Montgomery's diaries as 'an enormous help in my research for Eliza's journal,' and she recommends *Rilla* for those who 'want to know more about how it felt to be young and living in Canada during that agonizing war' (217). She even writes Montgomery into her novel. Eliza, whose father is a Presbyterian minister in Uxbridge, notes that 'Mrs Macdonald, who wrote *Anne of Green Gables* under her maiden name of Lucy Maud Montgomery, is a great reciter and she works for the Red Cross and knits. She is the Presbyterian minister's wife at Leaskdale which is near Uxbridge, so we see her now and again' (78).

4 This description seems based on the recollections of one survivor, Arthur Raley: 'The only visible sign that the men knew they were

under this terrific fire … was that they all instinctively tucked their
chins into an advanced shoulder as they had so often done when
fighting their way home against a blizzard in some little outpost in
far off Newfoundland' (quoted in 'Newfoundland and the Great
War'). After the battle, the divisional commander was to write
of the Newfoundlanders' effort that 'it was a magnificent display
of trained and disciplined valour, and its assault failed of success
because dead men can advance no further' (quoted in Fairbairn).

5  In the First World War, conscientious objectors could be assigned
non-combatant duties in the military, but a program of alternate
civilian service, which seems to be implied by David's farm work,
did not exist.

6  See Roberts for profiles of four Canadian feminist pacifists: Laura
Hughes, Francis Marion Beynon, Violet McNaughton, and Ger-
trude Richardson. See also the materials about Julia Grace Wales at
'Women Pacifists' at the Library and Archives Canada website.

7  In 'I want to join your club': Letters from Rural Children, 1900–1920,
Norah Lewis includes two anti-war letters. John Wilson, aged thirteen, of Milnerton, Alberta, wrote a prize story entitled 'War,' in
which he declared that 'war is a curse to the world' (218). His arguments against war were largely economic, not moral. Fourteen-
year-old Heidmar Bjornson of Vidar, Manitoba, inveighed against
war's human cost: '… to think of all the sorrow in the homes
where a father or a husband had heard the call to duty, gone to
the battlefield, never to return again, makes many regret that war
had ever existed' (217).

8  The Canadian Letters and Images Project (www.canadianletters.
ca), a collaboration of Vancouver Island University and the University of Western Ontario, offers an on-line archive of hundreds of
letters written by Canadian soldiers.

9  See, for example, Adrienne Kertzer's article 'Anxiety of Trauma,'
which discusses three Canadian books about the First World War
in the context of a larger examination of trauma and its secondary
manifestations in Holocaust fiction.

10  This experience seems akin to that of Robertson Davies's protagonist in Fifth Business: Dunstable Ramsay also has a spiritual awaken-
ing on a First World War battlefield (74).

11  Lawrence is Canadian – he was born in Sault Ste Marie and lives
in British Columbia – but the novel is based 'in part … on family
stories of his grandfather,' an Englishman who served as a gunner

(213). *Lord of the Nutcracker Men* does not deal explicitly with the Canadian experience of war, either on the battlefields or on the home front.

12  Granfield's most recent book is a biography of McCrae: *Remembering John McCrae: Soldier, Doctor, Poet* (2009).

13  Granfield's second book draws heavily on the first: the opening page and a half of text is reproduced verbatim from *In Flanders Fields*.

14  I have borrowed the term 'stylization' from Margaret Higonnet's discussion of how, in children's toys and books, combat is reduced to a kind of game ('War Games' 3–4).

15  See 'Toys and Models.'

16  This illustration is reminiscent of Eric Kennington's *The Conquerors*, in which 'the dead and the living walk together through the shattered, symbol-littered landscape of the western front' (Oliver and Brandon 27).

## Conclusion

1  In part, this was simply the consequence of a delayed revision schedule: 'The seven-year contracts for the books prepared between 1907 and 1911 expired during the years 1914 to 1918, and the Department found it more practical to extend contracts than to attempt preparation of new books' (Parvin 96).

2  See, for example, George M. Wrong's *History of Canada* (1920), Isaac Gammel's *History of Canada* (1922), Duncan McArthur's *History of Canada for High Schools* (1927), Arthur Doughty's *Under the Lily and the Rose: A Short History of Canada for Children* (1928), and W. Stewart Wallace's *A First Book of Canadian History* (1928).

3  See Flothow for a discussion of First World War children's fiction produced in Britain during the inter-war period.

4  From 1923 to 1931, Armistice Day was on the Monday of the week in which November 11 fell; this day was also Thanksgiving. In 1931, a bill was passed in Parliament making November 11 a permanent public holiday, to be renamed Remembrance Day. Thanksgiving was moved to October. See 'Facts on Remembrance Day.'

5  A child soldier is defined as 'any person below the age of 18 who is a member of or attached to government armed forces or any other regular or irregular armed force or armed political group, whether or not an armed conflict exists' ('Child Soldiers' 9).

# Works Cited

## Journals and Other Serial Publications

British Columbia. Superintendent of Education. *Annual Reports on the Public Schools of British Columbia.* Victoria: The Superintendent. 1871/2–1943/4.

*Canadian Forward.* Toronto: Social Democratic Party of Canada, 1916–18.

*Canadian Girl's Annual.* London: Cassell, 1916(?)–32(?).

*Catholic Register.* Toronto: 1893–1942.

*Child's Own.* Toronto: Sunday School Commission of the Church of England in Canada, 1909(?)–20.

*Christian Guardian.* Toronto: Methodist Church of Canada, 1829–1925.

Department of Indian Affairs. *Annual Reports,* 1864–1990. *Library and Archives Canada.* Jan. 2004. Web. 21 Aug. 2009.

Eaton's Catalogue. Toronto: T. Eaton Co., 1884–1976. (For 1918 edition, see 'Canadian Mail Order Catalogues.' *Library and Archives Canada.* 1 May 2007. Web. 25 Oct. 2008.)

Manitoba Department of Education. *Empire Day Annuals.* Winnipeg: Department of Education, 1908(?)-31.

*King's Own.* Toronto: Presbyterian Church of Canada, 1900–25.

*Letter Leaflet.* Toronto: Woman's Auxiliary to the Missionary Society of the Church of England in Canada, 1893(?)–19–.

*New Young Soldier.* Toronto: Sunday School Commission of the Church of England in Canada, 1916–60.

*Ontario Library Review and Book Selection Guide.* Toronto: Provincial Library Service, 1916–47.

*Playmate.* Toronto: William Briggs, 1907–35.

*School.* Toronto: Faculty of Education, University of Toronto, 1912–48.

*School Days.* Vancouver: Vancouver Board of Education, 1919–24(?).

*Sunday School Banner.* Toronto: Wesleyan Book Room, 1869–192?.

*Trail Makers Boys' Annual: An Annual Volume of Stories and Articles for Canadian Boys by Canadian Boys' Men.* Toronto: Musson, 1920–3.

*Victoria: The Public School Magazine.* Victoria: Thos. R. Cusack, 1919–?.

*Western School Journal.* Winnipeg: Western School Journal Company, 1906–38.

*Young Canada: An Illustrated Annual for Boys throughout the English-Speaking World.* Toronto: W. Briggs, 1879(?)–1918(?).

*Young Soldier.* Toronto: The Salvation Army, 1888–2000.

**Books, Articles, and Electronic Sources**

'About Us: Our History.' *The Blue Cross.* Web. 1 Oct. 2007.

Agnew, Kate, and Geoff Fox. *Children at War: From the First World War to the Gulf.* London: Continuum, 2001. Print.

'Agrippa von Nettesheim, Henry Cornelius.' *Encyclopedia Britannica.* 1911 ed. Print.

Allen, Richard. *The Social Passion: Religion and Social Reform in Canada, 1914–28.* Toronto: U of Toronto P, 1973. Print.

Altick, Richard D. *The English Common Reader: A Social History of the Mass Reading Public, 1800–1900.* Chicago: Phoenix-U of Chicago P, 1963. Print.

*Annals of Valour.* Toronto: Ontario Department of Education, 1919. Print.

Atwood, Margaret. 'The Boys' Own Annual, 1911.' *Murder in the Dark: Short Fictions and Prose Poems.* Toronto: Coach House, 1983. 11. Print.

Audoin-Rouzeau, Stéphane. *La Guerre des enfants, 1914–1918: essai d'histoire culturelle.* Paris: Armand Colin, 1993. Print.

Baden-Powell, Lieut.-General Sir Robert S. *The Canadian Boy Scout: A Handbook for Instruction in Good Citizenship.* Toronto: Morang, 1911. Microfiche CIHM 71367.

Baker, Peter Shaw. *Animal War Heroes.* London: A. and C. Black, 1933. Print.

Bedard, Michael. *Redwork.* Toronto: Lester, 1990. Print.

Berger, Carl. 'Introduction.' *Imperialism and Nationalism, 1884–1914: A Conflict in Canadian Thought.* Ed. Carl Berger. Toronto: Copp Clark, 1969. 1–5. Print. Issues in Canadian History.

– *The Sense of Power: Studies in the Ideas of Canadian Imperialism, 1867–1914.* Toronto: U of Toronto P, 1970. Print.

Beveridge, Cathy. *Chaos in Halifax*. Vancouver: Ronsdale, 2004. Print.

Beynon, Francis Marion. *Aleta Dey*. 1919. Peterborough, ON: Broadview, 2000. Print.

Bird, Kym. '"I want riches and position and standing among the other nations of the world": The Creation of National Subjects in Edith Lelean Groves's World War One Drama for Children, *The Wooing of Miss Canada*.' *Proceedings of the 2006 Hawaii International Conference on Education*. 6943–56. 26 June 2007. Web. 8 Sept. 2008.

Bittel, Helen. 'Required Reading for "Revolting Daughters"? The New Girl Fiction of L.T. Meade.' *Nineteenth-Century Studies* 2.2 (2006): 36 pars. Web. 15 Nov. 2008.

Blenkhorn, Deborah. 'Hale, Katherine.' *Encyclopedia of Literature in Canada*. Ed. W.H. New. Toronto: U of Toronto P, 2002. Print.

Blewett, Jean. 'The Little Refugee.' *Heart Stories*. Toronto: Warwick Bros. and Rutter, 1919. 27–9. Print.

Bloomfield, Anne. 'Drill and Dance as Symbols of Imperialism.' *Making Imperial Mentalities*. Ed. J.A. Mangan. Manchester: Manchester UP, 1990. 74–95. Print.

Borthwick, J. Douglas. *Poems and Songs of the South African War: An Anthology from England, Africa, Australia, United States, but Chiefly Canada*. Montreal: n.p., 1901. Print.

Botsford, Charles A. *Joining the Colors*. 1918. Philadelphia: Penn, 1929. Print.

Bratton, J[acqueline] S. 'British Imperialism and the Reproduction of Femininity in Girls' Fiction, 1900–1930.' *Imperialism and Juvenile Literature*. Ed. Jeffrey Richards. Manchester: Manchester UP, 1989. 195–215. Print. Studies in Imperialism.

– *The Impact of Victorian Children's Fiction*. London: Croom Helm, 1981. Print.

Brazil, Angela. *The Madcap of the School*. London: Blackie, [1917?]. Print.

– *A Patriotic Schoolgirl*. London: Blackie, [1918?]. Print.

Brereton, Captain Frederick Sadleir. *On the Road to Bagdad: A Story of the British Expeditionary Force in Mesopotamia*. London: Blackie, 1917. Print.

– *With French at the Front: A Story of the Great European War down to the Battle of the Aisne*. London: Blackie, [1916?]. Print.

Brewster, Hugh. *At Vimy Ridge: Canada's Greatest World War I Victory*. Toronto: Scholastic, 2006. Print.

Bristow, Joseph. *Empire Boys: Adventures in a Man's World*. London: Unwin Hyman, 1991. Print.

British Columbia Department of Education. Correspondence. British Columbia Archives GR-1446; Reel B-2033.

*British Columbia Readers: A Beginner's Reader.* Toronto: Gage, 1915. Print.

Brown, Gerald H. 'Introduction Respecting the Growth of the Movement in Canada to 1912.' *Canadian Boy Scouts: Report of the Contingent at Coronation and at the King's Rally, Windsor Park England, June-July 1911.* [Montreal?]: [1912]. N.pag. Microfiche CIHM 77596.

Brown, Judy. '"How the World Burns": Adults Writing War for Children.' *Canadian Literature* 179 (2003): 39–54. Print.

Bruce, Lorne, and Elizabeth Hanson. 'The Rise of the Public Library in English Canada.' *History of the Book in Canada, Vol. 3: 1918–1980.* Ed. Carole Gerson and Jacques Michon. Toronto: U of Toronto P, 2007. 429–35. Print.

Buitenhuis, Peter. *The Great War of Words: British, American, and Canadian Propaganda and Fiction, 1914–1933.* Vancouver: U of British Columbia P, 1987. Print.

Cadogan, Mary, and Patricia Craig. *Women and Children First: The Fiction of Two World Wars.* London: Victor Gollancz, 1978. Print.

– *You're a Brick, Angela! The Girls' Story, 1839–1985.* London: Victor Gollancz, 1986. Print.

'Canada's Last Known First World War Veteran.' *Veterans Affairs Canada.* 17 July 2007. Web. 29 Jan. 2010.

*Canada's Part in the Present War.* Toronto: Department of Education, 1918. Print.

*The Canada War Book.* Np: National War Savings Committee and the Department of Education of the Province of New Brunswick, 1919. Microfiche CIHM 79476.

'Canadian Posters from the First World War.' *Archives of Ontario.* 29 Jan. 2010. Web. 29 Jan. 2010.

Careless, J.M.S. *Toronto to 1918: An Illustrated History.* Toronto: Lorimer; Ottawa: National Museum of Man, National Museums of Canada, 1984. Print.

Castle, Kathryn. *Britannia's Children: Reading Colonialism through Children's Books and Magazines.* Manchester: Manchester UP, 1996. Print. Studies in Imperialism.

Chalou, Barbara Smith. *Struwwelpeter: Humor or Horror: 160 Years Later.* Lanham, MD: Lexington, 2007. Print.

'Child Soldiers Global Report 2008.' *Coalition to Stop the Use of Child Soldiers and Human Rights Watch.* 20 May 2008. Web. 16 May 2010.

Clark, Penney. 'The Publishing of School Books in English.' Lamonde et al. 335–40.

Clarkson, Stuart, and Daniel O'Leary. 'Books and Periodicals for an Expanding Community.' Lamonde et al. 354–60. Print.

Coates, Donna. 'The Best Soldiers of All: Unsung Heroines in Canadian Women's Great War Fictions.' *Canadian Literature* 151 (Winter 1996): 66–99. Print.

– 'War.' *Encyclopedia of Literature in Canada.* Ed. W.H. New. Toronto: U of Toronto P, 2002. Print.

Cockerill, A.W. *Sons of the Brave: The Story of Boy Soldiers.* London: Leo Cooper; Martin, Secker and Warburg, 1984. Print.

Connor, Ralph [Charles William Gordon]. *The Major.* New York: George Doran, 1917. Print.

– *The Sky Pilot in No Man's Land.* Toronto: McClelland, 1919. Print.

Cook, Ramsay. 'Francis Marion Beynon and the Crisis of Christian Reformism.' *The West and the Nation: Essays in Honour of W.L. Morton.* Ed. Carl Berger and Ramsay Cook. Toronto: McClelland and Stewart, 1976. 187–208. Print.

Cook, Tim. '"He was determined to go": Underage Soldiers in the Canadian Expeditionary Force.' *Histoire sociale / Social History* 41.81 (2008): 41–74. *Project Muse.* Web. 10 Feb. 2010.

Cooper, Jilly. Foreword. *The Animals' War: Animals in Wartime from the First World War to the Present Day.* By Juliet Gardiner. London: Portrait-Piatkus; Imperial War Museum, 2006. 6–9. Print.

Cosslett, Tess. *Talking Animals in British Children's Fiction, 1786–1914.* Aldershot: Ashgate, 2006. Print.

Crerar, Adam. 'Ontario and the Great War.' MacKenzie 230–71.

Davies, Gwendolyn. 'Marshall Saunders and the Urbanization of the Animal.' *Other Selves: Animals in the Canadian Literary Imagination.* Ed. Janice Fiamengo. Ottawa: U of Ottawa P, 2007. 170–83. Print. Reappraisals: Canadian Writers.

Davies, Robertson. *Fifth Business.* 1970. Toronto: Penguin, 1996. Print.

Dawson, Graham. *Soldier Heroes: British Adventure, Empire, and the Imagining of Masculinities.* London: Routledge, 1994. Print.

Debon, Nicolas. *A Brave Soldier.* Vancouver: Groundwood-Douglas and McIntyre, 2002. Print.

Dempsey, L. James. *Warriors of the King: Prairie Indians in World War I.* Regina: Canadian Plains Research Center, U of Regina, 1999. Print.

Desai, Christina M. 'Picture Book Soldiers: Men and Messages.' *Reading Horizons* 42.2 (2001): 77–98. Print.

'Directing America's Generosity to Belgium.' *The Independent* (New York) 82 (April 1915): 148. Print.

Djebabla, Mourad, and Samy Mesli. 'L'étude de la Première Guerre mondiale dans les manuels scolaires ontariens and québécois de l'entre-deux-guerres (1919–1939).' *Bulletin d'histoire politique* 17.2 (Winter 2009): 125–40. Print.

Dominion Institute. 'Annual Remembrance Day Survey: Is Our World War One Heritage and Remembrance Day Fading away?' 10 Nov. 2006. Web. 20 July 2007.

Dunae, Patrick A. 'Boys' Literature and the Idea of Empire, 1870–1914.' *Victorian Studies: A Journal of the Humanities, Arts and Sciences* 24 (1980): 105–21. Print.

– 'The Strathcona Trust and Physical Education in B.C. Public Schools.' *The Homeroom.* 11 Oct. 2008. Web. 28 Aug. 2008.

Dutil, Patrice A. 'Against Isolationism: Napoléon Belcourt, French Canada, and "La grande guerre."' MacKenzie 96–137.

Dyer, Walter A[lden]. *Pierrot, Dog of Belgium.* Ill. Gordon Grant. Toronto: McClelland, Goodchild and Stewart, [1915]. Print.

Edwards, Owen Dudley. 'L.M. Montgomery's *Rilla of Ingleside*: Intention, Inclusion, Implosion.' *Harvesting Thistles: The Textual Garden of L.M. Montgomery: Essays on Her Novels and Journals.* Ed. Mary Henley Rubio. Guelph, ON: Canadian Children's Press, 1994. 126–36. Print.

Egoff, Sheila. *The Republic of Childhood: A Critical Guide to Canadian Children's Literature in English.* Toronto: Oxford UP, 1975. Print.

Egoff, Sheila, and Judith Saltman. *The New Republic of Childhood: A Critical Guide to Canadian Children's Literature in English.* Toronto: Oxford UP, 1990. Print.

Ellis, Deborah. *Three Wishes: Palestinian and Israeli Children Speak.* Toronto: Groundwood-Douglas and McIntyre, 2004. Print.

Emerson, Alice B. *Ruth Fielding at the War Front; or, The Hunt for the Lost Soldier.* New York: Cupples and Leon, 1918. Print.

– *Ruth Fielding in the Red Cross: or, Doing Her Best for Uncle Sam.* New York: Cupples and Leon, 1918. Print.

Epperly, Elizabeth R. *The Fragrance of Sweet-Grass: L.M. Montgomery's Heroines and the Pursuit of Romance.* Toronto: U of Toronto P, 1992. Print.

Evans, Suzanne. *Mothers of Heroes, Mothers of Martyrs: World War I and the Politics of Grief.* Montreal and Kingston: McGill-Queen's UP, 2007. Print.

'Facts on Remembrance Day.' Teachers' Resources. *Veterans Affairs Canada.* 21 Oct. 1991. Web. 27 Jan. 2010.

Fairbairn, Bill. 'Memoirs and Pilgrimages: On Liberation's Trail.' *Legion Magazine* Nov. 1997. Web. 29 Jan. 2010.

Fass, Paula S. *Children of a New World: Society, Culture, and Globalization.* New York: New York UP, 2007. Print.

Fellman, Anita Clair. *Little House, Long Shadow: Laura Ingalls Wilder's Impact on American Culture.* Columbia: U of Missouri P, 2008. Print.

Ferguson, Niall. *The Pity of War: Explaining World War I.* New York: Basic, 1998. Print.

Flothow, Dorothea. 'Popular Children's Literature and the Memory of the First World War, 1919–1939.' *The Lion and the Unicorn* 31.2 (2007): 147–61. *Project Muse.* Web. 29 Jan. 2010.

Foster, Shirley, and Judy Simons. *What Katy Read: Feminist Re-Readings of 'Classic' Stories for Girls.* Iowa City: U of Iowa P, 1995. Print.

Fox, Carol. 'What the Children's Literature of War Is Telling the Children.' *Reading* 33.3 (1999): 126–31. Print.

'Front Lines.' *National Film Board.* 26 Jan. 2010. Web. 29 Jan. 2010.

Gaffen, Fred. *Cross-border Warriors: Canadians in American Forces, Americans in Canadian Forces: From the Civil War to the Gulf.* Toronto: Dundurn, 1995. Print.

Galway, Elizabeth. 'Fact, Fiction, and the Tradition of Historical Narratives in Nineteenth-Century Canadian Children's Literature.' *Canadian Children's Literature* 102 [27.2] (2001): 20–32. Print.

Gardiner, Juliet. *The Animals' War: Animals in Wartime from the First World War to the Present Day.* London: Portrait-Piatkus; Imperial War Museum, 2006. Print.

Garvin, John W., ed. *Canadian Poems of the Great War.* Toronto: McClelland and Stewart, 1918. Print.

Gauch, Patricia Lee. 'Why Writers Write of War: Looking into the Eye of Historical Fiction.' *ALAN Review* 21.1 (Fall 1993): 12–16. Print.

'Generals Die in Bed.' *Annick Press Catalog.* Web. 19 Sept. 2009.

'German Atrocities.' Union Government Publicity Bureau, Ottawa, [1917]. N.pag. Microfiche CIHM 84424.

Gerson, Carole. '"Dragged at Anne's Chariot Wheels": L.M. Montgomery and the Sequels to *Anne of Green Gables.*' *Papers of the Bibliographic Society of Canada* 35.2 (1997): 143–60. Web. 15 Feb. 2010.

Goldberg, Susan. *Times of War and Peace: Dealing with Kids' Concerns.* Toronto: Annick, 1991. Print.

Goodenough, Elizabeth, and Andrea Immel, eds. *Under Fire: Childhood in the Shadow of War.* Detroit: Wayne State UP, 2008. Print. Land-scapes of Childhood.

Granatstein, J.L. 'Conscription in the Great War.' MacKenzie 62–75.

Granfield, Linda. 'In Flanders Fields.' *Canadian Children's Literature* 84 [22.4] (1996): 84–7. Print.

– *In Flanders Fields: The Story of the Poem by John McCrae.* Ill. Janet Wilson. Toronto: Lester, 1995. Print

– *Remembering John McCrae: Soldier, Doctor, Poet.* Toronto: Scholastic, 2009. Print.

– *The Unknown Soldier.* Toronto: Northwinds-Scholastic: 2008. Print.

– *Where Poppies Grow: A World War I Companion.* Toronto: Stoddart, 2001. Print.

Green, Martin. *Seven Types of Adventure Tale: An Etiology of a Major Genre.* University Park: Pennsylvania State UP, 1991. Print.

Groves, Edith Lelean. *Britannia.* Toronto: McClelland, Goodchild and Stewart, 1917. Microfiche CIHM 74282. All Canadian Entertainment series.

– *Canada Calls: A Timely Patriotic Play.* Toronto: McClelland, Goodchild and Stewart, 1918. Microfiche CIHM 74283. All Canadian Entertainment series.

– *Canada, Our Homeland.* Toronto: Briggs, 1900. Microfiche CIHM 27516. Canadian Drills and Exercises.

– *Fancy Flag Drill, Rule Britannia.* Toronto: McClelland, Goodchild and Stewart, 1917. Microfiche CIHM 74328. All Canadian Entertainment series.

– *Fancy Flag Drill, We'll Fight for the Grand Old Flag.* Toronto: McClelland, Goodchild and Stewart, 1917. Microfiche CIHM 74331. All Canadian Entertainment series.

– *A Patriotic Auction.* Toronto: McClelland, Goodchild and Stewart, 1918. Microfiche CIHM 74285. All Canadian Entertainment series.

– *Patriotic Scarf Drill.* Toronto: Briggs, 1901. Microfiche CIHM 74332. Canadian Drills and Exercises.

– *Primary Pieces.* Toronto: McClelland, Goodchild and Stewart, 1918. Microfiche CIHM 76938. All Canadian Entertainment series.

– *Saluting the Canadian Flag.* Toronto: McClelland, Goodchild and Stewart, 1917. Microfiche CIHM 74837. All Canadian Entertainment series.

– *The Soldiers of the Soil and the Farmerettes: A Dramatic Drill.* Toronto: McClelland, Goodchild and Stewart, 1918. Microfiche CIHM 74334. All Canadian Entertainment series.

– *A Spring Fantasy*. Toronto: McClelland, Goodchild and Stewart, 1918. Microfiche CIHM 74288. All Canadian Entertainment series.

– *The War on the Western Front: A Patriotic Play*. Toronto: Briggs, 1916. Microfiche CIHM 74289.

– *The Wooing of Miss Canada: A Play*. Toronto: McClelland, Goodchild and Stewart, 1917. Microfiche CIHM 74281. All Canadian Entertainment series.

Gwyn, Sandra. *Tapestry of War: A Private View of Canadians in the Great War*. Toronto: Harper-Collins, 1992. Print.

Hale, Katherine [Amelia Warnock Garvin]. *Grey Knitting and Other Poems*. Toronto: Briggs, 1914. Print.

Harper, Stephen. 'PM at the Lighting of the Christmas Lights across Canada, 4 December 2008.' *Media Centre, Office of the Prime Minister*. Web. 8 Dec. 2008.

Harris, Eiran. Archivist emeritus, Jewish Public Library of Montreal. Letter to the author. 7 Oct. 2008.

Haworth-Attard, Barbara. *Flying Geese*. Toronto: HarperCollins, 2001. Print.

Hayes, Clair W. *The Boy Allies at Liège; or, Through Lines of Steel*. New York: A.L. Burt, 1915. Print.

– *The Boy Allies in Great Peril; or, With the Italian Army in the Alps*. New York: A.L. Burt, 1916. Print.

– *The Boy Allies in the Trenches; or, Midst Shot and Shell along the Aisne*. New York: A.L. Burt, 1915. Print.

– *The Boy Allies on the Firing Line; or, Twelve Days Battle along the Marne*. New York, 1915. *Project Gutenberg*. 9 July 2004. Project Gutenberg Literary Archive Foundation. Web. 29 Oct. 2008.

– *The Boy Allies under the Stars and Stripes*. New York: A.L. Burt, n.d. [1918]. Print.

– *The Boy Allies with Haig in Flanders; or, The Fighting Canadians of Vimy Ridge*. New York, 1918. *Project Gutenberg*. 1 July 2004. Project Gutenberg Literary Archive Foundation. Web. 20 Oct. 2008.

Heathorn, Stephen. 'Representations of War and Martial Heroes in English Elementary School Reading.' Marten 103–15.

Heffernan, Colleen. *A Kind of Courage*. Victoria: Orca, 2005. Print.

Higonnet, Margaret R. 'War Games.' *The Lion and the Unicorn* 22.1 (1998): 1–17. *Project Muse*. Web. 29 Jan. 2010.

– 'War Toys: Breaking and Remaking in Great War Narratives.' *The Lion and the Unicorn* 31.2 (2007): 116–31. *Project Muse*. Web. 29 Jan. 2010.

Higonnet, Margaret R., and Barbara Rosen, eds. *Children's Literature* 15 (1987). Annual of the Modern Language Association's Division on Children's Literature and the Children's Literature Association. New Haven: Yale UP, 1987. Print.

Hobson, J.A. [John Atkinson]. *The Psychology of Jingoism.* London: Grant Richards, 1901. *Internet Archive.* Web. 24 Jan. 2010.

Hoffmann, Heinrich. *The English Struwwelpeter; or, Pretty Stories and Funny Pictures.* [London]: Routledge and Sons, [1909]. Print.

'Hoover's Legacy in Belgium.' Remembering Herbert Hoover. *U.S. Embassy Brussels Office of Public Diplomacy.* Web. 26 June 2007.

Hopkins, J. Castell. 'The Origin and History of Empire Day.' [Toronto?]: n.p., 1910. Microfiche CIHM 75098.

Horne, John, and Alan Kramer. *German Atrocities, 1914: A History of Denial.* New Haven: Yale UP, 2001. Print.

Hou, Charles, and Cynthia Hou. *Great Canadian Political Cartoons, 1915–1945.* Vancouver: Moody's Lookout, 2002. Print.

Ibbotson, John. 'Parallel between Vimy Ridge, Afghanistan Only Goes So Far.' *Globe and Mail,* 11 July 2006, national ed.: A4. Print.

Innes, Stephanie, and Harry Endrulat. *A Bear in War.* Ill. Brian Deines. Toronto: Key Porter Kids, 2008. Print.

Itani, Frances. 'Hear, Overhear, Observe, Remember: A Dialogue with Frances Itani.' Interview with Susan Fisher. *Canadian Literature* 183 (2004): 40–56. Print.

Janfelt, Monika. 'War in the Twentieth Century.' *Encyclopedia of Children and Childhood in History and Society.* Ed. Paula S. Fass. 3 vols. New York: Macmillan Reference, 2004. Print.

Johnson, Deidre. 'From Paragraphs to Pages: The Writing and Development of the Stratemeyer Syndicate Series.' *Rediscovering Nancy Drew.* Ed. Carolyn Stewart Dyer and Nancy Tillman Romalov. Iowa City: U of Iowa P, 1995. 29–40. Print.

Johnson, Eric J. 'Under Ideological Fire: Illustrated Wartime Propaganda for Children.' Goodenough and Immel 59–76.

Jones, Lynne. *Then They Started Shooting: Growing Up in Wartime Bosnia.* Cambridge, MA: Harvard UP, 2004. Print.

Kaminski, Winfred. 'War and Peace in Recent German Children's Literature.' Trans. J.D. Stahl. *Children's Literature* 15 (1987). Annual of the Modern Language Association's Division on Children's Literature and the Children's Literature Association. New Haven: Yale UP, 1987. 55–66. Print.

Kelly, M.F. 'We'll Never Let the Old Flag Fall.' 1915. Digital Collections: Music. *National Library of Australia*. http://nla.gov.au/nla. mus-an6054106. Web. 22 Jan. 2010.

Kelly, R., Gordon. *Mother Was a Lady: Self and Society in Selected American Children's Periodicals, 1865–1890*. Westport, CT: Greenwood, 1974. Print. Contributions in American Studies 12.

Kertzer, Adrienne. 'The Anxiety of Trauma in Children's War Fiction.' Goodenough and Immel 207–20.

Keshen, Jeffrey A. *Propaganda and Censorship during Canada's Great War*. Edmonton: U of Alberta P, 1996. Print.

'Key Economic Events.' '1914–1918 World War I: Effects on the Canadian Economy.' *Government of Canada*. Web. 31 July 2007.

Kidd, Kenneth. '*A* is for Auschwitz: Psychoanalysis, Trauma Theory, and the "Children's Literature of Atrocity."' Goodenough and Immel 161–84.

Kilpatrick, T.B. 'The War and the Christian Church.' Report for the General Assembly's Commission on the War and the Spiritual Life of the Church. Toronto: Presbyterian Church in Canada, 1917. Microfiche CIHM 86529.

Kingston, Brian [Percy Longhurst]. *Sons of the Empire! A Complete Adventure Story*. London: Fleetway, [1917?]. Print. Boys' Friend Library.

Kirk, Dylan. *Canada at War*. Calgary: Weigl, 2004. Print.

Kirk, Heather. 'No Home or Native Land: How Canadian History Got Left out of Recent Historical Fiction for Children by Canadians.' *Canadian Children's Literature* 83 [22.3] (1996): 8–25. Print.

Kitzan, Laurence. *Victorian Writers and the Image of Empire: The Rose-Colored Vision*. Westport, CT: Greenwood, 2001. Print.

Lackenbauer, P. Whitney, and Katharine McGowan. 'Competing Loyalties in a Complex Community: Enlisting the Six Nations in the Canadian Expeditionary Force, 1914–1917.' *Aboriginal Peoples and the Canadian Military: Historical Perspectives*. Ed. P. Whitney Lackenbauer and Craig Leslie Mantle. Winnipeg: Canadian Defence Academy Press, 2007. 89–115. Print.

Lamonde, Yvan, Patricia Lockhart Fleming, and Fiona A. Black, eds. *History of the Book in Canada. Vol. 2: 1840–1918*. Toronto: U of Toronto P, 2005. Print.

Lawrence, Iain. *Lord of the Nutcracker Men*. New York: Delacorte-Random, 2001. Print.

Lawson, Julie. *No Safe Harbour: The Halifax Explosion Diary of Charlotte Blackburn*. Toronto: Scholastic, 2006. Print. Dear Canada.

Leach, Norman. *Passchendaele: Canada's Triumph and Tragedy on the*

*Fields of Flanders. An Illustrated History.* Foreword Paul Gross. Regina: Coteau, 2008. Print.

Lerer, Seth. *Children's Literature: A Reader's History from Aesop to Harry Potter.* Chicago: U of Chicago P, 2008. Print.

'Letter from the Editor.' 'About Us.' *Our Canadian Girl.* Penguin Group Canada, 2009. Web. 16 Jan. 2010.

Levstik, Linda S. 'The Relationship between Historical Response and Narrative in a Sixth-Grade Classroom.' *Theory and Research in Social Education* 14.1 (1986): 1–19. Print.

Levstik, Linda S., and Keith C. Barton. *Doing History: Investigating with Children in Elementary and Middle Schools.* 3rd ed. Mahwah, NJ: Lawrence Erlbaum, 2005. Print.

Lewis, Norah. '"Isn't this a terrible war?": The Attitudes of Children to Two World Wars.' *Historical Studies in Education* 7.2 (1995): 193–215. Print.

– ed. *'I want to join your club': Letters from Rural Children, 1900–1920.* Waterloo, ON: Wilfrid Laurier UP, 1996. Print. Life Writing Series 2.

Lewis, Susan Ingalls. 'Girls to the Rescue: The Impact of World War I on Girls' Series Books.' *Dime Novel Round-up* 77.4 (August 2008): 131–40. Print.

Litt, Paul. 'Canada Invaded! The Great War, Mass Culture, and Canadian Cultural Nationalism.' MacKenzie 323–49.

Little, Jean. *Brothers Far from Home: The World War I Diary of Eliza Bates.* Markham, ON: Scholastic, 2003. Print. Dear Canada.

– *If I Die before I Wake: The Flu Epidemic Diary of Fiona Macgregor.* Toronto: Scholastic, 2007. Print. Dear Canada.

*Little Folks Alphabet.* Toronto: Canada Games Co., 1919. Microfiche CIHM 77325.

Livesey, Robert, and A.G. Smith. *The Great War.* Ill. A.G. Smith. Toronto: Fitzhenry and Whiteside, 2006. Print. Discovering Canada.

Lowe, Matt. Archivist, Canadian Baptist Archives, McMaster Divinity College. Message to the author. 28 Oct. 2008. E-mail.

Lowrey, Harold C. *Young Canada Boys with the S.O.S. on the Frontier.* Toronto: Thomas Allen, 1918. Print.

Lucas, E.V. *Swollen-headed William: Painful Stories and Funny Pictures after the German!* 4th ed. London: Methuen; Toronto: Musson, 1914. Microfiche CIHM 84229.

Lyman, Edward Branch. *Me'ow Jones, Belgian Refugee Cat: His Own True Tale.* New York: George Doran and Company, 1917. Print.

Lynne, Hobb. 'My Daddy's Gone to War (Has Your Daddy Gone Too?).' Toronto: Hawkes and Harris, 1916. Print.

MacCallum-Stewart, Esther. '"If they ask us why we died": Children's Literature and the First World War, 1970–2005.' *The Lion and the Unicorn* 31 (2007): 176–88. *Project Muse*. Web. 29 Jan. 2010.

MacDonald, Laura M. *Curse of the Narrows: The Halifax Explosion, 1917.* Toronto: HarperCollins, 2005. Print.

MacKenzie, David, ed. *Canada and the First World War: Essays in Honour of Robert Craig Brown.* Toronto: U of Toronto P, 2005. Print.

MacKenzie, John M. *Propaganda and Empire: The Manipulation of British Public Opinion, 1880–1960.* Manchester: Manchester UP, 1984. Print.

Macksoud, Mona. *Helping Children Cope with the Stresses of War: A Manual for Parents and Teachers.* 1993. New York: UNICEF, 2000. Print.

MacLeod, Anne Scott. *American Childhood: Essays on Children's Literature of the Nineteenth and Twentieth Centuries.* Athens, GA: U of Georgia P, 1994. Print.

– 'Writing Backward: Modern Models in Historical Fiction.' *Horn Book* 74.1 (1998): 26–33. *Academic Search Premier*. Web. 1 Aug. 2006.

MacLeod, Elizabeth. *Kids Book of Canada at War.* Ill. John Mantha. Toronto: Kids Can, 2007. Print.

MacMurchy, Helen. Introduction. *Everyday Children: A Book of Poems.* By Edith Lelean Groves. Toronto: Committee in Charge of the Edith L. Groves Memorial Fund for Underprivileged Children, 1932. 12–27. Print.

Major, Kevin. *No Man's Land.* Toronto: Doubleday, 1995. Print.

Mangan, J.A. 'Noble Specimens of Manhood: Schoolboy Literature and the Creation of a Colonial Chivalric Code.' *Imperialism and Juvenile Literature.* Ed. Jeffrey Richards. Manchester: Manchester UP, 1989. 173–94. Print. Studies in Imperialism.

Manley, Morris. 'Good Luck to the Boys of the Allies.' Toronto: Morris Manley, 1915. Print.

Maroney, Paul. '"The Great Adventure": The Context and Ideology of Recruiting in Ontario, 1914–17.' *Canadian Historical Review* 77.1 (1996): 62–98. Print.

Marshall, Dominique. 'Humanitarian Sympathy for Children in Times of War and the History of Children's Rights, 1919–1959.' Marten 184–99.

Marten, James, ed. *Children and War: A Historical Anthology.* New York: New York UP, 2002. Print.

Maw, Martin. Archivist, Oxford University Press. Message to the author. 19 July 2007. E-mail.

McArthur, Duncan A. *History of Canada for High Schools.* Toronto: Gage, 1927. Print.

McGrath, Leslie. 'Print for Young Readers.' Lamonde et al. 401–8.

McKay, Sharon E. *Charlie Wilcox.* Toronto: Stoddart, 2000. Print.

– *Charlie Wilcox's Great War.* Toronto: Penguin, 2003. Print.

– *Penelope: An Irish Penny.* Toronto: Penguin, 2003. Print. Our Canadian Girl.

McKenzie, Andrea. 'The Children's Crusade: American Children Writing War.' *The Lion and the Unicorn* 31 (2007): 87–102. *Project Muse.* Web. 29 Jan. 2010.

McKinnon, Ruth. 'How Can the Ontario High School Boy by Working on a Farm This Summer Help Himself, the Farmer, and the Empire.' B. Wilson 148–9.

Meisel, Martin. *Realizations: Narrative, Pictorial, and Theatrical Arts in Nineteenth-Century England.* Princeton: Princeton UP, 1983. Print.

Merivale, J[oy]. *The Fallen Flyer; or, Camping in Canada.* London: Society for Promoting Christian Knowledge; Toronto: Macmillan, 1919. Print.

Merton, Madge, and the editor. 'Our Children and Their Reading.' *Canadian Magazine,* January 1896: 282–7. Print.

Miller, Carman. *Painting the Map Red: Canada and the South African War, 1899–1902.* Montreal: Canadian War Museum and McGill-Queen's UP, 1993. Print. Canadian War Museum Historical Publication 28.

Miller, Ian Hugh Maclean. *Our Glory and Our Grief: Torontonians and the Great War.* Toronto: U of Toronto P, 2002. Print.

Minifie, James M. *Homesteader: A Prairie Boyhood Recalled.* Toronto: Macmillan, 1972. Print.

Montgomery, Lucy Maud. *Anne of Green Gables.* 1908. Toronto: Bantam: Skylark, 1976. Print.

– *Rainbow Valley.* Toronto: McClelland and Stewart, 1919. Print.

– *Rilla of Ingleside.* 1920. Toronto: Seal-McClelland and Stewart, 1996. Print.

Morton, Desmond. *Fight or Pay: Soldiers' Families in the Great War.* Vancouver: U of British Columbia P, 2004. Print. Studies in Canadian Military History.

– '"Kicking and Complaining": Demobilization Riots in the Canadian Expeditionary Force, 1918–19.' *Canadian Historical Review* 61.3 (1980): 334–60. *Canadian Reference Centre.* Web. 4 Jan. 2009.

– 'Supporting Soldiers' Families: Separation Allowance, Assigned Pay, and the Unexpected.' MacKenzie 194–229.

– *When Your Number's Up: The Canadian Soldier in the First World War.* Toronto: Random House, 1993. Print.

Moses, Lisa F., Jerry Aldridge, Anarella Cellitti, and Gwenyth Mc-Corquodale. *Children's Fears of War and Terrorism: A Resource for Teachers and Parents.* Olney, MD: Association for Childhood Education International, 2003. Print.

Moss, Mark. *Manliness and Militarism: Educating Young Boys in Ontario for War.* Toronto: Oxford UP, 2001. Print. Canadian Social History.

Mosse, George L. *Fallen Soldiers: Reshaping the Memory of the World Wars.* New York: Oxford UP, 1990. Print.

Moyles, R.G. [R. Gordon]. *The Blood and Fire in Canada: A History of the Salvation Army in the Dominion, 1882–1976.* Toronto: Peter Martin, 1977. Print.

– 'Young Canada: An Index to Canadian Materials in Major British and American Juvenile Periodicals, 1870–1950.' *Canadian Children's Literature* 78 (1995): 6–63. Print.

Moyles, R.G., and Doug Owram. *Imperial Dreams and Colonial Realities: British Views of Canada, 1880–1914.* Toronto: U of Toronto P, 1988. Print.

Myers, Mitzi. 'Storying War: A Capsule Overview.' *The Lion and the Unicorn* 24 (2000): 327–36. *Project Muse.* Web. 29 Jan. 2010.

National Association of School Psychologists. 'Children and Fear of War and Terrorism: Tips for Parents and Teachers.' 2002. Web. 29 Jan. 2010.

*New Canadian Readers: Book IV.* 20th Century ed. Toronto: Educational Book Company, 1900. Print.

'Newfoundland and the Great War: The Somme, 1916.' *Newfoundland and Labrador Heritage Web Project.* June 2008. Web. 29 Jan. 2010.

Nodelman, Perry, and Mavis Reimer. *The Pleasures of Children's Literature.* 3rd ed. Boston: Allyn and Bacon, 2003. Print.

Nora, Pierre. 'Between Memory and History: Les Lieux de Mémoire.' *Representations* 26. Special issue: Memory and Counter-Memory (Spring 1989): 7–12. *JSTOR.* Web. 9 Jan. 2009.

Oliver, Dean, and Laura Brandon. *Canvas of War: Painting the Canadian Experience: 1914–1945.* Vancouver: Douglas and McIntyre; Ottawa: Canadian War Museum and the Canadian Museum of Civilization, 2000. Print.

*Ontario Readers: Third Book.* Toronto: T. Eaton, 1909. Print.

Orwell, George. 'Boys' Weeklies.' 1939. *Inside the Whale and Other Essays.* Harmondsworth, UK: Penguin, 1957. 175–203. Print.

Paris, Michael. *Over the Top: The Great War and Juvenile Literature in Britain.* Westport, CT: Praeger, 2004. Print.

Parker, George L. 'Publishing Industry.' *Encyclopedia of Literature in Canada.* Ed. W.H. New. Toronto: U of Toronto P, 2002. 905–14. Print.

Parrott, Edward. *The Children's Story of the War.* Toronto: Nelson, 1915–19. Microfiche CIHM 79925–79974.

Parvin, Viola. *Authorization of Textbooks for the Schools of Ontario, 1846–1958.* Toronto: U of Toronto P; Canadian Textbook Publishers' Institute, 1964. Print.

Patterson, Heather. *A Poppy Is to Remember.* Ill. Ron Lightburn. Markham, ON: North Winds-Scholastic, 2004. Print.

Patteson, Susanna Louise. *Pussy Meow: The Autobiography of a Cat.* Philadelphia: George W. Jacobs, 1901. Print.

Peritz, Ingrid. 'One Dashing Quebecker Signs On to Play Another.' *Globe and Mail,* 13 July 2006, national ed.: A1+. Print.

Perkins, Lucy Fitch. *The Belgian Twins.* Boston: Houghton Mifflin-Riverside Press, 1917. Print.

– *The French Twins.* Boston: Houghton Mifflin, 1918. Print.

Phillipps-Wolley, Clive. 'A Short Record of the Work of the Imperial Order of the Daughters of the Empire since the Declaration of War.' [Victoria, BC]: Colonist Presses, [1915]. Microfiche CIHM 9–91023.

Phillips, C.E. *The Development of Education in Canada.* Toronto: Gage, 1957. Print.

'Piper Findlater VC.' 5 Oct. 2003. *Findlater.* Web. 14 Aug. 2007.

Power, F.J. Editor, *Canadian Messenger of the Sacred Heart.* Message to the author. 22 July 2009. E-mail.

Prost, Antoine, and Jay Winter. *Penser la Grande Guerre: un essai d'historiographie.* Paris: Seuil, 2004. Print. L'histoire en débats.

*Raise the Flag and Other Patriotic Canadian Songs and Poems.* Toronto: Rose, 1891. *Ontario Time Machine.* 2008. Web. 21 August 2009.

Raynsford, William, and Jeannette Raynsford. *Silent Casualties: Veterans' Families in the Aftermath of the Great War.* Madoc: Merribrae, 1986. Print.

Read, Daphne, ed. *The Great War and Canadian Society: An Oral History.* Toronto: New Hogtown, 1978. Print.

'Report of the Sunday School Commission.' The General Synod of the

Church of England in the Dominion of Canada. *Journal of Proceedings of the Eighth Session, Sept. 11–21 1918.* Toronto, 1919. Print.

Reynolds, Kimberley. *Girls Only? Gender and Popular Children's Fiction in Britain, 1880–1910.* New York: Harvester Wheatsheaf, 1990. Print.

Roberts, Barbara. "'Why do women do nothing to end the war?'": Canadian Feminist-Pacifists and the Great War.' Ottawa: CRIAW/ICREF, 1985. Print. CRIAW Papers 13.

Robinson, Laura. 'Bosom Friends: Lesbian Desire in L.M. Montgomery's Anne Books.' *Canadian Literature* 180 (2004): 12–28. Print.

Rochman, Hazel. 'What Makes a Good Holocaust Book? Beyond Oral History.' *Horn Book,* Sept./Oct. 2006: 547–51. Print.

Rubio, Mary, and Elizabeth Waterston, eds. *The Selected Journals of L.M. Montgomery.* Vols. 1–5. Toronto: Oxford UP, 1985–2004. Print.

Russell, Ruth Weber, Delbert Wayne Russell, and Rea Wilmshurst. *Lucy Maud Montgomery: A Preliminary Bibliography.* Waterloo, ON: U of Waterloo Library, 1986. Print.

Sangster, Joan. 'Mobilizing Women for War.' MacKenzie 157–93.

Saunders, Doug. 'From Symbol of Despair to Source of Inspiration.' *Globe and Mail,* 10 April 2007: A5. Print.

Saunders, Marshall. *Beautiful Joe: An Autobiography.* 1894. Halifax: Formac, 2001. Print.

– *The Wandering Dog: Adventures of a Fox-Terrier.* Toronto: Copp, Clark, 1916. Print.

Semple, Neil. *The Lord's Dominion: The History of Canadian Methodism.* Montreal and Kingston: McGill-Queen's UP, 1996. Print. McGill-Queen's Studies in the History of Religion 21.

Sheehan, Nancy. 'The IODE, the Schools and World War I.' *History of Education Review* 13.1 (1984): 29–44. Print.

Sime, J.G. 'Munitions!' 1919. *A New Anthology of Canadian Literature in English.* Ed. Donna Bennett and Russell Brown. Toronto: Oxford UP, 2002. 218–22. Print.

Simmons, Dale. 'Finding the Facts in Historical Fiction.' *Archivist* 121 (2003): 14–18. Print.

Sinclair, Bertrand W. *Burned Bridges.* 1919. New York: Grosset and Dunlap, 1920. Print.

Slade, Arthur. *Megiddo's Shadow.* Toronto: HarperTrophyCanada-HarperCollins, 2006. Print.

Smith, Lillian. 'A List of Books for Boys and Girls.' *Ontario Library Review and Book Selection Guide* 2.1 (August 1917): 11–33. Print.

Socknat, Thomas P. 'Canada's Liberal Pacifists and the Great War.'
    *Readings in Canadian History.* Ed. R. Douglas Francis and Donald
    B. Smith. Vol. 2. 4th ed. Toronto: Harcourt Brace Canada, 1994.
    335–50. Print.
– *Witness against War: Pacifism in Canada, 1900–1945.* Toronto: U of
    Toronto P, 1987. Print.
Spadoni, Carl, and Judy Donnelly. *Bibliography of McClelland and Stewart
    Imprints, 1909–1985: A Publisher's Legacy.* Toronto: ECW Press, 1994.
    Print.
Spence, Nellie. *The Schoolboy in the War.* Toronto: Musson, 1919. Print.
Stamp, Robert. 'Empire Day in the Schools of Ontario: The Training
    of Young Imperialists.' *Journal of Canadian Studies* 8.3 (1973): 33–42.
    Print.
– *The Schools of Ontario, 1876–1976.* Toronto: U of Toronto P, 1982.
    Print. Ontario Historical Studies.
Stanley, Timothy J. 'White Supremacy and the Rhetoric of Educa-
    tional Indoctrination: A Canadian Case Study.' *Children, Teachers and
    Schools in the History of British Columbia.* 2nd ed. Ed. Jean Barman and
    Mona Gleason. Calgary: Detselig, 2003. 113–31. Print.
*Star War Album: For Freedom and Right.* Montreal: Montreal Daily Star /
    Family Herald and Weekly Star, [1918?]. Microfiche CIHM 78818.
Stevenson, A[ndrew.] 'The Teacher as a Missionary of Peace.' [Phila-
    delphia?: s.n., 1904?]. Microfiche CIHM 99706.
Stirling, Helen. *A Soldier of the King: A True Story of a Young Canadian
    Hero.* Toronto: Oxford UP, [1915?]. Print.
Summerby, Janice. *Native Soldiers, Foreign Battlefields.* Ottawa: Veterans
    Affairs Canada, 2005. Print. Remembrance series.
Sutherland, Neil. *Growing Up: Childhood in English Canada from the
    Great War to the Age of Television.* Toronto: U of Toronto P, 1997.
    Print.
*Syllabus of Physical Exercises for Schools.* Executive Council, Strathcona
    Trust. Toronto: Copp Clark, 1911. Print.
Tatar, Maria. '"Appointed Journeys": Growing Up with War Stories.'
    Goodenough and Immel 237–50.
Thompson, John Herd. 'Canada and the "Third British Empire,"
    1901–1939.' *Canada and the British Empire.* Ed. Phillip Buckner. Ox-
    ford: Oxford UP, 2008. 87–106. Print. Oxford History of the British
    Empire Companion series.
*The Thrift Campaign in the Schools of Ontario, with a Brief Sketch of What
    Ontario Has Done in the War.* [Toronto]: Department of Education of
    Ontario, 1919. Print.

Tiessen, Hildi Froese, and Paul Gerard Tiessen, eds. *After Green Gables: L.M. Montgomery's Letters to Ephraim Weber, 1916–1941*. Toronto: U of Toronto P, 2006. Print.

Tomkins, George S. *A Common Countenance: Stability and Change in the Canadian Curriculum*. Scarborough, ON: Prentice-Hall, 1986. Print.

Tooth, John (Coordinator / Copyright Consultant, Instructional Resources Unit, Educational Resources Branch, Manitoba Education, Citizenship and Youth). 'Re: Researcher in Winnipeg.' Message to the author. 16 Nov. 2007. E-mail.

'Toys and Models.' 'Objects and Photos of the First World War: Art and Culture,' *Canada and the First World War*. Online Exhibitions, Canadian War Museum. 20 June 2008. Web. 22 Jan. 2009.

Trent, Martha. *Marieken de Bruin: Somewhere in Belgium*. New York: Barse and Hopkins, 1918. Print.

– *Phoebe Marshall: Somewhere in Canada*. New York: Barse and Hopkins, 1919. Print.

– *Valerie Duval: Somewhere in France*. New York: Barse and Hopkins, 1918. Print.

Turner, James. *Reckoning with the Beast: Animals, Pain, and Humanity in the Victorian Mind*. Baltimore: Johns Hopkins UP, 1980. Print.

Valpy, Michael. 'Invisible No More.' *Globe and Mail*, 21 Nov. 2009: F1+. Print.

Van Brummelen, Harro. 'Shifting Perspectives: Early British Columbia Textbooks from 1872 to 1925.' *BC Studies* 60 (Winter 1983–4): 3–27. Print.

Vance, Jonathan F. *Death So Noble*. Vancouver: U of British Columbia P, 1997. Print.

– 'The Soldier as Novelist: Literature, History and the Great War.' *Canadian Literature* 179 (Winter 2003): 22–37. Print.

Vandercook, Margaret. *The Red Cross Girls in the British Trenches*. Philadelphia: John C. Winston, 1916. Print.

– *The Red Cross Girls on the French Firing Line*. Philadelphia: John C. Winston, 1916. Print.

– *The Red Cross Girls under the Stars and Stripes*. Philadelphia: John C. Winston, 1917. Print.

– *The Red Cross Girls with the Russian Army*. Philadelphia: John C. Winston, 1916. *Project Gutenberg*. 2007. Project Gutenberg Literary Archive Foundation. Web. 30 Oct. 2008.

'Victoria Day and Empire Day: A Canadian Tradition.' Archives. *Instructional Resources Unit, Manitoba Education, Citizenship and Youth*. 2003. Web. 24 Aug. 2007.

*Victorian Readers: Fifth Reader.* Toronto: Copp, Clark and W.J. Gage, 1898. Print.

'Vigile 1914–1918 Vigil.' Canada's National History Society. Web. 16 Dec. 2008.

Vipond, Mary. 'Best Sellers in English Canada, 1899–1918: An Overview.' *Journal of Canadian Fiction* 24 (1979): 96–119. Print.

Walford, Jonathan. 'The Fashions of L.M. Montgomery.' *The Lucy Maud Montgomery Album.* Comp. Kevin McCabe. Toronto: Fitzhenry and Whiteside, 1999. 70–9. Print.

Wallace, W. Stewart. *The Ryerson Imprint: A Check-list of the Books and Pamphlets Published by the Ryerson Press since the Foundation of the House in 1829.* Toronto: Ryerson, [1954?]. Print.

Warner, Marina. *Monuments and Maidens: The Allegory of the Female Form.* London: Weidenfeld and Nicolson, 1985. Print.

Waterston, Elizabeth. 'Margaret Marshall Saunders: A Voice for the Silent.' *Silenced Sextet: Six Nineteenth-Century Canadian Women Novelists.* Ed. Carrie MacMillan, Lorraine McMullen, and Elizabeth Waterston. Montreal and Kingston: McGill-Queen's UP, 1992. 137–68. Print.

Watters, Reginald Eyre. *A Checklist of Canadian Literature and Background Materials, 1628–1960.* 2nd ed. Toronto: U of Toronto P, 1972. Print.

Webb, Jean. 'War, Heroism and Humanity in the Novels of Michael Morpurgo.' *Michael Morpurgo.* Home page. September 2005. Web. 18 Dec. 2009.

Webb, Peter. '"At War with Nature": Animals in Timothy Findley's *The Wars.*' *Other Selves: Animals in the Canadian Imagination.* Ed. Janice Fiamengo. Ottawa: U of Ottawa P, 2007. 227–44. Print. Reappraisals: Canadian Writers.

Weller, Joan. 'Canadian English-Language Juvenile Periodicals: An Historical Overview, 1847–1990.' *Canadian Children's Literature* 59 (1990): 38–69. Print.

Wetherell, J.E., ed. *The Great War in Verse and Prose.* Toronto: Minister of Education for Ontario, 1919. Print.

Wilson, Barbara, ed. *Ontario and the First World War, 1914–1918: A Collection of Documents.* Toronto: Champlain Society for the Government of Ontario; U of Toronto P, 1977. Print.

Wilson, John. *And in the Morning.* Toronto: Kids Can, 2003. Print.

– *Desperate Glory: The Story of WW I.* Toronto: Napoleon, 2008. Print.

– *Red Goodwin.* Vancouver: Ronsdale, 2006. Print.

Wilson, Richard. *The Post of Honour: Stories of Daring Deeds Done by Men of the British Empire in the Great War*. London and Toronto: Dent, 1917. Microfiche CIHM 65166.

'Winnie the Pooh.' *White River.* Corporation of the Township of White River. 2009. Web. 15 Feb. 2009.

'Women Pacifists.' *We Were There: Canada and the First World War. Library and Archives Canada.* 7 Nov. 2008. Web. 22 Jan. 2009.

Women's Canadian Club of St John, NB. 'Suggested Programme for Empire Day Celebration 1915 in the Schools of New Brunswick.' St John, NB: Women's Canadian Club of St John, 1915. Microfiche CIHM 79596.

Woodsworth, J.S. 'My Convictions about War.' *Vox,* July 1940: 5–7. Print.

Young, Andrew. 'Inspiration for Young Men.' *Archivist* 121 (2003): 19–24. Print.

Zipes, Jack. 'The Perverse Delight of Shockheaded Peter.' *Theater* 30.2 (2000): 128–43. *Project Muse Premium.* Web. 15 Feb. 2010.

# Index

aboriginal Canadians: children and war, 45–9, 92, 101; enlistment and home-front war work, 46–8; stereotypes in war stories, 162–3, 172, 202
Abraham and Isaac, 86, 120, 214–16
adventure tale of war: American 151–2, 164–75; boy-hero in, 153, 164–5, 171; British, 16–17, 154–64; Canadian, 160–4, 175–82; in *Children's Story of the War*, 68–9; effect on enlistment, 173–5; G.A. Henty as originator of, 150–1; nationalism in, 153, 164–5, 175, 178; national stereotypes in, 162–5, 169–70, 172; and popular militarism in Canada, 16–17, 150–1
Agnew, Kate, 229
*Aleta Dey* (Beynon), 224–5
Alger, Horatio (series), 19
All Canadian Entertainment series, 96, 266nn5–6. *See also* Groves, Edith Lelean
allegory: in animal stories, 133–

4, 146; as mode of treating war, 122–3, 180, 233, 235–6, 243
Altick, Richard, 264n8
Americans: representations of in children's war literature, 124–5, 164–70, 172, 198, 200
*And in the Morning* (Wilson), 218, 238, 273n2
Anderson, Dr Louisa Garrett. *See* Garrett Anderson, Dr Louisa
animal story. *See under* children's literature, genres of
animal welfare, 132–3, 141
animals in war: Blue Cross, 137, 270n3; fidelity of, 137–8; mascots, 138–40; parallels with child victims, 133–5; as victims and casualties, 130–1, 136, 147; working animals 130, 135–7. *See also Me'ow Jones; Pierrot; Wandering Dog*
Animals in War Memorial, 133, 269n1
*Annals of Valour*, 88, 247, 249
Annick Press, 24, 264n10
annuals. *See Boys' Own Annual;*

Thompson, Robert Clarence
(boy soldier), 4
*Three Wishes* (Ellis), 254
thrift, 43–5, 193–4
TOKO (The Order of the King's
Own), 20, 40, 117, 269n6
Tomkins, George, 52, 81, 89–90
*Trail Makers Boys' Annual* (Mac-
beth, ed.), 178–82
Trent, Martha (Somewhere in
series), 201–5, 206–7
Turner, James, 132
*Tyndareus*, 70

underage soldiers. *See* boy soldiers
uniforms for children, 108,
110–11
Union Jack, 83, 87, 88
*Unknown Soldier, The* (Granfield),
242

VAD (Voluntary Aid Detach-
ment), 272n5
*Valerie Duval Somewhere in France*
(Trent), 206
Valpy, Michael, 253
Vance, Jonathan, 3, 180
Vandercook, Margaret, 195–201,
211
Vaux, Patrick, 160
*Victoria* (magazine for Victoria
school district), 164
Victoria Cross, 66–7, 87
Victory Bond campaign, 10–11,
12, 45
Vigil Project, 251
Vimy Ridge, Battle of, 44, 60,
140, 166, 168, 169, 171, 213,
218, 231–2, 244–5, 248, 251

*Wandering Dog, The* (Saunders),
145–8, 270n7
war: domestication of, 112,
142; impact on children, 4–7,
254
'War and the Christian Church,
The' (Presbyterian report),
119, 215
*War Horse* (Morpurgo), 134,
272–3n1
War Measures Act, 225
War of 1812, 52, 53, 149, 176. *See
also* Brock, Isaac
war toys and games, 25, 107–8;
parental concern about,
108–10
*Wars, The* (Findley), 133, 220
Wartime Elections Act, 271n9
Webb, Jean, 134
Webb, Peter, 133
Weber, Ephraim, 208
*Western School Journal*, 101,
264n3, 265n10
Wetherell, J.E.: *The Great War in
Verse and Prose*, 11–13, 247–8
*Where Poppies Grow* (Granfield),
242
Wilson, Barbara, 264n1 (ch..1)
Wilson, David (head of BC Free
Textbook Branch), 63
Wilson, Janet (illustrator), 241
Wilson, John: *And in the Morn-
ing*, 218, 238, 273n2; *Desperate
Glory*, 242–3; *Red Goodwin*, 226
Wilson, Richard: *The Post of Hon-
our*, 74
Winnie-the-Pooh, 138
Winter, Jay. *See* Prost, Antoine
'With Chin Up' (Frame), 183,
189–91, 272n3